Hegel's Philosophy of Mind
By Georg Wilhelm Friedrich Hegel
Edited by Anthony Uyl

Devoted Publishing
Woodstock, Ontario, 2017

Hegel's Philosophy of Mind
By Georg Wilhelm Friedrich Hegel
Translated From The Encyclopaedia of the Philosophical Sciences
With Five Introductory Essays
By William Wallace, M.A., LL.D.
Fellow of Merton College, and Whyte's Professor of Moral Philosophy in the University of Oxford
Oxford; Clarendon Press; 1894
Edited by Anthony Uyl

Let us hear your stories and thoughts!

Contact us at: devotedpub@hotmail.com
Visit us on Facebook: Devoted Publishing
Visit our website: www.devotedpublishing.com
Published in Woodstock, Ontario, Canada 2017.

ISBN: 978-1-988297-83-5

Table of Contents

PREFACE

I here offer a translation of the third or last part of Hegel's encyclopaedic sketch of philosophy,—the Philosophy of Mind. The volume, like its subject, stands complete in itself. But it may also be regarded as a supplement or continuation of the work begun in my version of his Logic. I have not ventured upon the Philosophy of Nature which lies between these two. That is a province, to penetrate into which would require an equipment of learning I make no claim to,—a province, also, of which the present-day interest would be largely historical, or at least bound up with historical circumstances.

The translation is made from the German text given in the Second Part of the Seventh Volume of Hegel's Collected Works, occasionally corrected by comparison with that found in the second and third editions (of 1827 and 1830) published by the author. I have reproduced only Hegel's own paragraphs, and entirely omitted the Zusätze of the editors. These addenda—which are in origin lecture-notes—to the paragraphs are, in the text of the Collected Works, given for the first section only. The psychological part which they accompany has been barely treated elsewhere by Hegel: but a good popular exposition of it will be found in Erdmann's Psychologische Briefe. The second section was dealt with at greater length by Hegel himself in his Philosophy of Law (1820). The topics of the third section are largely covered by his lectures on Art, Religion, and History of Philosophy.

I do not conceal from myself that the text offers a hard nut to crack. Yet here and there, even through the medium of the translation, I think some light cannot fail to come to an earnest student. Occasionally, too, as, for instance, in §§ 406, 459, 549, and still more in §§ 552, 573, at the close of which might stand the words Liberavi animam meam, the writer really "lets himself go," and gives his mind freely on questions where speculation comes closely in touch with life.

In the Five Introductory Essays I have tried sometimes to put together, and sometimes to provide with collateral elucidation, some points in the Mental Philosophy. I shall not attempt to justify the selection of subjects for special treatment further than to hope that they form a more or less connected group, and to refer for a study of some general questions of system and method to my Prolegomena to the Study of Hegel's Philosophy which appear almost simultaneously with this volume.

OXFORD, December, 1893.

FIVE INTRODUCTORY ESSAYS IN PSYCHOLOGY AND ETHICS

Essay I - On The Scope Of A Philosophy Of Mind

The art of finding titles, and of striking out headings which catch the eye or ear, and lead the mind by easy paths of association to the subject under exposition, was not one of Hegel's gifts. A stirring phrase, a vivid or picturesque turn of words, he often has. But his lists of contents, when they cease to be commonplace, are apt to run into the bizarre and the grotesque. Generally, indeed, his rubrics are the old and (as we may be tempted to call them) insignificant terms of the text-books. But, in Hegel's use of them, these conventional designations are charged with a highly individualised meaning. They may mean more—they may mean less—than they habitually pass for: but they unquestionably specify their meaning with a unique and almost personal flavour. And this can hardly fail to create and to disappoint undue expectations.

(i.) *Philosophy and its Parts.*

Even the main divisions of his system show this conservatism in terminology. The names of the three parts of the Encyclopaedia are, we may say, non-significant of their peculiar contents. And that for a good reason. What Hegel proposes to give is no novel or special doctrine, but the universal philosophy which has passed on from age to age, here narrowed and there widened, but still essentially the same. It is conscious of its continuity and proud of its identity with the teachings of Plato and Aristotle.

The earliest attempts of the Greek philosophers to present philosophy in a complete and articulated order—attempts generally attributed to the Stoics, the schoolmen of antiquity—made it a tripartite whole. These three parts were Logic, Physics, and Ethics. In their entirety they were meant to form a cycle of unified knowledge, satisfying the needs of theory as well as practice. As time went on, however, the situation changed: and if the old names remained, their scope and value suffered many changes. New interests and curiosities, due to altered circumstances, brought other departments of reality under the focus of investigation besides those which had been primarily discussed under the old names. Inquiries became more specialised, and each tended to segregate itself from the rest as an independent field of science. The result was that in modern times the territory still marked by the ancient titles had shrunk to a mere phantom of its former bulk. Almost indeed things had come to such a pass that the time-honoured figures had sunk into the misery of rois fainéants; while the real business of knowledge was discharged by the younger and less conventional lines of research which the needs and fashions of the time had called up. Thus Logic, in the narrow formal sense, was turned into an "art" of argumentation and a system of technical rules for the analysis and synthesis of academical discussion. Physics or Natural Philosophy restricted itself to the elaboration of some metaphysical postulates or hypotheses regarding the general modes of physical operation. And Ethics came to be a very unpractical discussion of subtleties regarding moral faculty and moral standard. Meanwhile a theory of scientific method and of the laws governing the growth of intelligence and formation of ideas grew up, and left the older logic to perish of formality and inanition. The successive departments of physical science, each in turn asserting its independence, finally left Natural Philosophy no alternative between clinging to its outworn hypotheses and abstract generalities, or identifying itself (as Newton in his great book put it) with the Principia Mathematica of the physical sciences. Ethics, in its turn, saw itself, on one hand, replaced by psychological inquiries into the relations between the feelings and the will and the intelligence; while, on the other hand, a host of social, historical, economical, and other researches cut it off from the real facts of human life, and left it no more than the endless debates on the logical and metaphysical issues involved in free-will and conscience, duty and merit.

It has sometimes been said that Kant settled this controversy between the old departments of philosophy and the new branches of science. And the settlement, it is implied, consisted in assigning to the philosopher a sort of police and patrol duty in the commonwealth of science. He was to see that boundaries were duly respected, and that each science kept strictly to its own business. For this purpose each branch of philosophy was bound to convert itself into a department of criticism—an examination of first principles in the several provinces of reality or experience—with a view to get a distinct conception of what they were, and thus define exactly the lines on which the structures of more detailed science could be put up solidly and safely. This plan offered tempting lines to research, and sounded well. But on further reflection there emerge one or two difficulties, hard to get over. Paradoxical though it may seem, one cannot rightly estimate the capacity and range of foundations, before one has had some familiarity with the buildings erected upon them. Thus you are involved in a circle: a circle which is probably inevitable, but which for that reason it is well to recognise at once. Then—what is only another way of saying the same thing—it is impossible to draw an inflexible line between premises of principle and conclusions of detail. There is no spot at which criticism can stop, and, having done its business well, hand on the remaining task to dogmatic system. It was an instinctive feeling of this implication of system in what professed only to be criticism which led the aged Kant to ignore his own previous professions that he offered as yet no system, and when Fichte maintained himself to be erecting the fabric for which Kant had prepared the ground, to reply by the counter-declaration that the criticism was the system—that "the curtain was the picture."

The Hegelian philosophy is an attempt to combine criticism with system, and thus realise what Kant had at least foretold. It is a system which is self-critical, and systematic only through the absoluteness of its criticism. In Hegel's own phrase, it is an immanent and an incessant dialectic, which from first to last allows finality to no dogmatic rest, but carries out Kant's description of an Age of Criticism, in which nothing, however majestic and sacred its authority, can plead for exception from the all-testing Elenchus. Then, on the other hand, Hegel refuses to restrict philosophy and its branches to anything short of the totality. He takes in its full sense that often-used phrase—the Unity of Knowledge. Logic becomes the all-embracing research of "first principles,"—the principles which regulate physics and ethics. The old divisions between logic and metaphysic, between induction and deduction, between theory of reasoning and theory of knowledge,—divisions which those who most employed them were never able to show the reason and purpose of—because indeed they had grown up at various times and by "natural selection" through a vast mass of incidents: these are superseded and merged in one continuous theory of real knowledge considered under its abstract or formal aspect,—of organised and known reality in its underlying thought-system. But these first principles were only an abstraction from complete reality—the reality which nature has when unified by mind—and they presuppose the total from which they are derived. The realm of pure thought is only the ghost of the Idea—of the unity and reality of knowledge, and it must be reindued with its flesh and blood. The logical world is (in Kantian phrase) only the possibility of Nature and Mind. It comes first—because it is a system of First Principles: but these first principles could only be elicited by a philosophy which has realised the meaning of a mental experience, gathered by interpreting the facts of Nature.

Natural Philosophy is no longer—according to Hegel's view of it—merely a scheme of mathematical ground-work. That may be its first step. But its scope is a complete unity (which is not a mere aggregate) of the branches of natural knowledge, exploring both the inorganic and the organic world. In dealing with this endless problem, philosophy seems to be baulked by an impregnable obstacle to its progress. Every day the advance of specialisation renders any comprehensive or synoptic view of the totality of science more and more impossible. No doubt we talk readily enough of Science. But here, if anywhere, we may say there is no Science, but only sciences. The generality of science is a proud fiction or a gorgeous dream, variously told and interpreted according to the varying interest and proclivity of the scientist. The sciences, or those who specially expound them, know of no unity, no philosophy of science. They are content to remark that in these days the thing is impossible, and to pick out the faults in any attempts in that direction that are made outside their pale. Unfortunately for this contention, the thing is done by us all, and, indeed, has to be done. If not as men of science, yet as men—as human beings—we have to put together things and form some total estimate of the drift of development, of the unity of nature. To get a notion, not merely of the general methods and principles of the sciences, but of their results and teachings, and to get this not as a mere lot of fragments, but with a systematic unity, is indispensable in some degree for all rational life. The life not founded on science is not the life of man. But he will not find what he wants in the text-books of the specialist, who is obliged to treat his subject, as Plato says, "under the pressure of necessity," and who dare not look on it in its quality "to draw the soul towards truth, and to form the philosophic intellect so as to uplift what we now unduly keep down[1]." If the philosopher in this province does his work but badly, he may plead the novelty of the task to which he comes as a pioneer or even an architect. He finds little that he can directly utilise. The materials have been gathered and prepared for very special aims; and the great aim of science—that human life may be made a higher, an ampler, and happier thing,—has hardly been kept in view at all, except in its more materialistic aspects. To the philosopher the supreme interest of the physical sciences is that man also belongs to the physical universe, or that Mind and Matter as we know them are (in Mr. Spencer's language) "at once antithetical and inseparable." He wants to find the place of Man,—but of Man as Mind—in Nature.

If the scope of Natural Philosophy be thus expanded to make it the unity and more than the synthetic aggregate of the several physical sciences—to make it the whole which surpasses the addition of all their fragments, the purpose of Ethics has not less to be deepened and widened. Ethics, under that title, Hegel knows not. And for those who cannot recognise anything unless it be clearly labelled, it comes natural to record their censure of Hegelianism for ignoring or disparaging ethical studies. But if we take the word in that wide sense which common usage rather justifies than adopts, we may say that the whole philosophy of Mind is a moral philosophy. Its subject is the moral as opposed to the physical aspect of reality: the inner and ideal life as opposed to the merely external and real materials of it: the world of intelligence and of humanity. It displays Man in the several stages of that process by which he expresses the full meaning of nature, or discharges the burden of that task which is implicit in him from the first. It traces the steps of that growth by which what was no better than a fragment of nature—an intelligence located (as it seemed) in one piece of matter—comes to realise the truth of it and of himself. That truth is his ideal and his obligation: but it is also—such is the mystery of his birthright—his idea and possession. He—like the natural universe—is (as the Logic has shown) a principle of unification, organisation, idealisation: and his history (in its ideal completeness) is the history of the process by which he, the typical man, works the fragments of reality (and such mere reality must be always a collection of fragments) into the perfect unity of a many-sided character. Thus the philosophy of mind, beginning with man as a sentient organism, the focus in which the universe gets its first dim confused expression through mere feeling, shows how he "erects himself above himself" and realises what ancient thinkers called his kindred with the divine.

In that total process of the mind's liberation and self-realisation the portion specially called Morals is but one, though a necessary, stage. There are, said Porphyry and the later Platonists, four degrees in the path of perfection and self-accomplishment. And first, there is the career of honesty and worldly prudence, which makes the duty of the citizen. Secondly, there is the progress in purity which casts earthly things behind, and reaches the angelic height of passionless serenity. And the third step is the divine life which by intellectual energy is turned to behold the truth of things. Lastly, in the fourth grade, the mind, free and sublime in self-sustaining wisdom, makes itself an "exemplar" of virtue, and is even a "father of Gods." Even so, it may be said, the human mind is the subject of a complicated Teleology,—the field ruled by a multifarious Ought, psychological, aesthetical, social and religious. To adjust their several claims cannot be the object of any science, if adjustment means to supply a guide in practice. But it is the purpose of such a teleology to show that social requirements and moral duty as ordinarily conceived do not exhaust the range of obligation,—of the supreme ethical Ought. How that can best be done is however a question of some difficulty. For the ends under examination do not fall completely into a serial order, nor does one involve others in such a way as to destroy their independence. You cannot absolve psychology as if it stood independent of ethics or religion, nor can aesthetic considerations merely supervene on moral. Still, it may be said, the order followed by Hegel seems on the whole liable to fewer objections than others.

Mr. Herbert Spencer, the only English philosopher who has even attempted a System of Philosophy, may in this point be compared with Hegel. He also begins with a First Principles,—a work which, like Hegel's Logic, starts by presenting Philosophy as the supreme arbiter between the subordinate principles of Religion and Science, which are in it "necessary correlatives." The positive task of philosophy is (with some inconsistency or vagueness) presented, in the next place, as a "unification of knowledge." Such a unification has to make explicit the implicit unity of known reality: because "every thought involves a whole system of thoughts." And such a programme might again suggest the Logic. But unfortunately Mr. Spencer does not (and he has Francis Bacon to justify him here) think it worth his while to toil up the weary, but necessary, mount of Purgatory which is known to us as Logic. With a naïve realism, he builds on Cause and Power, and above all on Force, that "Ultimate of Ultimates," which seems to be, however marvellously, a denizen both of the Known and the Unknowable world. In the known world this Ultimate appears under two forms, matter and motion, and the problem of science and philosophy is to lay down in detail and in general the law of their continuous redistribution, of the segregation of motion from matter, and the inclusion of motion into matter.

Of this process, which has no beginning and no end,—the rhythm of generation and corruption, attraction and repulsion, it may be said that it is properly not a first principle of all knowledge, but the general or fundamental portion of Natural Philosophy to which Mr. Spencer next proceeds. Such a philosophy, however, he gives only in part: viz. as a Biology, dealing with organic (and at a further stage and under other names, with supra-organic) life. And that the Philosophy of Nature should take this form, and carry both the First Principles and the later portions of the system with it, as parts of a philosophy of evolution, is what we should have expected from the contemporaneous interests of science[2]. Even a one-sided attempt to give speculative unity to those researches, which get—for reasons the scientific specialist seldom asks—the title of biological, is however worth noting as a recognition of the necessity of a Natur-philosophie,—a speculative science of Nature.

The third part of the Hegelian System corresponds to what in the Synthetic Philosophy is known as Psychology, Ethics, and Sociology. And here Mr. Spencer recognises that something new has turned up. Psychology is "unique" as a science: it is a "double science," and as a whole quite sui generis. Whether perhaps all these epithets would not, mutatis mutandis, have to be applied also to Ethics and Sociology, if these are to do their full work, he does not say. In what this doubleness consists he even finds it somewhat difficult to show. For, as his fundamental philosophy does not on this point go beyond noting some pairs of verbal antitheses, and has no sense of unity except in the imperfect shape of a "relation"" between two things which are "antithetical and inseparable," he is perplexed by phrases such as "in" and "out of" consciousness, and stumbles over the equivocal use of "inner" to denote both mental (or non-spatial) in general, and locally sub-cuticular in special. Still, he gets so far as to see that the law of consciousness is that in it neither feelings nor relations have independent subsistence, and that the unit of mind does not begin till what he calls two feelings are made one. The phraseology may be faulty, but it shows an inkling of the a priori. Unfortunately it is apparently forgotten; and the language too often reverts into the habit of what he calls the "objective," i.e. purely physical, sciences.

Mr. Spencer's conception of Psychology restricts it to the more general physics of the mind. For its more concrete life he refers us to Sociology. But his Sociology is yet unfinished: and from the plan of its inception, and the imperfect conception of the ends and means of its investigation, hardly admits of completion in any systematic sense. To that incipiency is no doubt due its excess in historical or anecdotal detail—detail, however, too much segregated from its social context, and in general its tendency to neglect normal and central theory for incidental and peripheral facts. Here, too, there is a weakness in First Principles and a love of catchwords, which goes along with the fallacy that illustration is proof. Above all, it is evident that the great fact of religion overhangs Mr. Spencer with the attraction of an unsolved and unacceptable problem. He cannot get the religious ideas of men into co-ordination with their scientific, aesthetic, and moral doctrines; and only betrays his sense of the high importance of the former by placing them in the forefront of inquiry, as due to the inexperience and limitations of the so-called primitive man. That is hardly adequate recognition of the religious principle: and the defect will make itself seriously felt, should he ever come to carry out the further stage of his prospectus dealing with "the growth and correlation of language, knowledge, morals, and aesthetics."

(ii.) *Mind and Morals.*

A Mental Philosophy—if we so put what might also be rendered a Spiritual Philosophy, or Philosophy of Spirit—may to an English reader suggest something much narrower than it actually contains. A Philosophy of the Human Mind—if we consult English specimens—would not imply much more than a psychology, and probably what is called an inductive psychology. But as Hegel understands it, it covers an unexpectedly wide range of topics, the whole range from Nature to Spirit. Besides Subjective Mind, which would seem on first thoughts to exhaust the topics of psychology, it goes on to Mind as Objective, and finally to Absolute mind. And such combinations of words may sound either self-contradictory or meaningless.

The first Section deals with the range of what is usually termed Psychology. That term indeed is employed by Hegel, in a restricted sense, to denote the last of the three sub-sections in the discussion of Subjective Mind. The Mind, which is the topic of psychology proper, cannot be assumed as a ready-made object, or datum. A Self, a self-consciousness, an intelligent and volitional agent, if it be the birthright of man, is a birthright which he has to realise for himself, to earn and to make his own. To trace the steps by which mind in its stricter acceptation, as will and intelligence, emerges from the general animal sensibility which is the crowning phase of organic life, and the final problem of biology, is the work of two preliminary sub-sections—the first entitled Anthropology, the second the Phenomenology of Mind.

The subject of Anthropology, as Hegel understands it, is the Soul—the raw material of consciousness, the basis of all higher mental life. This is a borderland, where the ground is still debateable between Nature and Mind: it is the region of feeling, where the sensibility has not yet been differentiated to intelligence. Soul and body are here, as the phrase goes, in communion: the inward life is still imperfectly disengaged from its natural co-physical setting. Still one with nature, it submits to natural influences and natural vicissitudes: is not as yet master of itself, but the half-passive receptacle of a foreign life, of a general vitality, of a common soul not yet fully differentiated into individuality. But it is awaking to self-activity: it is emerging to Consciousness,—to distinguish itself, as aware and conscious, from the facts of life and sentiency of which it is aware.

From this region of psychical physiology or physiological psychology, Hegel in the second sub-section of his first part takes us to the "Phenomenology of Mind,"—to Consciousness. The sentient soul is also conscious—but in a looser sense of that word[4]: it has feelings, but can scarcely be said itself to know that it has them. As consciousness, the Soul has come to separate what it is from what it feels. The distinction emerges of a subject which is conscious, and an object of which it is conscious. And the main thing is obviously the relationship between the two, or the Consciousness itself, as tending to distinguish itself alike from its subject and its object. Hence, perhaps, may be gathered why it is called Phenomenology of Mind. Mind as yet is not yet more than emergent or apparent: nor yet self-possessed and self-certified. No longer, however, one with the circumambient nature which it feels, it sees itself set against it, but only as a passive recipient of it, a tabula rasa on which external nature is reflected, or to which phenomena are presented. No longer, on the other hand, a mere passive instrument of suggestion from without, its instinct of life, its nisus of self-assertion is developed, through antagonism to a like nisus, into the consciousness of self-hood, of a Me and Mine as set against a Thee and Thine. But just in proportion as it is so developed in opposition to and recognition of other equally self-centred selves, it has passed beyond the narrower characteristic of Consciousness proper. It is no longer mere intelligent perception or reproduction of a world, but it is life, with perception (or apperception) of that life. It has returned in a way to its original unity with nature, but it is now the sense of its self-hood—the consciousness of itself as the focus in which subjective and objective are at one. Or, to put it in the language of the great champion of Realism[5], the standpoint of Reason or full-grown Mind is this: "The world which appears to us is our percept, therefore in us. The real world, out of which we explain the phenomenon, is our thought: therefore in us."

The third sub-section of the theory of Subjective Mind—the Psychology proper—deals with Mind. This is the real, independent Psyché—hence the special appropriation of the term Psychology. "The Soul," says Herbart, "no doubt dwells in a body: there are, moreover, corresponding states of the one and the other: but nothing corporeal occurs in the Soul, nothing purely mental, which we could reckon to our Ego, occurs in the body: the affections of the body are no representations of the Ego, and our pleasant and unpleasant feelings do not immediately lie in the organic life they favour or hinder." Such a Soul, so conceived, is an intelligent and volitional self, a being of intellectual and "active" powers or phenomena: it is a Mind. And "Mind," adds Hegel[6], "is just this elevation above Nature and physical modes and above the complication with an external object." Nothing is external to it: it is rather the internalising of all externality. In this psychology proper, we are out of any immediate connexion with physiology. "Psychology as such," remarks Herbart, "has its questions common to it with Idealism"— with the doctrine that all reality is mental reality. It traces, in Hegel's exposition of it, the steps of the way by which mind realises that independence which is its characteristic stand-point. On the intellectual side that independence is assured in language,—the system of signs by which the intelligence stamps external objects as its own, made part of its inner world. A science, some one has said, is after all only une langue bien faite. So, reversing the saying, we may note that a language is an inwardised and mind-appropriated world. On the active side, the independence of mind is seen in self-enjoyment, in happiness, or self-content, where impulse and volition have attained satisfaction in equilibrium, and the soul possesses itself in fullness. Such a mind[7], which has made the world its certified possession in language, and which enjoys itself in self-possession of soul, called happiness, is a free Mind. And that is the highest which Subjective Mind can reach.

At this point, perhaps, having rounded off by a liberal sweep the scope of psychology, the ordinary mental philosophy would stop. Hegel, instead of finishing, now goes on to the field of what he calls Objective Mind. For as yet it has been only the story of a preparation, an inward adorning and equipment, and we have yet to see what is to come of it in actuality. Or rather, we have yet to consider the social forms on which this preparation rests. The mind, self-possessed and sure of itself or free, is so only through the objective shape which its main development runs parallel with. An intelligent Will, or a practical reason, was the last word of the psychological development. But a reason which is practical, or a volition which is intelligent, is realised by action which takes regular shapes, and by practice which transforms the world. The theory of Objective Mind delineates the new form which nature assumes under the sway of intelligence and will. That intellectual world realises itself by transforming the physical into a social and political world, the given natural conditions of existence into a freely-instituted system of life, the primitive struggle of kinds for subsistence into the ordinances of the social state. Given man as a being possessed of will and intelligence, this inward faculty, whatever be its degree, will try to impress itself on nature and to reproduce itself in a legal, a moral, and social world. The kingdom of deed replaces, or rises on the foundation of, the kingdom of word: and instead of the equilibrium of a well-adjusted soul comes the harmonious life of a social organism. We are, in short, in the sphere of Ethics and Politics, of Jurisprudence and Morals, of Law and Conscience.

Here,—as always in Hegel's system—there is a triad of steps. First the province of Law or Right. But if we call it Law, we must keep out of sight the idea of a special law-giver, of a conscious imposition of laws, above all by a political superior. And if we call it Right, we must remember that it is neutral, inhuman, abstract right: the right whose principle is impartial and impassive uniformity, equality, order;—not moral right, or the equity which takes cognisance of circumstances, of personal claims, and provides against its own hardness. The intelligent will of Man, throwing itself upon the mere gifts of nature as their appointed master, creates the world of Property—of things instrumental, and regarded as adjectival, to the human personality. But the autonomy of Reason (which is latent in the will) carries with it certain consequences. As it acts, it also, by its inherent quality of uniformity or universality, enacts for itself a law and laws, and creates the realm of formal equality or order-giving law. But this is a mere equality: which is not inconsistent with what in other respects may be excess of inequality. What one does, if it is really to be treated as done, others may or even must do: each act creates an expectation of continuance and uniformity of behaviour. The doer is bound by it, and others are entitled to do the like. The material which the person appropriates creates a system of obligation. Thus is constituted—in the natural give and take of rational Wills—in the inevitable course of human action and reaction,—a system of rights and duties. This law of equality—the basis of justice, and the seed of benevolence—is the scaffolding or perhaps rather the rudimentary framework of society and moral life. Or it is the bare skeleton which is to be clothed upon by the softer and fuller outlines of the social tissues and the ethical organs.

And thus the first range of Objective Mind postulates the second, which Hegel calls "Morality." The word is to be taken in its strict sense as a protest against the quasi-physical order of law. It is the morality of conscience and of the good will, of the inner rectitude of soul and purpose, as all-sufficient and supreme. Here is brought out the complementary factor in social life: the element of liberty, spontaneity, self-consciousness. The motto of mere inward morality (as opposed to the spirit of legality) is (in Kant's words): "There is nothing without qualification good, in heaven or earth, but only a good will." The essential condition of goodness is that the action be done with purpose and intelligence, and in full persuasion of its goodness by the conscience of the agent. The characteristic of Morality thus described is its essential inwardness, and the sovereignty of the conscience over all heteronomy. Its justification is that it protests against the authority of a mere external or objective order, subsisting and ruling in separation from the subjectivity. Its defect is the turn it gives to this assertion of the rights of subjective conscience: briefly in the circumstance that it tends to set up a mere individualism against a mere universalism, instead of realising the unity and essential interdependence of the two.

The third sub-section of the theory of Objective Mind describes a state of affairs in which this antithesis is explicitly overcome. This is the moral life in a social community. Here law and usage prevail and provide the fixed permanent scheme of life: but the law and the usage are, in their true or ideal conception, only the unforced expression of the mind and will of those who live under them. And, on the other hand, the mind and will of the individual members of such a community are pervaded and animated by its universal spirit. In such a community, and so constituting it, the individual is at once free and equal, and that because of the spirit of fraternity, which forms its spiritual link. In the world supposed to be governed by mere legality the idea of right is exclusively prominent; and when that is the case, it may often happen that summum jus summa injuria. In mere morality, the stress falls exclusively on the idea of inward freedom, or the necessity of the harmony of the judgment and the will, or the dependence of conduct upon conscience. In the union of the two, in the moral community as normally constituted, the mere idea of right is replaced, or controlled and modified, by the idea of equity—a balance as it were between the two preceding, inasmuch as motive and purpose are employed to modify and interpret strict right. But this effect—this harmonisation—is brought about by the predominance of a new idea—the principle of benevolence,—a principle however which is itself modified by the fundamental idea of right or law[8] into a wise or regulated kindliness.

But what Hegel chiefly deals with under this head is the interdependence of form and content, of social order and personal progress. In the picture of an ethical organisation or harmoniously-alive moral community he shows us partly the underlying idea which gave room for the antithesis between law and conscience, and partly the outlines of the ideal in which that conflict becomes only the instrument of progress. This organisation has three grades or three typical aspects. These are the Family, Civil Society, and the State. The first of these, the Family, must be taken to include those primary unities of human life where the natural affinity of sex and the natural ties of parentage are the preponderant influence in forming and maintaining the social group. This, as it were, is the soul-nucleus of social organisation: where the principle of unity is an instinct, a feeling, an absorbing solidarity. Next comes what Hegel has called Civil Society,—meaning however by civil the antithesis to political, the society of those who may be styled bourgeois, not citoyens:—and meaning by society the antithesis to community. There are other natural influences binding men together besides those which form the close unities of the family, gens, tribe, or clan. Economical needs associate human beings within a much larger radius—in ways capable of almost indefinite expansion—but also in a way much less intense and deep. Civil Society is the more or less loosely organised aggregate of such associations, which, if, on one hand, they keep human life from stagnating in the mere family, on another, accentuate more sharply the tendency to competition and the struggle for life. Lastly, in the Political State comes the synthesis of family and society. Of the family; in so far as the State tends to develope itself on the nature-given unit of the Nation (an extended family, supplementing as need arises real descent by fictitious incorporations), and has apparently never permanently maintained itself except on the basis of a predominant common nationality. Of society; in so far as the extension and dispersion of family ties have left free room for the differentiation of many other sides of human interest and action, and given ground for the full development of individuality. In consequence of this, the State (and such a state as Hegel describes is essentially the idea or ideal of the modern State)[9] has a certain artificial air about it. It can only be maintained by the free action of intelligence: it must make its laws public: it must bring to consciousness the principles of its constitution, and create agencies for keeping up unity of organisation through the several separate provinces or contending social interests, each of which is inclined to insist on the right of home mis-rule.

The State—which in its actuality must always be a quasi-national state—is thus the supreme unity of Nature and Mind. Its natural basis in land, language, blood, and the many ties which spring therefrom, has to be constantly raised into an intelligent unity through universal interests. But the elements of race and of culture have no essential connexion, and they perpetually incline to wrench themselves asunder. Blood and judgment are for ever at war in the state as in the individual[10]: the cosmopolitan interest, to which the maxim is Ubi bene, ibi patria, resists the national, which adopts the patriotic watchword of Hector[11]. The State however has another source of danger in the very principle that gave it birth. It arose through antagonism: it was baptised on the battlefield, and it only lives as it is able to assert itself against a foreign foe. And this circumstance tends to intensify and even pervert its natural basis of nationality:—tends to give the very conception of the political a negative and superficial look. But, notwithstanding all these drawbacks, the State in its Idea is entitled to the name Hobbes gave it,—the Mortal God. Here in a way culminates the obviously objective,—we may almost say, visible and tangible—development of Man and Mind. Here it attains a certain completeness—a union of reality and of ideality: a quasi-immortality, a quasi-universality. What the individual person could not do unaided, he can do in the strength of his commonwealth. Much that in the solitary was but implicit or potential, is in the State actualised.

But the God of the State is a mortal God. It is but a national and a limited mind. To be actual, one must at least begin by restricting oneself. Or, rather actuality is rational, but always with a conditioned and a relative rationality[12]: it is in the realm of action and re-action,—in the realm of change and nature. It has warring forces outside it,—warring forces inside it. Its unity is never perfect: because it never produces a true identity of interests within, or maintains an absolute independence without. Thus the true and real State—the State in its Idea—the realisation of concrete humanity,—of Mind as the fullness and unity of nature—is not reached in any single or historical State: but floats away, when we try to seize it, into the endless progress of history. Always indeed the State, the historical and objective, points beyond itself. It does so first in the succession of times. Die Weltgeschichte ist das Weltgericht.[13] And in that doom of the world the eternal blast sweeps along the successive generations of the temporal, one expelling another from the stage of time—each because it is inadequate to the Idea which it tried to express, and has succumbed to an enemy from without because it was not a real and true unity within.

But if temporal flees away before another temporal, it abides in so far as it has, however inadequately, given expression and visible reality—as it points inward and upward—to the eternal. The earthly state is also the city of God; and if the republic of Plato seems to find scant admission into the reality of flesh and blood, it stands eternal as a witness in the heaven of idea. Behind the fleeting succession of consulates and dictatures, of aristocracy and empire, feuds of plebeian with patrician, in that apparent anarchy of powers which the so-called Roman constitution is to the superficial observer, there is the eternal Rome, one, strong, victorious, semper eadem: the Rome of Virgil and Justinian, the ghost whereof still haunts with memories the seven-hilled city, but which with full spiritual presence lives in the law, the literature, the manners of the modern world. To find fitter expression for this Absolute Mind than it has in the Ethical community—to reach that reality of which the moral world is but one-sidedly representative—is the work of Art, Religion, and Philosophy. And to deal with these efforts to find the truth and the unity of Mind and Nature is the subject of Hegel's third Section.

(iii.) *Religion and Philosophy.*

It may be well at this point to guard against a misconception of this serial order of exposition[14]. As stage is seen to follow stage, the historical imagination, which governs our ordinary current of ideas, turns the logical dependence into a time-sequence. But it is of course not meant that the later stage follows the earlier in history. The later is the more real, and therefore the more fundamental. But we can only understand by abstracting and then transcending our abstractions, or rather by showing how the abstraction implies relations which force us to go further and beyond our arbitrary arrest. Each stage therefore either stands to that preceding it as an antithesis, which inevitably dogs its steps as an accusing spirit, or it is the conjunction of the original thesis with the antithesis, in a union which should not be called synthesis because it is a closer fusion and true marriage of minds. A truth and reality, though fundamental, is only appreciated at its true value and seen in all its force where it appears as the reconciliation and reunion of partial and opposing points of view. Thus, e.g., the full significance of the State does not emerge so long as we view it in isolation as a supposed single state, but only as it is seen in the conflict of history, in its actual "energy" as a world-power among powers, always pointing beyond itself to a something universal which it fain would be, and yet cannot be. Or, again, there never was a civil or economic society which existed save under the wing of a state, or in one-sided assumption of state powers to itself: and a family is no isolated and independent unit belonging to a supposed patriarchal age, but was always mixed up with, and in manifold dependence upon, political and civil combinations. The true family, indeed, far from preceding the state in time, presupposes the political power to give it its precise sphere and its social stability: as is well illustrated by that typical form of it presented in the Roman state.

So, again, religion does not supervene upon an already existing political and moral system and invest it with an additional sanction. The true order would be better described as the reverse. The real basis of social life, and even of intelligence, is religion. As some thinkers quaintly put it, the known rests and lives on the bosom of the Unknowable. But when we say that, we must at once guard against a misconception. There are religions of all sorts; and some of them which are most heard of in the modern world only exist or survive in the shape of a traditional name and venerated creed which has lost its power. Nor is a religion necessarily committed to a definite conception of a supernatural—of a personal power outside the order of Nature. But in all cases, religion is a faith and a theory which gives unity to the facts of life, and gives it, not because the unity is in detail proved or detected, but because life and experience in their deepest reality inexorably demand and evince such a unity to the heart. The religion of a time is not its nominal creed, but its dominant conviction of the meaning of reality, the principle which animates all its being and all its striving, the faith it has in the laws of nature and the purpose of life. Dimly or clearly felt and perceived, religion has for its principle (one cannot well say, its object) not the unknowable, but the inner unity of life and knowledge, of act and consciousness, a unity which is certified in its every knowledge, but is never fully demonstrable by the summation of all its ascertained items. As such a felt and believed synthesis of the world and life, religion is the unity which gives stability and harmony to the social sphere; just as morality in its turn gives a partial and practical realisation to the ideal of religion. But religion does not merely establish and sanction morality; it also frees it from a certain narrowness it always has, as of the earth. Or, otherwise put, morality has to the keener inspection something in it which is more than the mere moral injunction at first indicates. Beyond the moral, in its stricter sense, as the obligatory duty and the obedience to law, rises and expands the beautiful and the good: a beautiful which is disinterestedly loved, and a goodness which has thrown off all utilitarian relativity, and become a free self-enhancing joy. The true spirit of religion sees in the divine judgment not a mere final sanction to human morality which has failed of its earthly close, not the re-adjustment of social and political judgments in accordance with our more conscientious inner standards, but a certain, though, for our part-by-part vision, incalculable proportion between what is done and suffered. And in this liberation of the moral from its restrictions, Art renders no slight aid. Thus in different ways, religion presupposes morality to fill up its vacant form, and morality presupposes religion to give its laws an ultimate sanction, which at the same time points beyond their limitations.

But art, religion, and philosophy still rest on the national culture and on the individual mind. However much they rise in the heights of the ideal world, they never leave the reality of life and circumstance behind, and float in the free empyrean. Yet there are degrees of universality, degrees in which they reach what they promised. As the various psychical nuclei of an individual consciousness tend through the course of experience to gather round a central idea and by fusion and assimilation form a complete mental organisation; so, through the march of history, there grows up a complication and a fusion of national ideas and aspirations, which, though still retaining the individuality and restriction of a concrete national life, ultimately present an organisation social, aesthetic, and religious which is a type of humanity in its universality and completeness. Always moving in the measure and on the lines of the real development of its social organisation, the art and religion of a nation tend to give expression to what social and political actuality at its best but imperfectly sets in existence. They come more and more to be, not mere competing fragments as set side by side with those of others, but comparatively equal and complete representations of the many-sided and many-voiced reality of man and the world. Yet always they live and flourish in reciprocity with the fullness of practical institutions and individual character. An abstractly universal art and religion is a delusion—until all diversities of geography and climate, of language and temperament, have been made to disappear. If these energies are in power and reality and not merely in name, they cannot be applied like a panacea or put on like a suit of ready-made clothes. If alive, they grow with individualised type out of the social situation: and they can only attain a vulgar and visible universality, so far as they attach themselves to some simple and uniform aspects,—a part tolerably identical everywhere—in human nature in all times and races.

Art, according to Hegel's account, is the first of the three expressions of Absolute Mind. But the key-note to the whole is to be found in Religion[15]: or Religion is the generic description of that phase of mind which has found rest in the fullness of attainment and is no longer a struggle and a warfare, but a fruition. "It is the conviction of all nations," he says[16], "that in the religious consciousness they hold their truth; and they have always regarded religion as their dignity and as the Sunday of their life. Whatever excites our doubts and alarms, all grief and all anxiety, all that the petty fields of finitude can offer to attract us, we leave behind on the shoals of time: and as the traveller on the highest peak of a mountain range, removed from every distinct view of the earth's surface, quietly lets his vision neglect all the restrictions of the landscape and the world; so in this pure region of faith man, lifted above the hard and inflexible reality, sees it with his mind's eye reflected in the rays of the mental sun to an image where its discords, its lights and shades, are softened to eternal calm. In this region of mind flow the waters of forgetfulness, from which Psyche drinks, and in which she drowns all her pain: and the darknesses of this life are here softened to a dream-image, and transfigured into a mere setting for the splendours of the Eternal.'"

If we take Religion, in this extended sense, we find it is the sense, the vision, the faith, the certainty of the eternal in the changeable, of the infinite in the finite, of the reality in appearance, of the truth in error. It is freedom from the distractions and pre-occupations of the particular details of life; it is the sense of permanence, repose, certainty, rounding off, toning down and absorbing the vicissitude, the restlessness, the doubts of actual life. Such a victory over palpable reality has no doubt its origin—its embryology—in phases of mind which have been already discussed in the first section. Religion will vary enormously according to the grade of national mood of mind and social development in which it emerges. But whatever be the peculiarities of its original swaddling-clothes, its cardinal note will be a sense of dependence on, and independence in, something more permanent, more august, more of a surety and stay than visible and variable nature and man,—something also which whether God or devil, or both in one, holds the keys of life and death, of weal and woe, and holds them from some safe vantage-ground above the lower realms of change. By this central being the outward and the inward, past and present and to come, are made one. And as already indicated, Religion, emerging, as it does, from social man, from mind ethical, will retain traces of the two foci in society: the individual subjectivity and the objective community. Retain them however only as traces, which still show in the actually envisaged reconciliation. For that is what religion does to morality. It carries a step higher the unity or rather combination gained in the State: it is the fuller harmony of the individual and the collectivity. The moral conscience rests in certainty and fixity on the religious.

But Religion (thus widely understood as the faith in sempiternal and all-explaining reality) at first appears under a guise of Art. The poem and the pyramid, the temple-image and the painting, the drama and the fairy legend, these are religion: but they are, perhaps, religion as Art. And that means that they present the eternal under sensible representations, the work of an artist, and in a perishable material of limited range. Yet even the carvers of a long-past day whose works have been disinterred from the plateaux of Auvergne knew that they gave to the perishable life around them a quasi-immortality: and the myth-teller of a savage tribe elevated the incident of a season into a perennial power of love and fear. The cynic may remind us that from the finest picture of the artist, readily

> *"We turn*
> *To yonder girl that fords the burn."*

And yet it may be said in reply to the cynic that, had it not been for the deep-imprinted lesson of the artist, it would have been but a brutal instinct that would have drawn our eyes. The artist, the poet, the musician, reveal the meaning, the truth, the reality of the world: they teach us, they help us, backward younger brothers, to see, to hear, to feel what our rude senses had failed to detect. They enact the miracle of the loaves and fishes, again and again: out of the common limited things of every day they produce a bread of life in which the generations continue to find nourishment.

But if Art embodies for us the unseen and the eternal, it embodies it in the stone, the colour, the tone, and the word: and these are by themselves only dead matter. To the untutored eye and taste the finest picture-gallery is only a weariness: when the national life has drifted away, the sacred book and the image are but idols and enigmas. "The statues are now corpses from which the vivifying soul has fled, and the hymns are words whence faith has departed: the tables of the Gods are without spiritual meat and drink, and games and feasts no longer afford the mind its joyful union with the being of being. The works of the Muse lack that intellectual force which knew itself strong and real by crushing gods and men in its winepress. They are now (in this iron age) what they are for us,—fair fruits broken from the tree, and handed to us by a kindly destiny. But the gift is like the fruits which the girl in the picture presents: she does not give the real life of their existence, not the tree which bore them, not the earth and the elements which entered into their substance, nor the climate which formed their quality, nor the change of seasons which governed the process of their growth. Like her, Destiny in giving us the works of ancient art does not give us their world, not the spring and summer of the ethical life in which they blossomed and ripened, but solely a memory and a suggestion of this actuality. Our act in enjoying them, therefore, is not a Divine service: were it so, our mind would achieve its perfect and satisfying truth. All that we do is a mere externalism, which from these fruits wipes off some rain-drop, some speck of dust, and which, in place of the inward elements of moral actuality that created and inspired them, tries from the dead elements of their external reality, such as language and historical allusion, to set up a tedious mass of scaffolding, not in order to live ourselves into them, but only to form a picture of them in our minds. But as the girl who proffers the plucked fruits is more and nobler than the natural element with all its details of tree, air, light, &c. which first yielded them, because she gathers all this together, in a nobler way, into the glance of the conscious eye and the gesture which proffers them; so the spirit of destiny which offers us those works of art is more than the ethical life and actuality of the ancient people: for it is the inwardising of that mind which in them was still self-estranged and self-dispossessed:—it is the spirit of tragic destiny, the destiny which collects all those individualised gods and attributes of substance into the one Pantheon. And that temple of all the gods is Mind conscious of itself as mind[17]."

Religion enters into its more adequate form when it ceases to appear in the guise of Art and realises that the kingdom of God is within, that the truth must be felt, the eternal inwardly revealed, the holy one apprehended by faith[18], not by outward vision. Eye hath not seen, nor ear heard, the things of God. They cannot be presented, or delineated: they come only in the witness of the spirit. The human soul itself is the only worthy temple of the Most High, whom heaven, and the heaven of heavens, cannot contain. Here in truth God has come down to dwell with men; and the Son of Man, caught up in the effusion of the Spirit, can in all assurance and all humility claim that he is divinified. Here apparently Absolute Mind is reached: the soul knows no limitation, no struggle: in time it is already eternal. Yet, there is, according to Hegel, a flaw,—not in the essence and the matter, but in the manner and mode in which the ordinary religious consciousness represents to itself, or pictures that unification which it feels and experiences.

"In religion then this unification of ultimate Being with the Self is implicitly reached. But the religious consciousness, if it has this symbolic idea of its reconciliation, still has it as a mere symbol or representation. It attains the satisfaction by tacking on to its pure negativity, and that externally, the positive signification of its unity with the ultimate Being: its satisfaction remains therefore tainted by the antithesis of another world. Its own reconciliation, therefore, is presented to its consciousness as something far away, something far away in the future: just as the reconciliation which the other Self accomplished appears as a far-away thing in the past. The one Divine Man had but an implicit father and only an actual mother; conversely the universal divine man, the community, has its own deed and knowledge for its father, but for its mother only the eternal Love, which it only feels, but does not behold in its consciousness as an actual immediate object. Its reconciliation therefore is in its heart, but still at variance with its consciousness, and its actuality still has a flaw. In its field of consciousness the place of implicit reality or side of pure mediation is taken by the reconciliation that lies far away behind: the place of the actually present, or the side of immediacy and existence, is filled by the world which has still to wait for its transfiguration to glory. Implicitly no doubt the world is reconciled with the eternal Being; and that Being, it is well known, no longer looks upon the object as alien to it, but in its love sees it as like itself. But for self-consciousness this immediate presence is not yet set in the full light of mind. In its immediate consciousness accordingly the spirit of the community is parted from its religious: for while the religious consciousness declares that they are implicitly not parted, this implicitness is not raised to reality and not yet grown to absolute self-certainty[19]."

Religion therefore, which as it first appeared in art-worship had yet to realise its essential inwardness or spirituality, so has now to overcome the antithesis in which its (the religious) consciousness stands to the secular. For the peculiarly religious type of mind is distinguished by an indifference and even hostility, more or less veiled, to art, to morality and the civil state, to science and to nature. Strong in the certainty of faith, or of its implicit rest in God, it resents too curious inquiry into the central mystery of its union, and in its distincter consciousness sets the foundation of faith on the evidence of a fact, which, however, it in the same breath declares to be unique and miraculous, the central event of the ages, pointing back in its reference to the first days of humanity, and forward in the future to the winding-up of the business of terrestrial life. Philosophy, according to Hegel's conception of it, does but draw the conclusion supplied by the premises of religion: it supplements and rounds off into coherence the religious implications. The unique events in Judea nearly nineteen centuries ago are for it also the first step in a new revelation of man's relationship to God: but while it acknowledges the transcendent interest of that age, it lays main stress on the permanent truth then revealed, and it insists on the duty of carrying out the principle there awakened to all the depth and breadth of its explication. Its task—its supreme task—is to explicate religion. But to do so is to show that religion is no exotic, and no mere revelation from an external source. It is to show that religion is the truth, the complete reality, of the mind that lived in Art, that founded the state and sought to be dutiful and upright: the truth, the crowning fruit of all scientific knowledge, of all human affections, of all secular consciousness. Its lesson ultimately is that there is nothing essentially common or unclean: that the holy is not parted off from the true and the good and the beautiful.

Religion thus expanded descends from its abstract or "intelligible" world, to which it had retired from art and science, and the affairs of ordinary life. Its God—as a true God—is not of the dead alone, but also of the living: not a far-off supreme and ultimate Being, but also a man among men. Philosophy thus has to break down the middle partition-wall of life, the fence between secular and sacred. It is but religion come to its maturity, made at home in the world, and no longer a stranger and a wonder. Religion has pronounced in its inmost heart and faith of faith, that the earth is the Lord's, and that day unto day shows forth the divine handiwork. But the heart of unbelief, of little faith, has hardly uttered the word, than it forgets its assurance and leans to the conviction that the prince of this world is the Spirit of Evil. The mood of Théodicée is also—but with a difference—the mood of philosophy. It asserts the ways of Providence: but its providence is not the God of the Moralist, or the ideal of the Artist, or rather is not these only, but also the Law of Nature, and more than that. Its aim is the Unity of History. The words have sometimes been lightly used to mean that events run on in one continuous flow, and that there are no abrupt, no ultimate beginnings, parting age from age. But the Unity of History in its full sense is beyond history: it is history "reduced" from the expanses of time to the eternal present: its thousand years made one day,—made even the glance of a moment. The theme of the Unity of History—in the full depth of unity and the full expanse of history—is the theme of Hegelian philosophy. It traces the process in which Mind has to be all-inclusive, self-upholding, one with the Eternal reality.

"That process of the mind's self-realisation" says Hegel in the close of his Phenomenology, "exhibits a lingering movement and succession of minds, a gallery of images, each of which, equipped with the complete wealth of mind, only seems to linger because the Self has to penetrate and to digest this wealth of its Substance. As its perfection consists in coming completely to know what it is (its substance), this knowledge is its self-involution in which it deserts its outward existence and surrenders its shape to recollection. Thus self-involved, it is sunk in the night of its self-consciousness: but in that night its vanished being is preserved, and that being, thus in idea preserved,—old, but now new-born of the spirit,—is the new sphere of being, a new world, a new phase of mind. In this new phase it has again to begin afresh and from the beginning, and again nurture itself to maturity from its own resources, as if for it all that preceded were lost, and it had learned nothing from the experience of the earlier minds. Yet is that recollection a preservation of experience: it is the quintessence, and in fact a higher form, of the substance. If therefore this new mind appears only to count on its own resources, and to start quite fresh and blank, it is at the same time on a higher grade that it starts. The intellectual and spiritual realm, which is thus constructed in actuality, forms a succession in time, where one mind relieved another of its watch, and each took over the kingdom of the world from the preceding. The purpose of that succession is to reveal the depth, and that depth is the absolute comprehension of mind: this revelation is therefore to uplift its depth, to spread it out in breadth, so negativing this self-involved Ego, wherein it is self-dispossessed or reduced to substance. But it is also its time: the course of time shows this dispossession itself dispossessed, and thus in its extension it is no less in its depth, the self. The way to that goal,—absolute self-certainty—or the mind knowing itself as mind—is the inwardising of the minds, as they severally are in themselves, and as they accomplish the organisation of their realm. Their conservation,—regarded on the side of its free and apparently contingent succession of fact—is history: on the side of their comprehended organisation, again, it is the science of mental phenomenology: the two together, comprehended history, form at once the recollection and the grave-yard of the absolute Mind, the actuality, truth, and certitude of his throne, apart from which he were lifeless and alone."

Such in brief outline—lingering most on the points where Hegel has here been briefest—is the range of the Philosophy of Mind. Its aim is to comprehend, not to explain: to put together in intelligent unity, not to analyse into a series of elements. For it psychology is not an analysis or description of mental phenomena, of laws of association, of the growth of certain powers and ideas, but a "comprehended history" of the formation of subjective mind, of the intelligent, feeling, willing self or ego. For it Ethics is part and only part of the great scheme or system of self-development; but continuing into greater concreteness the normal endowment of the individual mind, and but preparing the ground on which religion may be most effectively cultivated. And finally Religion itself, released from its isolation and other-world sacrosanctity, is shown to be only the crown of life, the ripest growth of actuality, and shown to be so by philosophy, whilst it is made clear that religion is the basis of philosophy, or that a philosophy can only go as far as the religious stand-point allows. The hierarchy, if so it be called, of the spiritual forces is one where none can stand alone, or claim an abstract and independent supremacy. The truth of egoism is the truth of altruism: the truly moral is the truly religious: and each is not what it professes to be unless it anticipate the later, or include the earlier.

(iv.) *Mind or Spirit.*

It may be said, however, that for such a range of subjects the term Mind is wretchedly inadequate and common-place, and that the better rendering of the title would be Philosophy of Spirit. It may be admitted that Mind is not all that could be wished. But neither is Spirit blameless. And, it may be added, Hegel's own term Geist has to be unduly strained to cover so wide a region. It serves—and was no doubt meant to serve—as a sign of the conformity of his system with the religion which sees in God no other-world being, but our very self and mind, and which worships him in spirit and in truth. And if the use of a word like this could allay the "ancient variance" between the religious and the philosophic mood, it would be but churlish perhaps to refuse the sign of compliance and compromise. But whatever may be the case in German,—and even there the new wine was dangerous to the old wine-skin—it is certain that to average English ears the word Spiritual would carry us over the medium line into the proper land of religiosity. And to do that, as we have seen, is to sin against the central idea: the idea that religion is of one blood with the whole mental family, though the most graciously complete of all the sisters. Yet, however the word may be chosen, the philosophy of Hegel, like the august lady who appeared in vision to the emprisoned Boëthius, has on her garment a sign which "signifies the life which is on earth," as also a sign which signifies the "right law of heaven"; if her right-hand holds the "book of the justice of the King omnipotent," the sceptre in her left is "corporal judgment against sin[20]."

There is indeed no sufficient reason for contemning the term Mind. If Inductive Philosophy of the Human Mind has—perhaps to a dainty taste—made the word unsavoury, that is no reason for refusing to give it all the wealth of soul and heart, of intellect and will. The mens aeterna which, if we hear Tacitus, expressed the Hebrew conception of the spirituality of God, and the Νοῦς which Aristotelianism set supreme in the Soul, are not the mere or abstract intelligence, which late-acquired habits of abstraction have made out of them. If the reader will adopt the term (in want of a better) in its widest scope, we may shelter ourselves under the example of Wordsworth. His theme is—as he describes it in the Recluse—"the Mind and Man": his

> *"voice proclaims*
> *How exquisitely the individual Mind*
> *(And the progressive powers perhaps no less*
> *Of the whole species) to the external World*
> *Is fitted;—and how exquisitely too*
> *The external World is fitted to the Mind;*
> *And the creation (by no lower name*
> *Can it be called) which they with blended might*
> *Accomplish."*

The verse which expounds that "high argument" speaks

> *"Of Truth, of Grandeur, Beauty, Love and Hope*
> *And melancholy Fear subdued by Faith."*

And the poet adds:

> *"As we look*
> *Into our Minds, into the Mind of Man—*
> *My haunt, and the main region of my song;*
> *Beauty—a living Presence of the earth*
> *Surpassing the most fair ideal forms*
> *... waits upon my steps."*

The reality duly seen in the spiritual vision

> *"That inspires*
> *The human Soul of universal earth*
> *Dreaming of things to come"*

will be a greater glory than the ideals of imaginative fiction ever fancied:

> *"For the discerning intellect of Man,*
> *When wedded to this goodly universe*
> *In love and holy passion, shall find these*
> *A simple produce of the common day."*

If Wordsworth, thus, as it were, echoing the great conception of Francis Bacon,

> *"Would chant, in lonely peace, the spousal verse*
> *Of this great consummation,"*

perhaps the poet and the essayist may help us with Hegel to rate the Mind—the Mind of Man—at its highest value.

Essay II - Aims And Methods Of Psychology

It is not going too far to say that in common estimation psychology has as yet hardly reached what Kant has called the steady walk of science—der sichere Gang der Wissenschaft. To assert this is not, of course, to throw any doubts on the importance of the problems, or on the intrinsic value of the results, in the studies which have been prosecuted under that name. It is only to note the obvious fact that a number of inquiries of somewhat discrepant tone, method, and tendency have all at different times covered themselves under the common title of psychological, and that the work of orientation is as yet incomplete. Such a destiny seems inevitable, when a name is coined rather as the title of an unexplored territory, than fixed on to describe an accomplished fact.

(i.) *Psychology as a Science and as a Part of Philosophy.*

The De Anima of Aristotle, gathering up into one the work of Plato and his predecessors, may be said to lay the foundation of psychology. But even in it, we can already see that there are two elements or aspects struggling for mastery: two elements not unrelated or independent, but hard to keep fairly and fully in unity. On one hand there is the conception of Soul as a part of Nature, as a grade of existence in the physical or natural universe,—in the universe of things which suffer growth and change, which are never entirely "without matter," and are always attached to or present in body. From this point of view Aristotle urged that a sound and realistic psychology must, e.g. in its definition of a passion, give the prominent place to its physical (or material) expression, and not to its mental form or significance. It must remember, he said, that the phenomena or "accidents" are what really throw light on the nature or the "substance" of the Soul. On the other hand, there are two points to be considered. There is, first of all, the counterpoising remark that the conception of Soul as such, as a unity and common characteristic, will be determinative of the phenomena or "accidents,"—will settle, as it were, what we are to observe and look for, and how we are to describe our observations. And by the conception of Soul, is meant not a soul, as a thing or agent (subject) which has properties attaching to it; but soul, as the generic feature, the universal, which is set as a stamp on everything that claims to be psychical. In other words, Soul is one, not as a single thing contrasted with its attributes, activities, or exercises of force (such single thing will be shown by logic to be a metaphysical fiction); but as the unity of form and character, the comprehensive and identical feature, which is present in all its manifestations and exercises. But there is a second consideration. The question is asked by Aristotle whether it is completely and strictly accurate to put Soul under the category of natural objects. There is in it, or of it, perhaps, something, and something essential to it, which belongs to the order of the eternal and self-active: something which is "form" and "energy" quite unaffected by and separate from "matter." How this is related to the realm of the perishable and changeable is a problem on which Aristotle has been often (and with some reason) believed to be obscure, if not even inconsistent[21].

In these divergent elements which come to the fore in Aristotle's treatment we have the appearance of a radical difference of conception and purpose as to psychology. He himself does a good deal to keep them both in view. But it is evident that here already we have the contrast between a purely physical or (in the narrower sense) "scientific" psychology, empirical and realistic in treatment, and a more philosophical—what in certain quarters would be called a speculative or metaphysical—conception of the problem. There is also in Aristotle the antithesis of a popular or superficial, and an accurate or analytic, psychology. The former is of a certain use in dealing, say, with questions of practical ethics and education: the latter is of more strictly scientific interest. Both of these distinctions—that between a speculative and an empirical, and that between a scientific and a popular treatment—affect the subsequent history of the study. Psychology is sometimes understood to mean the results of casual observation of our own minds by what is termed introspection, and by the interpretation of what we may observe in others. Such observations are in the first place carried on under the guidance of distinctions or points of view supplied by the names in common use. We interrogate our own consciousness as to what facts or relations of facts correspond to the terms of our national language. Or we attempt—what is really an inexhaustible quest—to get definite divisions between them, and clear-cut definitions. Inquiries like these which start from popular distinctions fall a long way short of science: and the inquirer will find that accidental and essential properties are given in the same handful of conclusions. Yet there is always much value in these attempts to get our minds cleared: and it is indispensable for all inquiries that all alleged or reported facts of mind should be realised and reproduced in our own mental experience. And this is especially the case in psychology, just because here we cannot get the object outside us, we cannot get or make a diagram, and unless we give it reality by re-constructing it,—by re-interrogating our own experience, our knowledge of it will be but wooden and mechanical. And the term introspection need not be too seriously taken: it means much more than watching passively an internal drama; and is quite as well describable as mental projection, setting out what was within, and so as it were hidden and involved, before ourselves in the field of mental vision. Here, as always, the essential point is to get ourselves well out of the way of the object observed, and to stand, figuratively speaking, quite on one side.

But even at the best, such a popular or empirical psychology has no special claim to be ranked as science. It may no doubt be said that at least it collects, describes, or notes down facts. But even this is not so certain as it seems. Its so-called facts are very largely fictions, or so largely interpolated with error, that they cannot be safely used for construction. If psychology is to accomplish anything valuable, it must go more radically to work. It must—at least in a measure—discard from its preliminary view the data of common and current distinctions, and try to get at something more primary or ultimate as its starting-point. And this it may do in two ways. It may, in the one case, follow the example of the physical sciences. In these it is the universal practice to assume that the explanation of complex and concrete facts is to be attained by (a) postulating certain simple elements (which we may call atoms, molecules, and perhaps units or monads), which are supposed to be clearly conceivable and to justify themselves by intrinsic intelligibility, and by (b) assuming that these elements are compounded and combined according to laws which again are in the last resort self-evident, or such that they seem to have an obvious and palpable lucidity. Further, such laws being always axioms or plain postulates of mechanics (for these alone possess this feature of self-evident intelligibility), they are subject to and invite all the aids and refinements of the higher mathematical calculus. What the primary and self-explicative bits of psychical reality may be, is a further question on which there may be some dispute. They may be, so to say, taken in a more physical or in a more metaphysical way: i.e. more as units of nerve-function or more as elements of ideative-function. And there may be differences as to how far and in what provinces the mathematical calculus may be applicable. But, in any case, there will be a strong tendency in psychology, worked on this plan, to follow, mutatis mutandis, and at some distance perhaps, the analogy of material physics. In both the justification of the postulated units and laws will be their ability to describe and systematise the observed phenomena in a uniform and consistent way.

The other way in which psychology gets a foundation and ulterior certainty is different, and goes deeper. After all, the "scientific" method is only a way in which the facts of a given sphere are presented in thoroughgoing interconnexion, each reduced to an exact multiple or fraction of some other, by an inimitably continued subtraction and addition of an assumed homogeneous element, found or assumed to be perfectly imaginable (conceivable). But we may also consider the province in relation to the whole sphere of reality, may ask what is its place and meaning in the whole, what reality is in the end driving at or coming to be, and how far this special province contributes to that end. If we do this, we attach psychology to philosophy, or, if we prefer so to call it, to metaphysics, as in the former way we established it on the principles generally received as governing the method of the physical sciences.

This—the relation of psychology to fundamental philosophy—is a question which also turns up in dealing with Ethics. There is on the part of those engaged in either of these inquiries a certain impatience against the intermeddling (which is held to be only muddling) of metaphysics with them. It is clear that in a very decided way both psychology and ethics can, up to some extent at least, be treated as what is called empirical (or, to use the more English phrase, inductive) sciences. On many hands they are actually so treated: and not without result. Considering the tendency of metaphysical inquiries, it may be urged that it is well to avoid preliminary criticism of the current conceptions and beliefs about reality which these sciences imply. Yet such beliefs are undoubtedly present and effective.

Schopenhauer has popularised the principle that the pure empiricist is a fiction, that man is a radically metaphysical animal, and that he inevitably turns what he receives into a part of a dogmatic creed—a conviction how things ought to be. Almost without effort there grows up in him, or flows in upon him, a belief and a system of beliefs as to the order and values of things. Every judgment, even in logic, rests on such an order of truth. He need not be able to formulate his creed: it will influence him none the less: nay, his faith will probably seem more a part of the solid earth and common reality, the less it has been reduced to a determinate creed or to a code of principles. For such formulation presupposes doubt and scepticism, which it beats back by mere assertion. Each human being has such a background of convictions which govern his actions and conceptions, and of which it so startles him to suggest the possibility of a doubt, that he turns away in dogmatic horror. Such ruling ideas vary, from man to man, and from man to woman—if we consider them in all their minuteness. But above all they constitute themselves in a differently organised system or aggregate according to the social and educational stratum to which an individual belongs. Each group, engaged in a common task, it may be in the study of a part of nature, is ideally bound and obliged by a common language, and special standards of truth and reality for its own. Such a group of ideas is what Bacon would have called a scientific fetich or idolum theatri. A scientific idolum is a traditional belief or dogma as to principles, values, and methods, which has so thoroughly pervaded the minds of those engaged in a branch of inquiry, that they no longer recognise its hypothetical character,—its relation of means to the main end of their function.

Such a collected and united theory of reality (it is what Hegel has designated the Idea) is what is understood by a natural metaphysic. It has nothing necessarily to do with a supersensible or a supernatural, if these words mean a ghostly, materialised, but super-finely-materialised nature, above and beyond the present. But that there is a persistent tendency to conceive the unity and coherence, the theoretic idea of reality, in this pseudo-sensuous (i.e. super-sensuous) form, is of course a well-known fact. For the present, however, this aberration—this idol of the tribe—may be left out of sight. By a metaphysic or fundamental philosophy, is, in the present instance, meant a system of first principles—a secular and cosmic creed: a belief in ends and values, a belief in truth—again premising that the system in question is, for most, a rudely organised and almost inarticulate mass of belief and hope, conviction and impression. It is, in short, a natural metaphysic: a metaphysic, that is, which has but an imperfect coherence, which imperfectly realises both its nature and its limits.

In certain parts, however, it is more and better than this crude background of belief. Each science—or at least every group of sciences—has a more definite system or aggregate of first principles, axioms, and conceptions belonging to it. It has, that is,—and here in a much distincter way—its special standard of reality, its peculiar forms of conceiving things, its distinctions between the actual and the apparent, &c. Here again it will probably be found that the scientific specialist is hardly conscious that these are principles and concepts: on the contrary, they will be supposed self-evident and ultimate facts, foundations of being. Instead of being treated as modes of conception, more or less justified by their use and their results, these categories will be regarded as fundamental facts, essential conditions of all reality. Like popular thought in its ingrained categories, the specialist cannot understand the possibility of any limitation to his radical ideas of reality. To him they are not hypotheses, but principles. The scientific specialist may be as convinced of the universal application of his peculiar categories, as the Chinese or the Eskimo that his standards are natural and final.

Under such metaphysical or extra-empirical presuppositions all investigation, whether it be crudely empirical or (in the physical sense) scientific, is carried on. And when so carried on, it is said to be prosecuted apart from any interference from metaphysic. Such a naïve or natural metaphysic, not raised to explicit consciousness, not followed as an imposed rule, but governing with the strength of an immanent faith, does not count for those who live under it as a metaphysic at all. M. Jourdain was amazed suddenly to learn he had been speaking prose for forty years without knowing it. But in the present case there is something worse than amazement sure to be excited by the news. For the critic who thus reveals the secrets of the scientist's heart is pretty sure to go on to say that a good deal of this naïve unconscious metaphysic is incoherent, contradictory, even bad: that it requires correction, revision, and readjustment, and has by criticism to be made one and harmonious. That readjustment or criticism which shall eliminate contradiction and produce unity, is the aim of the science of metaphysic—the science of the meta-physical element in physical knowledge: what Hegel has chosen to call the Science of Logic (in the wide sense of the term). This higher Logic, this science of metaphysic, is the process to revise and harmonise in systematic completeness the imperfect or misleading and partial estimates of reality which are to be found in popular and scientific thought.

In the case of the run of physical sciences this revision is less necessary; and for no very recondite reason. Every science by its very nature deals with a special, a limited topic. It is confined to a part or aspect of reality. Its propositions are not complete truths; they apply to an artificial world, to a part expressly cut off from the concrete reality. Its principles are generally cut according to their cloth,— according to the range in which they apply. The only danger that can well arise is if these categories are transplanted without due reservations, and made of universal application, i.e. if the scientist elects on his speciality to pronounce de omnibus rebus. But in the case of psychology and ethics the harmlessness of natural metaphysics will be less certain. Here a general human or universal interest is almost an inevitable coefficient: especially if they really rise to the full sweep of the subject. For as such they both seem to deal not with a part of reality, but with the very centre and purpose of all reality. In them we are not dealing with topics of secondary interest, but with the very heart of the human problem. Here the questions of reality and ideals, of unity and diversity, and of the evaluation of existence, come distinctly to the fore. If psychology is to answer the question, What am I? and ethics the question, What ought I to do? they can hardly work without some formulated creed of metaphysical character, without some preliminary criticisms of current first principles.

(ii.) *Herbart.*

The German thinker, who has given perhaps the most fruitful stimulus to the scientific study of psychology in modern times—Johann Friedrich Herbart—is after all essentially a philosopher, and not a mere scientist, even in his psychology. His psychological inquiry, that is, stands in intimate connexion with the last questions of all intelligence, with metaphysics and ethics. The business of philosophy, says Herbart, is to touch up and finish off conceptions (Bearbeitung der Begriffe)[22]. It finds, as it supervenes upon the unphilosophical world, that mere and pure facts (if there ever are or were such purisms) have been enveloped in a cloud of theory, have been construed into some form of unity, but have been imperfectly, inadequately construed: and that the existing concepts in current use need to be corrected, supplemented and readjusted. It has, accordingly, for its work to "reconcile experience with itself[23]," and to elicit "the hidden pre-suppositions without which the fact of experience is unthinkable."

Psychology, then, as a branch of this philosophic enterprise, has to readjust the facts discovered in inner experience. For mere uncritical experience or merely empirical knowledge only offers problems; it suggests gaps, which indeed further reflection serves at first only to deepen into contradictions. Such a psychology is "speculative": i.e. it is not content to accept the mere given, but goes forward and backward to find something that will make the fact intelligible. It employs totally different methods from the "classification, induction, analogy" familiar to the logic of the empirical sciences. Its "principles," therefore, are not given facts: but facts which have been manipulated and adjusted so as to lose their self-contradictory quality: they are facts "reduced," by introducing the omitted relationships which they postulate if they are to be true and self-consistent[24]. While it is far from rejecting or ignoring experience, therefore, psychology cannot strictly be said to build upon it alone. It uses experimental fact as an unfinished datum,—or it sees in experience a torso which betrays its imperfection, and suggests completing.

The starting-point, it may be said, of Herbart's psychology is a question which to the ordinary psychologist (and to the so-called scientific psychologist) has a secondary, if it have any interest. It was, he says, the problem of Personality, the problem of the Self or Ego, which first led to his characteristic conception of psychological method. "My first discovery," he tells us[25], "was that the Self was neither primitive nor independent, but must be the most dependent and most conditioned thing one can imagine. The second was that the elementary ideas of an intelligent being, if they were ever to reach the pitch of self-consciousness, must be either all, or at least in part, opposed to each other, and that they must check or block one another in consequence of this opposition. Though held in check, however, these ideas were not to be supposed lost: they subsist as endeavours or tendencies to return into the position of actual idea, as soon as the check became, for any reason, either in whole or in part inoperative. This check could and must be calculated, and thus it was clear that psychology required a mathematical as well as a metaphysical foundation."

The place of the conception of the Ego in Kant's and Fichte's theory of knowledge is well known. Equally well known is Kant's treatment of the soul-reality or soul-substance in his examination of Rational Psychology. Whereas the (logical) unity of consciousness, or "synthetic unity of apperception," is assumed as a fundamental starting-point in explanation of our objective judgments, or of our knowledge of objective existence, its real (as opposed to its formal) foundation in a "substantial" soul is set aside as an illegitimate interpretation of, or inference from, the facts of inner experience. The belief in the separate unity and persistence of the soul, said Kant, is not a scientifically-warranted conclusion. Its true place is as an ineffaceable postulate of the faith which inspires human life and action. Herbart did not rest content with either of these—as he believed—dogmatic assumptions of his master. He did not fall in cheerfully with the idealism which seemed ready to dispense with a soul, or which justified its acceptance of empirical reality by referring to the fundamental unity of the function of judgment. With a strong bent towards fully-differentiated and individualised experience Herbart conjoined a conviction of the need of logical analysis to prevent us being carried away by the first-come and inadequate generalities. The Ego which, in its extremest abstraction, he found defined as the unity of subject and object, did not seem to him to offer the proper guarantees of reality: it was itself a problem, full of contradictions, waiting for solution. On the other hand, the real Ego, or self of concrete experience, is very much more than this logical abstract, and differs widely from individual to individual, and apparently from time to time even in the same individual. Our self, of which we talk so fluently, as one and the self-same—how far does it really possess the continuity and identity with which we credit it? Does it not rather seem to be an ideal which we gradually form and set before ourselves as the standard for measuring our attainments of the moment,—the perfect fulfilment of that oneness of being and purpose and knowledge which we never reach? Sometimes even it seems no better than a name which we move along the varying phenomena of our inner life, at one time identifying it with the power which has gained the victory in a moral struggle, at another with that which has been defeated[26], according as the attitude of the moment makes us throw now one, now another, aspect of mental activity in the foreground.

The other—or logical Ego—the mere identity of subject and object,—when taken in its utter abstractness and simplicity, shrivels up to something very small indeed—to a something which is little better than nothing. The mere I which is not contra-distinguished by a Thou and a He—which is without all definiteness of predication (the I=I of Fichte and Schelling)—is only as it were a point of being cut off from all its connexions in reality, and treated as if it were or could be entirely independent. It is an identity in which subject and object have not yet appeared: it is not a real I, though we may still retain the name. It is—as Hegel's Logic will tell us—exactly definable as Being, which is as yet Nothing: the impossible edge of abstraction on which we try—and in vain—to steady ourselves at the initial point of thought. And to reach or stand at that intangible, ungraspable point, which slips away as we approach, and transmutes itself as we hold it, is not the natural beginning, but the result of introspection and reflection on the concrete self. But with this aspect of the question we are not now concerned.

That the unity of the Self as an intelligent and moral being, that the Ego of self-consciousness was an ideal and a product of development, was what Herbart soon became convinced of. The unity of Self is even as given in mature experience an imperfect fact. It is a fact, that is, which does not come up to what it promised, and which requires to be supplemented, or philosophically justified. Here and everywhere the custom of life carries us over gaps which yawn deep to the eye of philosophic reflection: even though accident and illness force them not unfrequently even upon the blindest. To trace the process of unification towards this unity—to trace, if you like, even the formation of the concept of such unity, as a governing and guiding principle in life and conduct, comes to be the problem of the psychologist, in the largest sense of that problem. From Soul (Seele) to Mind or Spirit (Geist) is for Herbart, as for Hegel, the course of psychology[27]. The growth and development of mind, the formation of a self, the realisation of a personality, is for both the theme which psychology has to expound. And Herbart, not less than Hegel, had to bear the censure that such a conception of mental reality as a growth would destroy personality[28].

But with so much common in the general plan, the two thinkers differ profoundly in their special mode of carrying out the task. Or, rather, they turn their strength on different departments of the whole. Herbart's great practical interest had been the theory of education: "paedagogic" is the subject of his first important writings. The inner history of ideas—the processes which are based on the interaction of elements in the individual soul—are what he specially traces. Hegel's interests, on the contrary, are more towards the greater process, the unities of historical life, and the correlations of the powers of art, religion, and philosophy that work therein. He turns to the macrocosm, almost as naturally as Herbart does to the microcosm. Thus, even in Ethics, while Herbart gives a delicate analysis of the distinct aspects or elements in the Ethical idea,—the diverse headings under which the disinterested spectator within the breast measures with purely aesthetic eye his approach to unity and strength of purpose, Hegel seems to hurry away from the field of moral sense or conscience to throw himself on the social and political organisation of the moral life. The General Paedagogic of Herbart has its pendant in Hegel's Philosophy of Law and of History.

At an early period Herbart had become impressed with the necessity of applying mathematics to psychology[29]. To the usual objection, that psychical facts do not admit of measurement, he had a ready reply. We can calculate even on hypothetical assumptions: indeed, could we measure, we should scarcely take the trouble to calculate[30]. To calculate (i.e. to deduce mathematically) is to perform a general experiment, and to perform it in the medium where there is least likelihood of error or disturbance. There may be anomalies enough apparent in the mental life: there may be the great anomalies of Genius and of Freedom of Will; but the Newton and the Kepler of psychology will show by calculation on assumed conditions of psychic nature that these aberrations can be explained by mechanical laws. "The human Soul is no puppet-theatre: our wishes and resolutions are no marionettes: no juggler stands behind; but our true and proper life lies in our volition, and this life has its rule not outside, but in itself: it has its own purely mental rule, by no means borrowed from the material world. But this rule is in it sure and fixed; and on account of this its fixed quality it has more similarity to (what is otherwise heterogeneous) the laws of impact and pressure than to the marvels of an alleged inexplicable freedom[31]."

Psychology then deals with a real, which exhibits phenomena analogous in several respects to those discussed by statics and mechanics. Its foundation is a statics and mechanics of the Soul,—as this real is called. We begin by presupposing as the ultimate reality, underlying the factitious and generally imperfect unity of self-consciousness and mind, an essential and primary unity—the unity of an absolutely simple or individual point of being—a real point which amongst other points asserts itself, maintains itself. It has a character of its own, but that character it only shows in and through a development conditioned by external influences. The specific nature of the soul-reality is to be representative, to produce, or manifest itself in, ideas (Vorstellungen). But the character only emerges into actuality in the conflict of the soul-atom with other ultimate realities in the congregation of things. A soul per se or isolated is not possessed of ideas. It is merely blank, undeveloped, formal unity, of which nothing can be said. But like other realities it defines and characterises itself by antithesis, by resistance: it shows what it is by its behaviour in the struggle for existence. It acts in self-defence: and its peculiar style or weapon of self-defence is an idea or representation. The way the Soul maintains itself is by turning the assailant into an idea[32]: and each idea is therefore a Selbsterhaltung of the Soul. The Soul is thus enriched—to appearance or incidentally: and the assailant is annexed. In this way the one Soul may develop or evolve or express an innumerable variety of ideas: for in response to whatever it meets, the living and active Soul ideates, or gives rise to a representation. Thus, while the soul is one, its ideas or representations are many. Taken separately, they each express the psychic self-conservation. But brought in relation with each other, as so many acts or self-affirmations of the one soul, they behave as forces, and tend to thwart or check each other. It is as forces, as reciprocally arresting or fostering each other, that ideas are objects of science. When a representation is thus held in check, it is reduced to a mere endeavour or active tendency to represent. Thus there arises a distinction between representations proper, and those imperfect states or acts which are partly or wholly held in abeyance.

But the latent phase of an idea is as essential to a thorough understanding of it as what appears. It is the great blunder of empirical psychology to ignore what is sunk below the surface of consciousness. And to Herbart consciousness is not the condition but rather the product of ideas, which are primarily forces.

But representations are not merely in opposition,—impinging and resisting. The same reason which makes them resist, viz. that they are or would fain be acts of the one soul, but are more or less incompatible, leads them in other circumstances to form combinations with each other. These combinations are of two sorts. They are, first, complications, or "complexions": a number of ideas combine by quasi-addition and juxtaposition to form a total. Second, there is fusion: ideas presenting certain degrees of contrast enter into a union where the parts are no longer separately perceptible. It is easy to see how the problems of psychology now assume the form of a statics and mechanics of the mind. Quantitative data are to be sought in the strength of each separate single idea, and the degree in which two or more ideas block each other: in the degree of combination between ideas, and the number of ideas in a combination: and in the terms of relation between the members of a series of ideas. A statical theory has to show the conditions required for what we may call the ideal state of equilibrium of the "idea-forces": to determine, that is, the ultimate degree of obscuration suffered by any two ideas of different strength, and the conditions of their permanent combination or fusion. A mechanics of the mind will, on the contrary, deal with the rate at which these processes are brought about, the velocity with which in the movement of mind ideas are obscured or reawakened, &c.

It is fortunately unnecessary, here, to go further into details. What Herbart proposes is not a method for the mathematical measurement of psychic facts: it is a theory of mechanics and statics specially adapted to the peculiarities of psychical phenomena, where the forces are given with no sine or cosine, where instead of gravitation we have the constant effort (as it were elasticity) of each idea to revert to its unchecked state. He claims—in short—practically to be a Kepler and Newton of the mind, and in so doing to justify the vague professions of more than one writer on mind—above all, perhaps of David Hume, who goes beyond mere professions—to make mental science follow the example of physics. And a main argument in favour of his enterprise is the declaration of Kant that no body of knowledge can claim to be a science except in such proportion as it is mathematical. And the peculiarity of this enterprise is that self-consciousness, the Ego, is not allowed to interfere with the free play of psychic forces. The Ego is—psychologically—the result, the product, and the varying product of that play. The play of forces is no doubt a unity: but its unity lies not in the synthesis of consciousness, but in the essential unity of Soul. And Soul is in its essence neither consciousness, nor self-consciousness, nor mind: but something on the basis of whose unity these are built up and developed[33]. The mere "representation" does not include the further supervenience of consciousness: it represents, but it is not as yet necessary that we should also be conscious that there is representation. It is, in the phrase of Leibniz, perception: but not apperception. It is mere straight-out, not as yet reflected, representation. Gradually there emerges through the operation of mechanical psychics a nucleus, a floating unity, a fixed or definite central aggregate.

The suggestion of mathematical method has been taken up by subsequent inquirers (as it was pursued even before Herbart's time), but not in the sense he meant. Experimentation has now taken a prominent place in psychology. But in proportion as it has done so, psychology has lost its native character, and thrown itself into the arms of physiology. What Herbart calculated were actions and reactions of idea-forces: what the modern experimental school proposes to measure are to a large extent the velocities of certain physiological processes, the numerical specification of certain facts. Such ascertainments are unquestionably useful; as numerical precision is in other departments. But, taken in themselves, they do not carry us one bit further on the way to science. As experiments, further,—to note a point discussed elsewhere[34]—their value depends on the point of view, on the theory which has led to them, on the value of the general scheme for which they are intended to provide a special new determination. In many cases they serve to give a vivid reality to what was veiled under a general phrase. The truth looks so much more real when it is put in figures: as the size of a huge tree when set against a rock; or as when Milton bodies out his fallen angel by setting forth the ratio between his spear and the tallest Norway pine. But until the general relationship between soul and body is more clearly formulated, such statistics will have but a value of curiosity.

(iii.) *The Faculty-Psychology and its Critics.*

What Herbart (as well as Hegel) finds perpetual ground for objecting to is the talk about mental faculties. This objection is part of a general characteristic of all the higher philosophy; and the recurrence of it gives an illustration of how hard it is for any class of men to see themselves as others see them. If there be anything the vulgar believe to be true of philosophy, it is that it deals in distant and abstruse generalities, that it neglects the shades of individuality and reality, and launches out into unsubstantial general ideas. But it would be easy to gather from the great thinkers an anthology of passages in which they hold it forth as the great work of philosophy to rescue our conceptions from the indefiniteness and generality of popular conception, and to give them real, as opposed to a merely nominal, individuality.

The Wolffian school, which Herbart (not less than Kant) found in possession of the field, and which in Germany may be taken to represent only a slight variant of the half-and-half attitude of vulgar thought, was entrenched in the psychology of faculties. Empirical psychology, said Wolff[35], tells the number and character of the soul's faculties: rational psychology will tell what they "properly" are, and how they subsist in soul. It is assumed that there are general receptacles or tendencies of mental operation which in course of time get filled or qualified in a certain way: and that when this question is disposed of, it still remains to fix on the metaphysical bases of these facts.

That a doctrine of faculties should fix itself in psychology is not so wonderful. In the non-psychical world objects are easily discriminated in space, and the individual thing lasts through a time. But a phase of mind is as such fleeting and indeterminate: its individual features which come from its "object" tend soon to vanish in memory: all freshness of definite characters wears off, and there is left behind only a vague "recept" of the one and same in many, a sort of hypostatised representative, faint but persistent, of what in experience was an ever-varying succession. We generalise here as elsewhere: but elsewhere the many singulars remain to confront us more effectually. But in Mind the immense variety of real imagination, memory, judgment is forgotten, and the name in each case reduced to a meagre abstract. Thus the identity in character and operation, having been cut off from the changing elements in its real action, is transmuted into a substantial somewhat, a subsistent faculty. The relationship of one to another of the powers thus by abstraction and fancy created becomes a problem of considerable moment, their causal relations in particular: till in the end they stand outside and independent of each other, engaged, as Herbart says, in a veritable bellum omnium contra omnes.

But this hypostatising of faculties becomes a source of still further difficulties when it is taken in connexion with the hypostasis of the Soul or Self or Ego. To Aristotle the Soul in its general aspect is Energy or Essence; and its individual phases are energies. But in the hands of the untrained these conceptions came to be considerably displaced. Essence or Substance came to be understood (as may be seen in Locke, and still more in loose talk) as a something,—a substratum,—or peculiar nature—(of which in itself nothing further could be said[36] but which notwithstanding was permanent and perhaps imperishable): this something subsistent exhibited certain properties or activities. There thus arose, on one hand, the Soul-thing,—a substance misunderstood and sensualised with a supernatural sensuousness,—a denizen of the transcendental or even of the transcendent world: and, on the other hand, stood the actual manifestations, the several exhibitions of this force, the assignable and describable psychic facts. We are accordingly brought before the problem of how this one substance or essence stands to the several entities or hypostases known as faculties. And we still have in the rear the further problem of how these abstract entities stand to the real and concrete single acts and states of soul and mind.

This hypostatising of faculties, and this distinction of the "Substantial" soul from its "accidentia" or phenomena, had grown—through the materialistic proclivities of popular conception—from the indications found in Aristotle. It attained its climax, perhaps in the Wolffian school in Germany, but it has been the resort of superficial psychology in all ages. For while it, on one hand, seemed to save the substantial Soul on whose incorruptibility great issues were believed to hinge, it held out, on the other, an open hand to the experimental inquirer, whom it bade freely to search amongst the phenomena. But if it was the refuge of pusillanimity, it was also the perpetual object of censure from all the greater and bolder spirits. Thus, the psychology of Hobbes may be hasty and crude, but it is at least animated by a belief that the mental life is continuous, and not cut off by abrupt divisions severing the mental faculties. The "image" (according to his materialistically coloured psychology) which, when it is a strong motion, is called sense, passes, as it becomes weaker or decays, into imagination, and gives rise, by its various complications and associations with others, to reminiscence, experience, expectation. Similarly, the voluntary motion which is an effect or a phase of imagination, beginning at first in small motions—called by themselves "endeavours," and in relation to their cause "appetites" or "desires[37]"—leads on cumulatively to Will, which is the "last appetite in deliberating." Spinoza, his contemporary, speaks in the same strain[38]. "Faculties of intellect, desire, love, &c., are either utterly fictitious, or nothing but metaphysical entities, or universals which we are in the habit of forming from particulars. Will and intellect are thus supposed to stand to this or that idea, this or that volition, in the same way as stoniness to this or that stone, or as man to Peter or Paul." They are supposed to be a general something which gets defined and detached. But, in the mind, or in the cogitant soul, there are no such things. There are only ideas: and by an "idea" we are to understand not an image on the retina or in the brain, not a "dumb something, like a painting on a panel[39]," but a mode of thinking, or even the act of intellection itself. The ideas are the mind: mind does not have ideas. Further, every "idea," as such, "involves affirmation or negation,"—is not an image, but an act of judgment—contains, as we should say, an implicit reference to actuality,—a reference which in volition is made explicit. Thus (concludes the corollary of Eth. ii. 49) "Will and Intellect are one and the same." But in any case the "faculties" as such are no better than entia rationis (i.e. auxiliary modes of representing facts).

Leibniz speaks no less distinctly and sanely in this direction. "True powers are never mere possibilities: they are always tendency and action." The "Monad"—that is the quasi-intelligent unit of existence,—is essentially activity, and its actions are perceptions and appetitions, i.e. tendencies to pass from one perceptive state or act to another. It is out of the variety, the complication, and relations of these miniature or little perceptions and appetitions, that the conspicuous phenomena of consciousness are to be explained, and not by supposing them due to one or other faculty. The soul is a unity, a self-developing unity, a unity which at each stage of its existence shows itself in a perception or idea,—each such perception however being, to repeat the oft quoted phrase, plein de l'avenir et chargé du passé:—each, in other words, is not stationary, but active and urgent, a progressive force, as well as a representative element. Above all, Leibniz has the view that the soul gives rise to all its ideas from itself: that its life is its own production, not a mere inheritance of ideas which it has from birth and nature, nor a mere importation into an empty room from without, but a necessary result of its own constitution acting in necessary (predetermined) reciprocity and harmony with the rest of the universe.

But Hobbes, Spinoza, and Leibniz, were most attentively heard in the passages where they favoured or combatted the dominant social and theological prepossessions. Their glimpses of truer insight and even their palpable contributions in the line of a true psychology were ignored or forgotten. More attention, perhaps, was attracted by an attempt of a very different style. This was the system of Condillac, who, as Hegel says (p. 61), made an unmistakable attempt to show the necessary interconnexion of the several modes of mental activity. In his Traité des Sensations (1754), following on his Essai sur l'origine des connaissances humaines (1746), he tried to carry out systematically the deduction or derivation of all our ideas from sense, or to trace the filiation of all our faculties from sensation. Given a mind with no other power than sensibility, the problem is to show how it acquires all its other faculties. Let us then suppose a sentient animal to which is offered a single sensation, or one sensation standing out above the others. In such circumstances the sensation "becomes" (devient) attention: or a sensation "is" (est) attention, either because it is alone, or because it is more lively than all the rest. Again: before such a being, let us set two sensations: to perceive or feel (apercevoir ou sentir) the two sensations is the same thing (c'est la même chose). If one of the sensations is not present, but a sensation made already, then to perceive it is memory. Memory, then, is only "transformed sensation" (sensation transformée). Further, suppose we attend to both ideas, this is "the same thing" as to compare them. And to compare them we must see difference or resemblance. This is judgment. "Thus sensation becomes successively attention, comparison, judgment." And—by further steps of the equating process—it appears that sensation again "becomes" an act of reflection. And the same may be said of imagination and reasoning: all are transformed sensations.

If this is so with the intelligence, it is equally the case with the Will. To feel and not feel well or ill is impossible. Coupling then this feeling of pleasure or pain with the sensation and its transformations, we get the series of phases ranging from desire, to passion, hope, will. "Desire is only the action of the same faculties as are attributed to the understanding." A lively desire is a passion: a desire, accompanied with a belief that nothing stands in its way, is a volition. But combine these affective with the intellectual processes already noticed, and you have thinking (penser)[40]. Thus thought in its entirety is, only and always, transformed sensation.

Something not unlike this, though scarcely so simply and directly doctrinaire, is familiar to us in some English psychology, notably James Mill's[41]. Taken in their literal baldness, these identifications may sound strained,—or trifling. But if we look beyond the words, we can detect a genuine instinct for maintaining and displaying the unity and continuity of mental life through all its modifications,—coupled unfortunately with a bias sometimes in favour of reducing higher or more complex states of mind to a mere prolongation of lower and beggarly rudiments. But otherwise such analyses are useful as aids against the tendency of inert thought to take every name in this department as a distinguishable reality: the tendency to part will from thought—ideas from emotion—and even imagination from reason, as if either could be what it professed without the other.

(iv.) *Methods and Problems of Psychology.*

The difficulties of modern psychology perhaps lie in other directions, but they are not less worth guarding against. They proceed mainly from failure or inability to grasp the central problem of psychology, and a disposition to let the pen (if it be a book on the subject) wander freely through the almost illimitable range of instance, illustration, and application. Though it is true that the proper study of mankind is man, it is hardly possible to say what might not be brought under this head. Homo sum, nihil a me alienum puto, it might be urged. Placed in a sort of middle ground between physiology (summing up all the results of physical science) and general history (including the contributions of all the branches of sociology), the psychologist need not want for material. He can wander into ethics, aesthetic, and logic, into epistemology and metaphysics. And it cannot be said with any conviction that he is actually trespassing, so long as the ground remains so ill-fenced and vaguely enclosed. A desultory collection of observations on traits of character, anecdotes of mental events, mixed up with hypothetical descriptions of how a normal human being may be supposed to develop his so-called faculties, and including some dictionary-like verbal distinctions, may make a not uninteresting and possibly bulky work entitled Psychology.

It is partly a desire of keeping up to date which is responsible for the copious extracts or abstracts from treatises on the anatomy and functions of the nerve-system, which, accompanied perhaps by a diagram of the brain, often form the opening chapter of a work on psychology. Even if these researches had achieved a larger number of authenticated results than they as yet have, they would only form an appendix and an illustration to the proper subject[42]. As they stand, and so long as they remain largely hypothetical, the use of them in psychology only fosters the common delusion that, when we can picture out in material outlines a theory otherwise unsupported, it has gained some further witness in its favour. It is quite arguable indeed that it may be useful to cut out a section from general human biology which should include the parts of it that were specially interesting in connexion with the expression or generation of thought, emotion, and desire. But in that case, there is a blunder in singling out the brain alone, and especially the organs of sense and voluntary motion,—except for the reason that this province of psycho-physics alone has been fairly mapped out. The preponderant half of the soul's life is linked to other parts of the physical system. Emotion and volition, and the general tone of the train of ideas, if they are to be connected with their expression and physical accompaniment (or aspect), would require a sketch of the heart and lungs, as well as the digestive system in general. Nor these alone. Nerve analysis (especially confined to the larger system), though most modern, is not alone important, as Plato and Aristotle well saw. So that if biology is to be adapted for psychological use (and if psychology deals with more than cognitive processes), a liberal amount of physiological information seems required.

Experimental psychology is a term used with a considerable laxity of content; and so too is that of physiological psychology, or psycho-physics. And the laxity mainly arises because there is an uncertainty as to what is principal and what secondary in the inquiry. Experiment is obviously a help to observation: and so far as the latter is practicable, the former would seem to have a chance of introduction. But in any case, experiment is only a means to an end and only practicable under the guidance of hypothesis and theory. Its main value would be in case the sphere of psychology were completely paralleled with one province of physiology. It was long ago maintained by Spinoza and (in a way by) Leibniz, that there is no mental phenomenon without its bodily equivalent, pendant, or correspondent. The ordo rerum (the molecular system of movements) is, he held, the same as the order of ideas. But it is only at intervals, under special conditions, or when they reach a certain magnitude, that ideas emerge into full consciousness. As consciousness presents them, they are often discontinuous, and abrupt: and they do not always carry with them their own explanation. Hence if we are confined to the larger phenomena of consciousness alone, our science is imperfect: many things seem anomalous; above all, perhaps, will, attention, and the like. We have seen how Herbart (partly following the hints of Leibniz), attempted to get over this difficulty by the hypothesis of idea-forces which generate the forms and matter of consciousness by their mutual impact and resistance. Physiological psychology substitutes for Herbart's reals and his idea-forces a more materialistic sort of reality; perhaps functions of nerve-cells, or other analogous entities. There, it hopes one day to discover the underlying continuity of event which in the upper range of consciousness is often obscured, and then the process would be, as the phrase goes, explained: we should be able to picture it out without a gap.

These large hopes may have a certain fulfilment. They may lead to the withdrawal of some of the fictitious mental processes which are still described in works of psychology. But on the whole they can only have a negative and auxiliary value. The value, that is, of helping to confute feigned connexions and to suggest truer. They will be valid against the mode of thought which, when Psyché fails us for an explanation, turns to body, and interpolates soul between the states of body: the mode which, in an older phraseology, jumps from final causes to physical, and from physical (or efficient) to final. Here, as elsewhere, the physical has its place: and here, more than in many places, the physical has been unfairly treated. But the whole subject requires a discussion of the so-called "relations" of soul and body: a subject on which popular conceptions and so-called science are radically obscure.

"But the danger which threatens experimental psychology," says Münsterberg, "is that, in investigating details, the connexion with questions of principle may be so lost sight of that the investigation finally lands at objects scientifically quite worthless[43]. Psychology forgets only too easily that all those numerical statistics which experiment allows us to form are only means for psychological analysis and interpretation, not ends in themselves. It piles up numbers and numbers, and fails to ask whether the results so formed have any theoretical value whatever: it seeks answers before a question has been clearly and distinctly framed; whereas the value of experimental answers always depends on the exactitude with which the question is put. Let me remind the reader, how one inquirer after another made many thousand experiments on the estimation of small intervals of time, without a single one of them raising the question what the precise point was which these experiments sought to measure, what was the psychological occurrence in the case, or what psychological phenomena were employed as the standard of time-intervals. And so each had his own arbitrary standard of measurement, each of them piled up mountains of numbers, each demonstrated that his predecessor was wrong; but neither Estel nor Mehner have carried the problem of the time-sense a single step further.

"This must be all changed, if we are not to drift into the barrenest scholastic.... Everywhere out of the correct perception that problems of principle demand the investigation of detailed phenomena, and that the latter investigation must proceed in comparative independence of the question of principles, there has grown the false belief that the description of detail phenomena is the ultimate aim of science. And so, side by side with details which are of importance to principles, we have others, utterly indifferent and theoretically worthless, treated with the same zeal. To the solution of their barren problems the old Schoolmen applied a certain acuteness; but in order to turn out masses of numbers from barren experiments, all that is needed is a certain insensibility to fits of ennui. Let numbers be less collected for their own sake: and instead, let the problems be so brought to a point that the answers may possess the character of principles. Let each experiment be founded on far more theoretical considerations, then the number of the experiments may be largely diminished[44]."

What is thus said of a special group of inquiries by one of the foremost of the younger psychologists, is not without its bearings on all the departments in which psychology can learn. For physiological, or what is technically called psychological, experiment, is co-ordinate with many other sources of information. Much, for instance, is to be learnt by a careful study of language by those who combine sound linguistic knowledge with psychological training. It is in language, spoken and written, that we find at once the great instrument and the great document of the distinctively human progress from a mere Psyche to a mature Nous, from Soul to Mind. Whether we look at the varieties of its structure under different ethnological influences, or at the stages of its growth in a nation and an individual, we get light from language on the differentiation and consolidation of ideas. But here again it is easy to lose oneself in the world of etymology, or to be carried away into the enticing questions of real and ideal philology.

"The human being of the psychologist," says Herbart[45], "is the social and civilised human being who stands on the apex of the whole history through which his race has passed. In him is found visibly together all the multiplicity of elements, which, under the name of mental faculties, are regarded as a universal inheritance of humanity. Whether they are originally in conjunction, whether they are originally a multiplicity, is a point on which the facts are silent. The savage and the new-born child give us far less occasion to admire the range of their mind than do the nobler animals. But the psychologists get out of this difficulty by the unwarranted assumption that all the higher mental activities exist potentially in children and savages—though not in the animals—as a rudimentary predisposition or psychical endowment. Of such a nascent intellect, a nascent reason, and nascent moral sense, they find recognisable traces in the scanty similarities which the behaviour of child or savage offers to those of civilised man. We cannot fail to note that in their descriptions they have before them a special state of man, and one which, far from accurately defined, merely follows the general impression made upon us by those beings we name civilised. An extremely fluctuating character inevitably marks this total impression. For there are no general facts:—the genuine psychological documents lie in the momentary states of individuals: and there is an immeasurably long way from these to the height of the universal concept of man in general."

And yet Man in general,—Man as man and therefore as mind—the concept of Man—normal and ideal man—the complete and adequate Idea of man—is the true terminus of the psychological process; and whatever be the difficulties in the way, it is the only proper goal of the science. Only it has to be built up, constructed, evolved, developed,—and not assumed as a datum of popular imagination. We want a concept, concrete and real, of Man and of Mind, which shall give its proper place to each of the elements that, in the several examples open to detailed observation, are presented with unfair or exaggerated prominence. The savage and the child are not to be left out as free from contributing to form the ideal: virtues here are not more important than vices, and are certainly not likely to be so informing: even the insane and the idiot show us what human intelligence is and requires: and the animals are also within the sweep of psychology. Man is not its theatre to the exclusion of woman; if it records the results of introspection of the Me, it will find vast and copious quarries in the various modes in which an individual identifies himself with others as We. And even the social and civilised man gets his designation, as usual, a potiori. He is more civilised and social than others: perhaps rather more civilised than not. But always, in some measure, he is at the same time unsocial or anti-social, and uncivilised. Each unit in the society of civilisation has to the outside observer—and sometimes even to his own self-detached and impartial survey—a certain oddity or fixity, a gleam of irrationality, which shows him to fall short of complete sanity or limpid and mobile intelligence. He has not wholly put off the savage,—least of all, says the cynic, in his relations with the other sex. He carries with him even to the grave some grains of the recklessness and petulance of childhood. And rarely, if ever, can it be said of him that he has completely let the ape and tiger die.

But that is only one way of looking at the matter—and one which, perhaps, is more becoming to the pathologist and the cynic, than to the psychologist. Each of these stages of psychical development, even if that development be obviously describable as degeneration, has something which, duly adjusted, has its place and function in the theory of the normally-complete human mind. The animal, the savage, and the child,—each has its part there. It is a mutilated, one-sided and superficial advance in socialisation which cuts off the civilised creature from the natural stem of his ancestry, from the large freedom, the immense insouciance, the childlikeness of his first estate. There is something, again, wanting in the man who utterly lacks the individualising realism and tenderness of the woman, as in the woman who can show no comprehension of view or bravery of enterprise. Even pathological states of mind are not mere anomalies and mere degenerations. Nature perhaps knows no proper degenerations, but only by-ways and intricacies in the course of development. Still less is the vast enormity or irregularity of genius to be ignored. It is all—to the philosophic mind—a question of degree and proportion,—though often the proportion seems to exceed the scale of our customary denominators. If an element is latent or quiescent (in arrest), that is no index to its absolute amount: "we know not what's resisted." Let us by all means keep proudly to our happy mediocrity of faculty, and step clear of insanity or idiotcy on one hand, and from genius or heroism on the other. But the careful observer will notwithstanding note how delicately graded and how intricately combined are the steps which connect extremes so terribly disparate. It is only vulgar ignorance which turns away in hostility or contempt from the imbecile and the deranged, and only a worse than vulgar sciolism which sees in genius and the hero nothing but an aberration from its much-prized average. Criminalistic anthropology, or the psychology of the criminal, may have indulged in much frantic exaggeration as to the doom which nature and heredity have pronounced over the fruit of the womb even before it entered the shores of light: yet they have at least served to discredit the free and easy assumption of the abstract averagist, and shown how little the penalties of an unbending law meet the requirements of social well-being.

Yet, if psychology be willing to learn in all these and other provinces of the estate of man, it must remember that, once it goes beyond the narrow range in which the interpretations of symbol and expression have become familiar, it is constantly liable to blunder in the inevitable effort to translate observation into theory. The happy mean between making too much of palpable differences and hurrying on to a similar rendering of similar signs is the rarest of gifts. Or, perhaps, it were truer to say it is the latest and most hardly won of acquirements. To learn to observe—observe with mind—is not a small thing. There are rules for it—both rules of general scope and, above all, rules in each special department. But like all "major premisses" in practice, everything depends on the power of judgment, the tact, the skill, the "gift" of applying them. They work not as mere rules to be conned by rote, but as principles assimilated into constituents of the mental life-blood: rules which serve only as condensed reminders and hints of habits of thought and methods of research which have grown up in action and reflection. To observe we must comprehend: yet we can only comprehend by observing. We all know how unintelligible—save for epochs of ampler reciprocity, and it may be even of acquired unity of interest—the two sexes are for each other. Parents can remember how mysteriously minded they found their own elders; and in most cases they have to experience the depth of the gulf which in certain directions parts them from their children's hearts. Even in civilised Europe, the ordinary member of each nation has an underlying conviction (which at moments of passion or surprise will rise and find harsh utterance) that the foreigner is queer, irrational, and absurd. If the foreigner, further, be so far removed as a Chinaman (or an Australian "black"), there is hardly anything too vile, meaningless, or inhuman which the European will not readily believe in the case of one who, it may be, in turn describes him as a "foreign devil." It can only be in a fit of noble chivalry that the British rank and file can so far temporise with its insular prejudice as to admit of "Fuzzy-wuzzy" that

> *"He's a poor benighted 'eathen—but a first-class fightin' man."*

Not every one is an observer who chooses to dub himself so, nor is it in a short lapse of time and with condescension for foreign habits, that any observer whatever can become a trustworthy reporter of the ideas some barbarian tribe holds concerning the things of earth and air, and the hidden things of spirits and gods. The "interviewer" no doubt is a useful being when it is necessary to find "copy," or when sharp-drawn characters and picturesque incidents are needed to stimulate an inert public, ever open to be interested in some new thing. But he is a poor contributor to the stored materials of science.

It is of other stuff that true science is made. And if even years of nominal intercourse and spatial juxtaposition sometimes leave human beings, as regards their inner selves, in the position of strangers still, what shall be said of the attempt to discern the psychic life of animals? Will the touch of curiosity which prompts us to watch the proceedings of the strange creatures,—will a course of experimentation on their behaviour under artificial conditions,—justify us in drawing liberal conclusions as to why they so behaved, and what they thought and felt about it? It is necessary in the first place to know what to observe, and how, and above all what for. But that presumed, we must further live with the animals not only as their masters and their examiners, but as their friends and fellow-creatures; we must be able—

and so lightly that no effort is discernable—to lay aside the burden and garb of civilisation; we must possess that stamp of sympathy and similarity which invites confidence, and breaks down the reserve which our poor relations, whether human or others, offer to the first approaches of a strange superior. It is probable that in that case we should have less occasion to wonder at their oddities or to admire their sagacity. But a higher and more philosophical wonder might, as in other cases when we get inside the heart of our subject, take the place of the cheap and childish love of marvels, or of the vulgar straining after comic traits.

Of all this mass of materials the psychologist proper can directly make only a sparing use. Even as illustrations, his data must not be presented too often in all their crude and undigested individuality, or he runs the risk of leaving one-sided impressions. Every single instance, individualised and historical,— unless it be exhibited by that true art of genius which we cannot expect in the average psychologist— narrows, even though it be but slightly, the complete and all-sided truth. Anecdotes are good, and to the wise they convey a world of meaning, but to lesser minds they sometimes suggest anything but the points they should accentuate. Without the detail of individual realistic study there is no psychology worth the name. History, story, we must have: but at the same time, with the philosopher, we must say, I don't give much weight to stories. And this is what will always—except in rare instances where something like genius is conjoined with it—make esoteric science hard and unpopular. It dare not—if it is true to its idea—rest on any amount of mere instances, as isolated, unreduced facts. Yet it can only have real power so far as it concentrates into itself the life-blood of many instances, and indeed extracts the pith and unity of all instances.

Nor, on the other hand, can it turn itself too directly and intently towards practical applications. All this theory of mental progress from the animate soul to the fullness of religion and science deals solely with the universal process of education: "the education of humanity" we may call it: the way in which mind is made true and real[46]. It is therefore a question of intricacy and of time how to carry over this general theory into the arena of education as artificially directed and planned. To try to do so at a single step would be to repeat the mistake of Plato, if Plato may be taken to suppose (which seems incredible) that a theoretical study of the dialectics of truth and goodness would enable his rulers, without the training of special experience, to undertake the supreme tasks of legislation or administration. All politics, like all education, rests on these principles of the means and conditions of mental growth: but the schooling of concrete life, though it may not develop the faculty of formulating general laws, will often train better for the management of the relative than a mere logical Scholastic in first or absolute principles.

In conclusion, there are one or two points which seem of cardinal importance for the progress of psychology. [1] Its difference from the physical sciences has to be set out: in other words, the peculiarity of psychical fact. It will not do merely to say that experience marks out these boundaries with sufficient clearness. On the contrary, the terms consciousness, feeling, mind, &c., are evidently to many psychologists mere names. In particular, the habits of physical research when introduced into mental study lead to a good deal of what can only be called mythology. [2] There should be a clearer recognition of the problem of the relations of mental unity to mental elements. But to get that, a more thorough logical and metaphysical preparation is needed than is usually supposed necessary. The doctrine of identity and necessity, of universal and individual, has to be faced, however tedious. [3] The distinction between first-grade and second-grade elements and factors in the mental life has to be realised. The mere idea as presentative or immediate has to be kept clear of the more logico-reflective, or normative ideas, which belong to judgment and reasoning. And the number of these grades in mental development seems endless. [4] But, also, a separation is required—were it but temporary—between what may be called principles, and what is detail. At present, in psychology, "principles" is a word almost without meaning. A complete all-explaining system is of course impossible at present and may always be so. Yet if an effort of thought could be concentrated on cardinal issues, and less padding of conventional and traditional detail were foisted in, much might thereby be done to make detailed research fruitful. [5] And finally, perhaps, if psychology be a philosophical study, some hint as to its purpose and problem would be desirable. If it is only an abstract branch of science, of course, no such hint is in place.

Essay III - On Some Psychological Aspects Of Ethics

Allusion has already been made to the question of the boundaries between logic and psychology, between logic and ethics, ethics and psychology, and psychology and epistemology. Each of these occasionally comes to cover ground that seems more appropriate to the others. Logic is sometimes restricted to denote the study of the conditions of derivative knowledge, of the canons of inference and the modes of proof. If taken more widely as the science of thought-form, it is supposed to imply a world of fixed or stereotyped relations between ideas, a system of stable thoughts governed by inflexible laws in an absolute order of immemorial or eternal truth. As against such fixity, psychology is supposed to deal with these same ideas as products—as growing out of a living process of thought—having a history behind them and perhaps a prospect of further change. The genesis so given may be either a mere chronicle-history, or it may be a philosophical development. In the former case, it would note the occasions of incident and circumstance, the reactions of mind and environment, under which the ideas were formed. Such a psychological genesis of several ideas is found in the Second Book of Locke's Essay. In the latter case, the account would be more concerned with the inner movement, the action and reaction in ideas themselves, considered not as due to casual occurrences, but as self-developing by an organic growth. But in either case, ideas would be shown not to be ready-made and independently existing kinds in a world of idea-things, and not to form an unchanging diagram or framework, but to be a growth, to have a history, and a development. Psychology in this sense would be a dynamical, as opposed to the supposed statical, treatment of ideas and concepts in logic. But it may be doubted how far it is well to call this psychology: unless psychology deals with the contents of the mental life, in their meaning and purpose, instead of, as seems proper, merely in their character of psychic events. Such psychology is rather an evolutionist logic,—a dialectic process more than an analytic of a datum.

In the same way, ethics may be brought into one kind of contact with psychology. Ethics, like logic, may be supposed to presuppose and to deal with a certain inflexible scheme of requirements, a world of moral order governed by invariable or universal law; an eternal kingdom of right, existing independently of human wills, but to be learned and followed out in uncompromising obedience. As against this supposed absolute order, psychology may be said to show the genesis of the idea of obligation and duty, the growth of the authority of conscience, the formation of ideals, the relativity of moral ideas. Here also it may reach this conclusion, by a more external or a more internal mode of argument. It may try to show, in other words, that circumstances give rise to these forms of estimating conduct, or it may argue that they are a necessary development in the human being, constituted as he is. It may again be doubted whether this is properly called psychology. Yet its purport seems ultimately to be that the objective order is misconceived when it is regarded as an external or quasi-physical order: as a law written up and sanctioned with an external authority—as, in Kant's words, a heteronomy. If that order is objective, it is so because it is also in a sense subjective: if it is above the mere individuality of the individual, it is still in a way identical with his true or universal self-hood. Thus "psychological" here means the recognition that the logical and the moral law is an autonomy: that it is not given, but though necessary, necessary by the inward movement of the mind. The metaphor of law is, in brief, misleading. For, according to a common, though probably an erroneous, analysis of that term, the essence of a law in the political sphere is to be a species of command. And that is rather a one-sidedly practical or aesthetic way of looking at it. The essence of law in general, and the precondition of every law in special, is rather uniformity and universality, self-consistency and absence of contradiction: or, in other words, rationality. Its essential opposite—or its contradiction in essence—is a privilege, an attempt at isolating a case from others. It need not indeed always require bare uniformity—require i.e. the same act to be done by different people: but it must always require that every thing within its operation shall be treated on principles of utter and thorough harmony and consistency. It requires each thing to be treated on public principles and with publicity: nothing apart and mere singular, as a mere incident or as a world by itself. Differently it may be treated, but always on grounds of common well-being, as part of an embracing system.

There is probably another sense, however, in which psychology comes into close relation with ethics. If we look on man as a microcosm, his inner system will more or less reproduce the system of the larger world. The older psychology used to distinguish an upper or superior order of faculties from a lower or inferior. Thus in the intellectual sphere, the intellect, judgment, and reason were set above the senses, imagination, and memory. Among the active powers, reasonable will, practical reason and conscience were ranked as paramount over the appetites and desires and emotions. And this use of the word "faculty" is as old as Plato, who regards science as a superior faculty to opinion or imagination. But this application—which seems a perfectly legitimate one—does not, in the first instance, belong to psychology at all. No doubt it is psychically presented: but it has an other source. It springs from an appreciation, a judgment of the comparative truth or reality of what the so-called psychical act means or expresses. Such faculties are powers in a hierarchy of means and ends and presuppose a normative or critical function which has classified reality. Psychically, the elements which enter into knowledge are not other than those which belong to opinion: but they are nearer an adequate rendering of reality, they are truer, or nearer the Idea. And in the main we may say, that is truer or more real which succeeds in more completely organising and unifying elements—which rises more and more above the selfish or isolated part into the thorough unity of all parts.

The superior faculty is therefore the more thorough organisation of that which is elsewhere less harmoniously systematised. Opinion is fragmentary and partial: it begins abruptly and casually from the unknown, and runs off no less abruptly into the unknown. Knowledge, on the contrary, is unified: and its unity gives it its strength and superiority. The powers which thus exist are the subjective counterparts of objectively valuable products. Thus, reason is the subjective counterpart of a world in which all the constituents are harmonised and fall into due relationship. It is a product or result, which is not psychologically, but logically or morally important. It is a faculty, because it means that actually its possessor has ordered and systematised his life or his ideas of things. Psychologically, it, like unreason, is a compound of elements: but in the case of reason the composition is unendingly and infinitely consistent; it is knowledge completely unified. The distinction then is not in the strictest sense psychological: for it has an aesthetic or normative character; it is logical or ethical: it denotes that the idea or the act is an approach to truth or goodness. And so, when Butler or Plato distinguishes reason or reflection from appetites and affections, and even from self-love or from the heart which loves and hates, this is not exactly a psychological division in the narrower sense. That is to say: these are, in Plato's words, not merely "parts," but quite as much "kinds" and "forms" of soul. They denote degrees in that harmonisation of mind and soul which reproduces the permanent and complete truth of things. For example, self-love, as Butler describes it, has but a partial and narrowed view of the worth of acts: it is engrossing and self-involved: it cannot take in the full dependence of the narrower interest on the larger and eternal self. So, in Plato, the man of heart is but a nature which by fits and starts, or with steady but limited vision, realises the larger life. These parts or kinds are not separate and co-existent faculties: but grades in the co-ordination and unification of the same one human nature.

(i.) *Psychology and Epistemology.*

Psychology however in the strict sense is extremely difficult to define. Those who describe it as the "science of mind," the "phenomenology of consciousness," seem to give it a wider scope than they really mean. The psychologist of the straiter sect tends, on the other hand, to carry us beyond mind and consciousness altogether. His, it has been said, is a psychology without a Psyché. For him Mind, Soul, and Consciousness are only current and convenient names to designate the field, the ground on which the phenomena he observes are supposed to transact themselves. But they must not on any account interfere with the operations; any more than Nature in general may interfere with strictly physical inquiries, or Life and vital force with the theories of biology. The so-called Mind is only to be regarded as a stage on which certain events represent themselves. In this field, or on this stage, there are certain relatively ultimate elements, variously called ideas, presentations, feelings, or states of consciousness. But these elements, though called ideas, must not be supposed more than mechanical or dynamical elements; consciousness is rather their product, a product which presupposes certain operations and relations between them. If we are to be strictly scientific, we must, it is urged, treat the factors of consciousness as not themselves conscious: we must regard them as quasi-objective, or in abstraction from the consciousness which surveys them. The Ego must sink into a mere receptacle or arena of psychic event; its independent meaning or purport is to be ignored, as beside the question.

When this line is once fixed upon, it seems inevitable to go farther. Comte was inclined to treat psychology as falling between two stools: it must, he thought, draw all its content either from physiology on the one hand, or from social factors on the other. The dominant or experimental psychology of the present day seems inclined, without however formulating any very definite statement, to pronounce for the former alternative. It does not indeed adopt the materialistic view that mind is only a function of matter. Its standpoint rather is that the psychical presents itself even to unskilled observation as dependent on (i.e. not independent of) or as concomitant with certain physical or corporeal facts. It adds that the more accurately trained the observer becomes, the more he comes to discover a corporeal aspect even where originally he had not surmised its existence, and to conclude that the two cycles of psychical and physical event never interfere with each other: that soul does not intervene in bodily process, nor body take up and carry on psychical. If it is said that the will moves the limbs, he replies that the will which moves is really certain formerly unnoticed movements of nerve and muscle which are felt or interpreted as a discharge of power. If the ocular impression is said to cause an impression on the mind, he replies that any fact hidden under that phrase refers to a change in the molecules of the brain. He will therefore conclude that for the study of psychical phenomena the physical basis, as it may be called, is all important. Only so can observation really deal with fact capable of description and measurement. Thus psychology, it may be said, tends to become a department of physiology. From another standpoint, biology may be said to receive its completion in psychology. How much either phrase means, however, will depend on the estimate we form of biology. If biology is only the study of mechanical and chemical phenomena on the peculiar field known as an organism, and if that organism is only treated as an environment which may be ignored, then psychology, put on the same level, is not the full science of mind, any more than the other is the full study of life. They both have narrowed their subject to suit the abstract scheme of the laboratory, where the victim of experiment is either altered by mutilation and artificial restrictions, or is dead. If, on the contrary, biology has a substantial unity of its own to which mechanical and chemical considerations are subordinate and instrumental, psychology may even take part with physiology without losing its essential rank. But in that case, we must, as Spinoza said[47], think less mechanically of the animal frame, and recognise (after the example of Schelling) something truly inward (i.e. not merely locally inside the skin) as the supreme phase or characteristic of life. We must, in short, recognise sensibility as the culmination of the physiological and the beginning of the psychological.

To the strictly scientific psychologist, as has been noted—or to the psychology which imitates optical and electrical science—ideas are only psychical events: they are not ideas of anything, relative, i.e. to something else; they have no meaning, and no reference to a reality beyond themselves. They are presentations;—not representations of something outside consciousness. They are appearances: but not appearances of something: they do not reveal anything beyond themselves. They are, we may almost say, a unique kind of physical phenomena. If we say they are presentations of something, we only mean that in the presented something, in the felt something, the wished something, we separate the quality or form or aspect of presentativeness, of feltness, of wishedness, and consider this aspect by itself. There are grades, relations, complications, of such presentations or in such presentedness: and with the description and explanation of these, psychology is concerned. They are fainter or stronger, more or less correlated and antithetical. Presentation (or ideation), in short, is the name of a train of event, which has its peculiarities, its laws, its systems, its history.

All reality, it may be said, subsists in such presentation; it is for a consciousness, or in a consciousness. All esse, in its widest sense, is percipi. And yet, it seems but the commonest of experiences to say that all that is presented is not reality. It is, it has a sort of being,—is somehow presumed to exist: but it is not reality. And this reference and antithesis to what is presented is implied in all such terms as "ideas," "feelings," "states of consciousness": they are distinguished from and related to objects of sense or external facts, to something, as it is called, outside consciousness. Thoughts and ideas are set against things and realities. In their primitive stage both the child and the savage seem to recognise no such difference. What they imagine is, as we might say, on the same plane with what they touch and feel. They do not, as we reproachfully remark, recognise the difference between fact and fiction. All of us indeed are liable to lapses into the same condition. A strong passion, a keen hope or fear, as we say, invests its objects with reality: even a sanguine moment presents as fact what calmer reflection disallows as fancy. With natural and sane intelligences, however, the recrudescence of barbarous imagination is soon dispelled, and the difference between hallucinations and realities is established. With the utterly wrecked in mind, the reality of hallucinations becomes a permanent or habitual state. With the child and the untrained it is a recurrent and a disturbing influence: and it need hardly be added that the circle of these decepti deceptores—people with the "lie in the Soul"—is a large one. There thus emerges a distinction of vast importance, that of truth and falsehood, of reality and unreality, or between representation and reality. There arise two worlds, the world of ideas, and the world of reality which it is supposed to represent, and, in many cases, to represent badly.

With this distinction we are brought across the problem sometimes called Epistemological. Strictly speaking, it is really part of a larger problem: the problem of what—if Greek compounds must be used—may be styled Aletheiology—the theory of truth and reality: what Hegel called Logic, and what many others have called Metaphysics. As it is ordinarily taken up, "ideas" are believed to be something in us which is representative or symbolical of something truly real outside us. This inward something is said to be the first and immediate object of knowledge[48], and gives us—in a mysterious way we need not here discuss—the mediate knowledge of the reality, which is sometimes said to cause it. Ideas in the Mind, or in the Subject, or in us, bear witness to something outside the mind,—trans-subjective— beyond us. The Mind, Subject, or Ego, in this parallelism is evidently in some way identified with our corporeal organism: perhaps even located, and provided with a "seat," in some defined space of that organism. It is, however, the starting-point of the whole distinction that ideas do not, no less than they do, conform or correspond to this supra-conscious or extra-conscious world of real things. Truth or falsehood arises, according to these assumptions, according as psychical image or idea corresponds or not to physical fact. But how, unless by some miraculous second-sight, where the supreme consciousness, directly contemplating by intuition the true and independent reality, turns to compare with this immediate vision the results of the mediate processes conducted along the organs of sense,— how this agreement or disagreement of copy and original, of idea and reality, can be detected, it is impossible to say.

As has been already noted, the mischief lies in the hypostatisation of ideas as something existing in abstraction from things—and, of things, in abstraction from ideas. They are two abstractions, the first by the realist, the second by the idealist called subjective and psychological. To the realist, things exist by themselves, and they manage to produce a copy of themselves (more or less exact, or symbolical) in our mind, i.e. in a materialistically-spiritual or a spiritualistically-material locus which holds "images" and ideas. To the psychological idealist, ideas have a substantive and primary right to existence, them alone do we really know, and from them we more or less legitimately are said (but probably no one takes this seriously) to infer or postulate a world of permanent things. Now ideas have no substantive existence as a sort of things, or even images of things anywhere. All this is pure mythology. It is said by comparative mythologists that in some cases the epithet or quality of some deity has been substantialised (hypostatised) into a separate god, who, however (so still to keep up the unity), is regarded as a relative, a son, or daughter, of the original. So the phrase "ideas of things" has been taken literally as if it was double. But to have an idea of a thing merely means that we know it, or think it. An idea is not given: it is a thing which is given in the idea. An idea is not an additional and intervening object of our knowledge or supposed knowledge. That a thing is our object of thought is another word for its being our idea, and that means we know it.

The distinction between truth and falsehood, between reality and appearance, is not arrived at by comparing what we have before us in our mind with some inaccessible reality beyond. It is a distinction that grows up with the growth and organisation of our presentations—with their gradual systematisation and unification in one consciousness. But this consciousness which thinks, i.e. judges and reasons, is something superior to the contrast of physical and psychical: superior, i.e. in so far as it includes and surveys the antithesis, without superseding it. It is the "transcendental unity of consciousness" of Kant—his synthetic unity of apperception. It means that all ideas ultimately derive their reality from their coherence with each other in an all-embracing or infinite idea. Real in a sense ideas always are, but with an imperfect reality. Thus the education to truth is not—such a thing would be meaningless— ended by a rough and ready recommendation to compare our ideas with facts: it must teach the art which discovers facts. And the teaching may have to go through many grades or provinces: in each of which it is possible to acquire a certain virtuosoship without being necessarily an adept in another. It is through what is called the development of intellect, judgment, and reasoning that the faculty of truth-detecting or truth-selecting comes. And the common feature of all of these is, so to say, their superiority to the psychological mechanism, not in the sense of working without it and directly, but of being the organising unity or unifier and controller and judge of that mechanism. The certainty and necessity of truth and knowledge do not come from a constraint from the external thing which forces the inner idea into submission; they come from the inner necessity of conformity and coherence in the organism of experience. We in fact had better speak of ideas as experience—as felt reality: a reality however which has its degrees and perhaps even its provinces. All truth comes with the reasoned judgment, i.e. the syllogism—i.e. with the institution or discovery of relations of fact or element to fact or element, immediate or derivative, partial and less partial, up to its ideal coherence in one Idea. It is because this coherence is so imperfectly established in many human beings that their knowledge is so indistinguishable from opinion, and that they separate so loosely truth from error. They have not worked their way into a definitely articulated system, where there are no gaps, no abrupt transitions: their mental order is so loosely put together that divergences and contradictions which vex another drop off ineffectual from them.

(ii.) *Kant, Fichte, and Hegel.*

This was the idealism which Kant taught and Fichte promoted. Of the other idealism there are no doubt abundant traces in the language of Kant: and they were greedily fastened on by Schopenhauer. To him the doctrine, that the world is my idea, is adequately represented when it is translated into the phrase that the world is a phantasmagoria of my brain; and escape from the subjective idealism thus initiated is found by him only through a supposed revelation of immediate being communicated in the experience of will. But according to the more consistently interpreted Kant, the problem of philosophy consists in laying bare the supreme law or conditions of consciousness on which depend the validity of our knowledge, our estimates of conduct, and our aesthetic standards. And these roots of reality are for Kant in the mind—or, should we rather say—in mind—in "Consciousness in General." In the Criticism of Pure Reason the general drift of his examination is to show that the great things or final realities which are popularly supposed to stand in self-subsistent being, as ultimate and all-comprehensive objects set up for knowledge, are not "things" as popularly supposed, but imperative and inevitable ideas. They are not objects to be known—(these are always finite): but rather the unification, the basis, or condition, and the completion of all knowledge. To know them—in the ordinary petty sense of knowledge—is as absurd and impossible as it would be, in the Platonic scheme of reality, to know the idea of good which is "on the further side of knowledge and being." God and the Soul—and the same would be true of the World (though modern speculators sometimes talk as if they had it at least within their grasp)—are not mere objects of knowledge. It would be truer to say they are that by which we know, and they are what in us knows: they make knowledge possible, and actual. Kant has sometimes spoken of them as the objects of a faith of reason. What he means is that reason only issues in knowledge because of and through this inevitable law of reason bidding us go on for ever in our search, because there can be nothing isolated and nowhere any ne plus ultra in science, which is infinite and yet only justified as it postulates or commands unity.

Kant's central idea is that truth, beauty, goodness, are not dependent on some qualities of the object, but on the universal nature or law of consciousness. Beauty is not an attribute of things in their abstractness: but of things as ideas of a subject, and depends on the proportion and symmetry in the play of human faculty. Goodness is not conformity to an outward law, but is obligatory on us through that higher nature which is our truer being. Truth is not conformity of ideas with supposed trans-subjective things, but coherence and stability in the system of ideas. The really infinite world is not out there, but in here—in consciousness in general, which is the denial of all limitation, of all finality, of all isolation. God is the essential and inherent unity and unifier of spirit and nature—the surety that the world in all its differentiations is one. The Soul is not an essential entity, but the infinite fruitfulness and freshness of mental life, which forbids us stopping at anything short of complete continuity and unity. The Kingdom of God—the Soul—the moral law—is within us: within us, as supreme, supra-personal and infinite intelligences, even amid all our littleness and finitude. Even happiness which we stretch our arms after is not really beyond us, but is the essential self which indeed we can only reach in detail. It is so both in knowledge and in action. Each knowledge and enjoyment in reality is limited and partial, but it is made stable, and it gets a touch of infinitude, by the larger idea which it helps to realise. Only indeed in that antithesis between the finite and the infinite does the real live. Every piece of knowledge is real, only because it assumes pro tempore certain premisses which are given: every actual beauty is set in some defect of aesthetic completeness: every actually good deed has to get its foil in surrounding badness. The real is always partial and incomplete. But it has the basis or condition of its reality in an idea—in a transcendental unity of consciousness, which is so to say a law, or a system and an order, which imposes upon it the condition of conformity and coherence; but a conformity which is essential and implicit in it.

Fichte has called his system a Wissenschaftslehre—a theory of knowledge. Modern German used the word Wissenschaft, as modern English uses the word Science, to denote the certified knowledge of piecemeal fact, the partial unification of elements still kept asunder. But by Wissen, as opposed to Erkennen, is meant the I know, am aware and sure, am in contact with reality, as opposed to the derivative and conditional reference of something to something else which explains it. The former is a wider term: it denotes all consciousness of objective truth, the certainty which claims to be necessary and universal, which pledges its whole self for its assertion. Fichte thus unifies and accentuates the common element in the Kantian criticisms. In the first of these Kant had begun by explaining the nature and limitation of empirical science. It was essentially conditioned by the given sensation—dependent i.e. on an unexplained and preliminary element. This is what makes it science in the strict or narrow sense of the term: its being set, as it were, in the unknown, the felt, the sense-datum. The side of reality is thus the side of limitation and of presupposition. But what makes it truth and knowledge in general, on the other hand,—as distinct from a truth (i.e. partial truth) and a knowledge,—is the ideal element— the mathematical, the logical, the rational law,—or in one word, the universal and formal character. So too every real action is on one hand the product of an impulse, a dark, merely given, immediate tendency to be, and without that would be nothing: but on the other hand it is only an intelligent and moral action in so far as it has its constitution from an intelligence, a formal system, which determine its place and function.

It is on the latter or ideal element that Kant makes the emphasis increasingly turn. Not truths, duties, beauties, but truth, duty, beauty, form his theme. The formal element—the logical or epistemological condition of knowledge and morality and of beauty—is what he (and still more Fichte) considers the prime question of fundamental philosophy. His philosophy is an attempt to get at the organism of our fundamental belief—the construction, from the very base, of our conception of reality, of our primary certainty. In technical language, he describes our essential nature as a Subject-object. It is the unity of an I am which is also I know that I am: an I will which is also I am conscious of my will[49]. Here there is a radical disunion and a supersession of that disunion. Action and contemplation are continually outrunning each other. The I will rests upon one I know, and works up to another: the I know reflects upon an I will, and includes it as an element in its idea.

Kant had brought into use the term Deduction, and Fichte follows him. The term leads to some confusion: for in English, by its modern antithesis to induction, it suggests a priori methods in all their iniquity. It means a kind of jugglery which brings an endless series out of one small term. Kant has explained that he uses it in the lawyer's sense in which a claim is justified by being traced step by step back to some acknowledged and accepted right[50]. It is a regressive method which shows us that if the original datum is to be accepted it carries along with it the legitimation of the consequence. This method Fichte applies to psychology. Begin, he says like Condillac, with the barest nucleus of soul-life; the mere sentiency, or feeling: the contact, as it were, with being, at a single point. But such a mere point is unthinkable. You find, as Mr. Spencer says, that "Thought" (or Consciousness) "cannot be framed out of one term only." "Every sensation to be known as one must be perceived." Such is the nature of the Ego—a subject which insists on each part being qualified by the whole and so transformed. As Mr. Spencer, again, puts it, the mind not merely tends to revive, to associate, to assimilate, to represent its own presentations, but it carries on this process infinitely and in ever higher multiples. Ideas as it were are growing in complexity by re-presenting: i.e. by embracing and enveloping elements which cannot be found existing in separation. In the mind there is no mere presentation, no bare sensation. Such a unit is a fiction or hypothesis we employ, like the atom, for purposes of explanation. The pure sensation therefore—which you admit because you must have something to begin with, not a mere nothing, but something so simple that it seems to stand out clear and indisputable—this pure sensation, when you think of it, forces you to go a good deal further. Even to be itself, it must be more than itself. It is like the pure or mere being of the logicians. Admit the simple sensation—and you have admitted everything which is required to make sensation a possible reality. But you do not—in the sense of vulgar logic— deduce what follows out of the beginning. From that, taken by itself, you will get only itself: mere being will give you only nothing, to the end of the chapter. But, as the phrase is, sensation is an element in a consciousness: it is, when you think of it, always more than you called it: there is a curious "continuity" about the phenomena, which makes real isolation impossible.

Of course this "deduction" is not history: it is logic. It says, if you posit sensation, then in doing so, you posit a good deal more. You have imagination, reason, and many more, all involved in your original assumption. And there is a further point to be noted. You cannot really stop even at reason, at intelligence and will, if you take these in the full sense. You must realise that these only exist as part and parcel of a reasonable world. An individual intelligence presupposes a society of intelligences. The successive steps in this argument are presented by Fichte in the chief works of his earlier period (1794-98). The works of that period form a kind of trilogy of philosophy, by which the faint outlines of the absolute selfhood is shown acquiring definite consistency in the moral organisation of society. First comes the "Foundation for the collective philosophy." It shows how our conception of reality and our psychical organisation are inevitably presupposed in the barest function of intelligence, in the abstractest forms of logical law. Begin where you like, with the most abstract and formal point of consciousness, you are forced, as you dwell upon it (you identifying yourself with the thought you realise), to go step by step on till you accept as a self-consistent and self-explanatory unity all that your cognitive and volitional nature claims to own as its birthright. Only in such an intelligent will is perception and sensation possible. Next came the "Foundation of Natural Law, on the principles of the general theory." Here the process of deduction is carried a step further. If man is to realise himself as an intelligence with an inherent bent to action, then he must be conceived as a person among persons, as possessed of rights, as incapable of acting without at the same moment claiming for his acts recognition, generality, and logical consecution. The reference, which in the conception of a practical intelligence was implicit,—the reference to fellow-agents, to a world in which law rules—is thus, by the explicit recognition of these references, made a fact patent and positive—gesetzt,—expressly instituted in the way that the nature and condition of things postulates. But this is not all: we step from the formal and absolute into the material and relative. If man is to be a real intelligence, he must be an intelligence served by organs. "The rational being cannot realise its efficient individuality, unless it ascribes to itself a material body": a body, moreover, in which Fichte believes he can show that the details of structure and organs are equally with the general corporeity predetermined by reason[51]. In the same way it is shown that the social and political organisation is required for the realisation—the making positive and yet coherent—of the rights of all individuals. You deduce society by showing it is required to make a genuine individual man. Thirdly came the "System of Ethics." Here it is further argued that, at least in a certain respect[52], in spite of my absolute reason and my absolute freedom, I can only be fully real as a part of Nature: that my reason is realised in a creature of appetite and impulse. From first to last this deduction is one process which may be said to have for its object to determine "the conditions of self-hood or egoity." It is the deduction of the concrete and empirical moral agent—the actual ego of actual life—from the abstract, unconditioned ego, which in order to be actual must condescend to be at once determining and determined.

In all of this Fichte makes—especially formally—a decided advance upon Kant. In Ethics Kant in particular, (—especially for readers who never got beyond the beginning of his moral treatise and were overpowered by the categorical imperative of duty) had found the moral initiative or dynamic apparently in the other world. The voice of duty seemed to speak from a region outside and beyond the individual conscience. In a sense it must do so: but it comes from a consciousness which is, and yet is more than, the individual. It is indeed true that appearances here are deceptive: and that the idea of autonomy, the self-legislation of reason, is trying to become the central conception of Kant's Ethics.

Still it is Fichte's merit to have seen this clearly, to have held it in view unfalteringly, and to have carried it out in undeviating system or deduction. Man, intelligent, social, ethical, is a being all of one piece and to be explained entirely immanently, or from himself. Law and ethics are no accident either to sense or to intelligence—nothing imposed by mere external or supernal authority[53]. Society is not a brand-new order of things supervening upon and superseding a state of nature, where the individual was entirely self-supporting. Morals, law, society, are all necessary steps (necessary i.e. in logic, and hence in the long run also inevitable in course of time) to complete the full evolution or realisation of a human being. The same conditions as make man intelligent make him social and moral. He does not proceed so far as to become intelligent and practical, under terms of natural and logical development, then to fall into the hands of a foreign influence, an accident ab extra, which causes him to become social and moral. Rather he is intelligent, because he is a social agent.

Hence, in Fichte, the absence of the ascetic element so often stamping its character on ethics, and representing the moral life as the enemy of the natural, or as mainly a struggle to subdue the sensibility and the flesh. With Kant,—as becomes his position of mere inquirer—the sensibility has the place of a predominant and permanent foreground. Reason, to his way of talking, is always something of an intruder, a stranger from a far-off world, to be feared even when obeyed: sublime, rather than beautiful. From the land of sense which we habitually occupy, the land of reason is a country we can only behold from afar: or if we can be said to have a standpoint in it, that is only a figurative way of saying that though it is really over the border, we can act—it would sometimes seem by a sort of make-believe—as if we were already there. But these moments of high enthusiasm are rare; and Kant commends sobriety and warns against high-minded Schwärmerei, or over-strained Mysticism. For us it is reserved to struggle with a recalcitrant selfhood, a grovelling sensibility: it were only fantastic extravagance, fit for "fair souls" who unfortunately often lapse into "fair sinners," should we fancy ourselves already anchored in the haven of untempted rest and peace.

When we come to Fichte, we find another spirit breathing. We have passed from the age of Frederick the Great to the age of the French Revolution; and the breeze that burst in the War of Liberation is already beginning to freshen the air. Boldly he pronounces the primacy of that faith of reason whereby not merely the just but all shall live. Your will shall show you what you really are. You are essentially a rational will, or a will-reason. Your sensuous nature, of impulse and appetite, far from being the given and found obstacle to the realisation of reason,—which Kant strictly interpreted might sometimes seem to imply—(and in this point Schopenhauer carries out the implications of Kant)—is really the condition or mode of being which reason assumes, or rises up to, in order to be a practical or moral being. Far from the body and the sensible needs being a stumbling-block to hamper the free fullness of rationality and morality, the truth rather is that it is only by body and sense, by flesh and blood, that the full moral and rational life can be realised[54]. Or, to put it otherwise, if human reason (intelligence and will) is to be more than a mere and empty inner possibility, if man is to be a real and concrete cognitive and volitional being, he must be a member of an ethical and actual society, which lives by bread, and which marries and has children.

(iii.) *Psychology in Ethics.*

In this way, for Fichte, and through Fichte still more decidedly for Hegel, both psychology and ethics breathe an opener and ampler air than they often enjoy. Psychology ceases to be a mere description of psychic events, and becomes the history of the self-organising process of human reason. Ethics loses its cloistered, negative, unnatural aspect, and becomes a name for some further conditions of the same development, essentially postulated to complete or supplement its shortcomings. Psychology—taken in this high philosophical acceptation—thus leads on to Ethics; and Ethics is parted by no impassable line from Psychology. That, at least, is what must happen if they are still to retain a place in philosophy: for, as Kant says[55], "under the government of reason our cognitions cannot form a rhapsody, but must constitute a system, in which alone can they support and further its essential aims." As parts of such a system, they carry out their special work in subordination to, and in the realisation of, a single Idea—and therefore in essential interconnexion. From that interconnecting band we may however in detail-enquiry dispense ourselves; and then we have the empirical or inductive sciences of psychology and ethics. But even with these, the necessity of the situation is such that it is only a question of degree how far we lose sight of the philosophical horizon, and entrench ourselves in special enquiry. Something of the philosophic largeness must always guide us; even when, to further the interests of the whole, it is necessary for the special enquirer to bury himself entirely in his part. So long as each part is sincerely and thoroughly pursued, and no part is neglected, there is an indwelling reason in the parts which will in the long run tend to constitute the total.

A philosophical psychology will show us how the sane intelligence and the rational will are, at least approximately, built up out of elements, and through stages and processes, which modify and complement, as they may also arrest and perplex, each other. The unity, coherence, and completeness of the intelligent self is not, as vulgar irreflectiveness supposes and somewhat angrily maintains, a full-grown thing or agent, of whose actions and modes of behaviour the psychologist has to narrate the history,—a history which is too apt to degenerate into the anecdotal and the merely interesting. This unity of self has to be "deduced," as Fichte would say: it has to be shown as the necessary result which certain elements in a certain order will lead to[56]. A normal mind, self-possessed, developed and articulated, yet thoroughly one, a real microcosm, or true and full monad, which under the mode of its individuality still represents the universe: that is, what psychology has to show as the product of factors and processes. And it is clearly something great and good, something valuable, and already possessing, by implication we may say, an ethical character.

In philosophy, at least, it is difficult, or rather impossible to draw a hard and fast line which shall demarcate ethical from non-ethical characters,—to separate them from other intellectual and reasonable motives. Kant, as we know, attempted to do so: but with the result that he was forced to add a doubt whether a purely moral act could ever be said to exist[57]; or rather to express the certainty that if it did it was for ever inaccessible to observation. All such designations of the several "factors" or "moments" in reality, as has been hinted, are only a potiori. But they are misused when it is supposed that they connote abrupt and total discontinuity. And Kant, after all, only repeated in his own terminology an old and inveterate habit of thought:—the habit which in Stoicism seemed to see sage and foolish utterly separated, and which in the straiter sects of Christendom fenced off saint absolutely from sinner. It is a habit to which Hegel, and even his immediate predecessors, are radically opposed. With Herder, he might say, "Ethics is only a higher physics of the mind[58]." This—the truth in Spinozism—no doubt demands some emphasis on the word "higher": and it requires us to read ethics (or something like it) into physics; but it is a step on the right road,—the step which Utilitarianism and Evolutionism had (however awkwardly) got their foot upon, and which "transcendent" ethics seems unduly afraid of committing itself to. Let us say, if we like, that the mind is more than mere nature, and that it is no proper object of a merely natural science. But let us remember that a merely natural science is only a fragment of science: let us add that the merely natural is an abstraction which in part denaturalises and mutilates the larger nature—a nature which includes the natural mind, and cannot altogether exclude the ethical.

What have been called "formal duties[59]" seem to fall under this range—the province of a philosophical psychology which unveils the conditions of personality. Under that heading may be put self-control, consistency, resolution, energy, forethought, prudence, and the like. The due proportion of faculty, the correspondence of head and heart, the vivacity and quickness of sympathy, the ease and simplicity of mental tone, the due vigour of memory and the grace of imagination, sweetness of temper, and the like, are parts of the same group[60]. They are lovely, and of good report: they are praise and virtue. If it be urged that they are only natural gifts and graces, that objection cuts two ways. The objector may of course be reminded that religion tones down the self-complacency of morality. Yet, first, even apart from that, it may be said that of virtues, which stand independent of natural conditions—of external supply of means (as Aristotle would say)—nothing can be known and nothing need be said. And secondly, none of these qualities are mere gifts;—all require exercise, habituation, energising, to get and keep them. How much and how little in each case is nature's and how much ours is a problem which has some personal interest—due perhaps to a rather selfish and envious curiosity. But on the broad field of experience and history we may perhaps accept the—apparently one-sided— proverb that "Each man is the architect of his own fortune." Be this as it may, it will not do to deny the ethical character of these "formal duties" on the ground e.g. that self-control, prudence, and even sweetness of temper may be used for evil ends,—that one may smile and smile, and yet be a villain. That—let us reply,—on one hand, is a fault (if fault it be) incidental to all virtues in detail (for every single quality has its defect): nay it may be a limitation attaching to the whole ethical sphere: and, secondly, its inevitable limitation does not render the virtue in any case one whit less genuine so far as it goes. And yet of such virtues it may be said, as Hume[61] would say (who calls them "natural," as opposed to the more artificial merits of justice and its kin), that they please in themselves, or in the mere contemplation, and without any regard to their social effects. But they please as entering into our idea of complete human nature, of mind and spirit as will and intellect.

The moralists of last century sometimes divided the field of ethics by assigning to man three grades or kinds of duty: duties to himself, duties to society, and duties to God. For the distinction there is a good deal to be said: there are also faults to be found with it. It may be said, amongst other things, that to speak of duties to self is a metaphorical way of talking, and that God lies out of the range of human duty altogether, except in so far as religious service forms a part of social obligation. It may be urged that man is essentially a social being, and that it is only in his relations to other such beings that his morality can find a sphere. The sphere of morality, according to Dr. Bain, embraces whatever "society has seen fit to enforce with all the rigour of positive inflictions. Positive good deeds and self-sacrifice ... transcend the region of morality proper and occupy a sphere of their own[62]." And there is little doubt that this restriction is in accordance with a main current of usage. It may even be said that there are tendencies towards a narrower usage still, which would restrict the term to questions affecting the relations of the sexes. But, without going so far, we may accept the standpoint which finds in the phrase "popular or social" sanction, as equivalent to the moral sanction, a description of the average level of common opinion on the topic. The morality of an age or country thus denotes, first, the average requirement in act and behaviour imposed by general consent on the members of a community, and secondly, the average performance of the members in response to these requirements. Generally speaking the two will be pretty much the same. If the society is in a state of equilibrium, there will be a palpable agreement between what all severally expect and what all severally perform. On the other hand, as no society is ever in complete equilibrium, this harmony will never be perfect and may often be widely departed from. In what is called a single community, if it reach a considerable bulk, there are (in other words) often a number of minor societies, more or less thwarting and modifying each other; and different observers, who belong in the main to one or other of these subordinate groups, may elicit from the facts before them a somewhat different social code, and a different grade of social observance. Still, with whatever diversity of detail, the important feature of such social ethics is that the stress is laid on the performance of certain acts, in accordance with the organisation of society. So long as the required compliance is given, public opinion is satisfied, and morality has got its due.

But in two directions this conception of morality needs to be supplementing. There is, on one hand, what is called duty to God. The phrase is not altogether appropriate: for it follows too closely the analogy of social requirement, and treats Deity as an additional and social authority,—a lord paramount over merely human sovereigns. But though there may be some use in the analogy, to press the conception is seriously to narrow the divine character and the scope of religion. As in similar cases, we cannot change one term without altering its correlative. And therefore to describe our relation to God under the name of duty is to narrow and falsify that relation. The word is no longer applicable in this connexion without a strain, and where it exists it indicates the survival of a conception of theocracy: of God regarded as a glorification of the magistrate, as king of kings and lord of lords. It is the social world—and indeed we may say the outside of the social world—that is the sphere of duties. Duty is still with these reductions a great august name: but in literal strictness it only rules over the medial sphere of life, the sphere which lies between the individual as such and his universal humanity[63]. Beyond duty, lies the sphere of conscience and of religion. And that is not the mere insistence by the individual to have a voice and a vote in determining the social order. It is the sense that the social order, however omnipotent it may seem, is limited and finite, and that man has in him a kindred with the Eternal.

It is not very satisfactory, either, as Aristotle and others have pointed out, to speak of man's duties to himself. The phrase is analogical, like the other. But it has the merit, like that of duty to God, of reminding us that the ordinary latitude occupied by morality is not all that comes under the larger scope of ethics. The "ethics of individual life" is a subject which Mr. Spencer has touched upon: and by this title, he means that, besides his general relationship to others, a human being has to mind his own health, food, and amusement, and has duties as husband and parent. But, after all, these are not matters of peculiarly individual interest. They rather refer to points which society at certain epochs leaves to the common sense of the agent,—apparently on an assumption that he is the person chiefly interested. And these points—as the Greeks taught long ago—are of fundamental importance: they are the very bases of life. Yet the comparative neglect in which so-called civilised societies[64] hold the precepts of wisdom in relation to bodily health and vigour, in regard to marriage and progeny, serve to illustrate the doctrine of the ancient Stoics that πάντα ὑπόληψις, or the modern idealist utterance that the World is my idea. More and more as civilisation succeeds in its disruption of man from nature, it shows him governed not by bare facts and isolated experiences, but by the systematic idea under which all things are subsumed. He loses the naïveté of the natural man, which takes each fact as it came, all alike good: he becomes sentimental, and artificial, sees things under a conventional point of view, and would rather die than not be in the fashion. And this tendency is apparently irresistible. Yet the mistake lies in the one-sidedness of sentiment and convention. Not the domination of the idea is evil; but the domination of a partial and fragmentary idea: and this is what constitutes the evil of artificiality. And the correction must lie not in a return to nature, but in the reconstruction of a wider and more comprehensive idea: an idea which shall be the unity and system of all nature; not a fantastic idealism, but an attempt to do justice to the more realist as well as the idealist sides of life.

There is however another side of individualist ethics which needs even more especial enforcement. It is the formation of

> *"The reason firm, the temperate will,*
> *Endurance, foresight, strength and skill:"*

the healthy mind in a healthy body. Ethics is only too apt to suppose that will and intelligence are assumptions which need no special justification. But the truth is that they vary from individual to individual in degree and structure. It is the business of ethical psychology to give to these vague attributions the definiteness of a normal standard: to show what proportions are required to justify the proper title of reason and will—to show what reason and will really are if they do what they are encouraged or expected to do. It talks of the diseases of will and personality: it must also set forth their educational ideal. The first problem of Ethics, it may be said, is the question of the will and its freedom. But to say this is of course not to say that, unless freedom of will be understood in some special sense, ethics becomes impossible. If the moral law is the ratio cognoscendi of freedom, then must our conception of morality and of freedom hang together. And it will clearly be indispensable to begin by some attempt to discover in what sense man may be in the most general way described as a moral agent—as an intelligent will, or (more briefly, yet synonymously) as a will. "The soil of law and morality," says Hegel[65], "is the intelligent life: and its more precise place and starting-point the will, which is free, in the sense that freedom is its substance and characteristic, and the system of law the realm of freedom realised, the world of intelligence produced out of itself as a second nature." Such a freedom is a freedom made and acquired, the work of the mind's self-realisation, not to be taken as a given fact of consciousness which must be believed[66]. To have a will—in other words, to have freedom, is the consummation—and let us add, only the formal or ideal consummation—of a process by which man raises himself out of his absorption in sensation and impulse, establishes within himself a mental realm, an organism of ideas, a self-consciousness, and a self.

The vulgar apprehension of these things seems to assume that we have by nature, or are born with, a general faculty or set of general faculties, which we subsequently fill up and embody by the aid of experience. We possess—they seem to imply—so many "forms" and "categories" latent in our minds ready to hold and contain the raw materials supplied from without. According to this view we have all a will and an intelligence: the difference only is that some put more into them, and some put less. But such a separation of the general form from its contents is a piece of pure mythology. It is perhaps true and safe to say that the human being is of such a character that will and intelligence are in the ordinary course inevitably produced. But the forms which grow up are the more and more definite and systematic organisation of a graded experience, of series of ideas, working themselves up again and again in representative and re-representative degree, till they constitute a mental or inner world of their own. The will is thus the title appropriate to the final stage of a process, by which sensation and impulse have polished and perfected themselves by union and opposition, by differentiation and accompanying redintegration, till they assume characters quite unsurmised in their earliest aspects, and yet only the consolidation or self-realisation of implications. Thus the mental faculties are essentially acquired powers,—acquired not from without, but by action which generates the faculties it seems to imply. The process of mind is a process which creates individual centres, raises them to completer independence;—which produces an inner life more and more self-centered and also more and more equal to the universe which it has embodied. And will and intelligence are an important stage in that process.

Herbart (as was briefly hinted at in the first essay) has analysed ethical appreciation (which may or may not be accompanied by approbation) into five distinct standard ideas. These are the ideas of inward liberty, of perfection, of right, benevolence, and equity. Like Hume, he regards the moral judgment as in its purity a kind of aesthetic pronouncement on the agreement or proportion of certain activities in relations to each other. Two of these standard ideas,—that of inward liberty and of perfection—seem to belong to the sphere at present under review. They emerge as conditions determining the normal development of human nature to an intelligent and matured personality. By inward freedom Herbart means the harmony between the will and the intellect: what Aristotle has named "practical truth or reality," and what he describes in his conception of wisdom or moral intelligence,—the power of discerning the right path and of pursuing it with will and temper: the unity, clear but indissoluble, of will and discernment. By the idea of perfection Herbart means the sense of proportion and of propriety which is awakened by comparing a progress in development or an increase in strength with its earlier stages of promise and imperfection. The pleasure such perception affords works in two ways: it is a satisfaction in achievement past, and a stimulus to achievement yet to come.

Such ideas of inward liberty and of growth in ability or in performance govern (at least in part) our judgment of the individual, and have an ethical significance. Indeed, if the cardinal feature of the ethical sentiment be the inwardness and independence of its approbation and obligation, these ideas lie at the root of all true morality. Inward harmony and inward progress, lucidity of conscience and the resolution which knows no finality of effort, are the very essence of moral life. Yet, if ethics is to include in the first instance social relationships and external utilities and sanctions, these conditions of true life must rather be described as pre-ethical. The truth seems to be that here we get to a range of ethics which is far wider than what is ordinarily called practice and conduct. At this stage logic, aesthetic, and ethic, are yet one: the true, the good, and the beautiful are still held in their fundamental unity. An ethics of wide principle precedes its narrower social application; and whereas in ordinary usage the social provinciality is allowed to prevail, here the higher ethics emerge clear and imperial above the limitations of local and temporal duty.

And though it is easy to step into exaggeration, it is still well to emphasise this larger conception of ethics. The moral principle of the "maximising of life," as it has been called[67], may be open to misconception (—so, unfortunately are all moral principles when stated in the effrontery of isolation): but it has its truth in the conviction that all moral evil is marked by a tendency to lower or lessen the total vitality. So too Friedrich Nietzsche's maxim, Sei vornehm[68], ensue distinction, and above all things be not common or vulgar (gemein), will easily lend itself to distortion. But it is good advice for all that, even though it may be difficult to define in a general formula wherein distinction consists, to mark the boundary between self-respect and vanity or obstinacy, or to say wherein lies the beauty and dignity of human nature. Kant has laid it down as the principle of duty to ask ourselves if in our act we are prepared to universalise the maxim implied by our conduct. And that this—which essentially bids us look at an act in the whole of its relations and context—is a safeguard against some forms of moral evil, is certain. But there is an opposite—or rather an apparently opposite—principle which bids us be individual, be true to our own selves, and never allow ourselves to be dismayed from our own unique responsibility. Perhaps the two principles are not so far apart as they seem. In any case true individuality is the last word and the first word in ethics; though, it may be added, there is a good deal to be said between the two termini.

(iv.) *An Excursus on Greek Ethics.*

It is in these regions that Greek ethics loves to linger; on the duty of the individual to himself, to be perfectly lucid and true, and to rise to ever higher heights of achievement. Ceteris paribus, there is felt to be something meritorious in superiority, something good:—even were it that you are master, and another is slave. Thus naïvely speaks Aristotle[69]. To a modern, set amid so many conflicting ideals, perhaps, the immense possibilities of yet further growth might suggest themselves with overpowering force. To him the idea of perfection takes the form of an idea of perfectibility: and sometimes it smites down his conceit in what he has actually done, and impresses a sense of humility in comparison with what yet remains unaccomplished. An ancient Greek apparently was little haunted by these vistas of possibilities of progress through worlds beyond worlds. A comparatively simple environment, a fixed and definite mental horizon, had its plain and definite standards, or at least seemed to have such. There were fewer cases of the man, unattached or faintly attached to any definite profession—moving about in worlds half realised—who has grown so common in a more developed civilisation. The ideals of the Greek were clearly descried: each man had his definite function or work to perform: and to do it better than the average, or than he himself habitually had done, that was perfection, excellence, virtue. For virtue to the Greek is essentially ability and respectability: promise of excellent performance: capacity to do better than others. Virtue is praiseworthy or meritorious character and quality: it is achievement at a higher rate, as set against one's past and against others' average.

The Greek moralists sometimes distinguish and sometimes combine moral virtue and wisdom, ἀρετή and φρόνησις: capacity to perform, and wisdom to guide that capacity. To the ordinary Greek perhaps the emphasis fell on the former, on the attainment of all recognised good quality which became a man, all that was beautiful and honourable, all that was appropriate, glorious, and fame-giving; and that not for any special reference to its utilitarian qualities. Useful, of course, such qualities were: but that was not in question at the time. In the more liberal commonwealths of ancient Greece there was little or no anxious care to control the education of its citizens, so as to get direct service, overt contribution to the public good. A suspicious Spartan legislation might claim to do that. But in the free air of Athens all that was required was loyalty, good-will—εὔνοια—to the common weal; it might be even a sentiment of human kindliness, of fraternity of spirit and purpose. Everything beyond and upon that basis was left to free development. Let each carry out to the full the development of his powers in the line which national estimation points out. He is—nature and history alike emphasise that fact beyond the reach of doubt, for all except the outlaw and the casual stranger—a member of a community, and as such has a governing instinct and ideal which animates him. But he is also a self-centered individual, with special endowments of nature, in his own person and in the material objects which are his. A purely individualist or selfish use of them is not—to the normal Greek—even dreamed of. He is too deeply rooted in the substance of his community for that: or it is on the ground and in the atmosphere of an assured community that his individuality is to be made to flourish. Nature has secured that his individuality shall rest securely in the presupposition of his citizenship. It seems, therefore, as if he were left free and independent in his personal search for perfection, for distinction. His place is fixed for him: Spartam nactus es; hanc orna: his duty is his virtue. That duty, as Plato expresses it, is to do his own deeds—and not meddle with others. Nature and history have arranged that others, in other posts, shall do theirs: that all severally shall energise their function. The very word "duty" seems out of place; if, at least, duty suggests external obligation, an order imposed and a debt to be discharged. If there be a task-master and a creditor, it is the inflexible order of nature and history:—or, to be more accurate, of nature, the indwelling and permanent reality of things. But the obligation to follow nature is scarcely felt as a yoke of constraint. A man's virtue is to perform his work and to perform it well: to do what he is specially capable of doing, and therefore specially charged to do.

Nowhere has this character of Greek ethics received more classical expression than in the

Republic of Plato. In the prelude to his subject—which is the nature of Right and Morality—Plato has touched briefly on certain popular and inadequate views. There is the view that Right has its province in performance of certain single and external acts—in business honesty and commercial straightforwardness. There is the view that it is rendering to each what is due to him; that it consists in the proper reciprocity of services, in the balance of social give and take. There is the critical or hyper-critical view which, from seeing so much that is called justice to be in harmony with the interest of the predominant social order, bluntly identifies mere force or strength as the ground of right. And there are views which regard it as due to social conventions and artifices, to the influence of education, to political arrangements and the operation of irrational prejudices. To all these views Plato objects: not because they are false—for they are all in part, often in large part, true—but because they are inadequate and do not go to the root of the matter. The foundations of right lie, he says, not in external act, but in the inner man: not in convention, but in nature: not in relation to others, but in the constitution of the soul itself. That ethical idea—the idea of right—which seems most obviously to have its centre outside the individual, to live and grow only in the relations between individuals, Plato selects in order to show the independent royalty of the single human soul. The world, as Hume afterwards, called justice artificial: Plato will prove it natural. In a way he joins company with those who bid us drive out the spectre of duty, of obligation coming upon the soul from social authority, from traditional idea, from religious sanctions. He preaches—or he is about to preach—the autonomy of the will.

The four cardinal virtues of Plato's list are the qualities which go to make a healthy, normal, natural human soul, fit for all activity, equipped with all arms for the battle of life. They tell us what such a soul is, not what it does. They are the qualities which unless a soul has, and has them each perfect, yet all co-operant, its mere outward and single acts have no virtue or merit, but are only lucky accidents at the best. On the other hand, if a man has these constitutive qualities, he will act in the social world, and act well. Plato has said scornful things of mere outward and verbal truthfulness, and has set at the very lowest pitch of degradation the "lie in the soul." His "temperance" or "self-restraint," if it be far from breathing any suggestion of self-suppression or self-assertion, is still farther from any suspicion of asceticism, or war against the flesh. It is the noble harmony of the ruling and the ruled, which makes the latter a partner of the sovereign, and takes from the dictates of the ruler any touch of coercion. It is literally sanity of soul, integrity and purity of spirit; it is what has been sometimes called the beautiful soul—the indiscerptible unity of reason and impulse. Plato's bravery, again, is fortitude and consistency of soul, the full-blooded heart which is fixed in reason, the zeal which is according to knowledge, unflinching loyalty to the idea, the spirit which burns in the martyrs to truth and humanity: yet withal with gentleness and courtesy and noble urbanity in its immediate train. And his truthfulness is that inner lucidity which cannot be self-deceived, the spirit which is a safeguard against fanaticism and hypocrisy, the sunlike warmth of intelligence without which the heart is a darkness full of unclean things.

The full development and crowning grace of such a manly nature Aristotle has tried to present in the character of the Great-souled man—him whom Plato has called the true king by divine right, or the autocrat by the patent of nature. Like all such attempts to delineate a type in the terms necessarily single and successive of abstract analysis, it tends occasionally to run into caricature, and to give partial aspects an absurd prominence. Only the greatest of artists could cope with such a task, though that artist may be found perhaps classed among the historians. Yet it is possible to form some conception of the ideal which Aristotle would set before us. The Great-souled man is great, and he dare not deny the witness of his spirit. He is one who does not quail before the anger and seek the applause of popular opinion: he holds his head as his own, and as high as his undimmed self-consciousness shows it is worth. There has been said to him by the reason within him the word that Virgil erewhile addressed to Dante:

> *"Libero, dritto, e sano è il tuo arbitrio*
> *E fallo fora non fare a suo cenno;*
> *Per ch' io te sopra te corono e mitrio."*

He is his own Emperor and his own Pope. He is the perfected man, in whom is no darkness, whose soul is utter clearness, and complete harmony. Calm in self-possessed majesty, he stands, if need be, contra mundum: but rather, with the world beneath his feet. The chatter of personality has no interest for him. Bent upon the best, lesser competitions for distinction have no attraction for him. To the vulgar he will seem cold, self-confined: in his apartness and distinction they will see the signs of a "prig." His look will be that of one who pities men—rather than loves them: and should he speak ill of a foe, it is rather out of pride of heart and unbroken spirit than because these things touch him. Such an one, in many ways, was the Florentine poet himself.

If the Greek world in general thus conceived ἀρετή as the full bloom of manly excellence (we all know how slightly—witness the remarks in the Periclean oration—Greeks, in their public and official utterances, rated womanliness), the philosophers had a further point to emphasise. That was what they variously called knowledge, prudence, reason, insight, intelligence, wisdom, truth. From Socrates to Aristotle, from Aristotle to the Stoics and Epicureans, and from the Stoics to the Neo-Platonists, this is the common theme: the supremacy of knowledge, its central and essential relation to virtue. They may differ—perhaps not so widely as current prejudice would suppose—as to how this knowledge is to be defined, what kind of knowledge it is, how acquired and maintained, and so on. But in essentials they are at one. None of them, of course, mean that in order to right conduct nothing more is needed than to learn and remember what is right, the precepts and commandments of ordinary morality. Memory is not knowledge, especially when it is out of mind. Even an ancient philosopher was not wholly devoid of common sense. They held—what they supposed was a fact of observation and reflection—that all action was prompted by feelings of the values of things, by a desire of something good or pleasing to self, and aimed at self-satisfaction and self-realisation, but that there was great mistake in what thus afforded satisfaction. People chose to act wrongly or erroneously, because they were, first, mistaken about themselves and what they wanted, and, secondly, mistaken in the means which would give them satisfaction. But this second point was secondary. The main thing was to know yourself, what you really were; in Plato's words, to "see the soul as it is, and know whether it have one form only or many, or what its nature is; to look upon it with the eye of reason in its original purity." Self-deception, confusion, that worst ignorance which is unaware of itself, false estimation—these are the radical evils of the natural man. To these critics the testimony of consciousness was worthless, unless corroborated. To cure this mental confusion, this blindness of will and judgment, is the task set for philosophy: to give inward light, to teach true self-measurement. In one passage, much misunderstood, Plato has called this philosophic art the due measurement of pleasures and pains. It should scarcely have been possible to mistake the meaning. But, with the catchwords of Utilitarianism ringing in their ears, the commentators ran straight contrary to the true teaching of the Protagoras, consentient as it is with that of the Phaedo and the Philebus. To measure, one must have a standard: and if Plato has one lesson always for us, it is that a sure standard the multitude have not, but only confusion. The so-called pleasures and pains of the world's experiences are so entitled for different reasons, for contrary aims, and with no unity or harmony of judgment. They are—not a fact to be accepted, but—a problem for investigation: their reality is in question, their genuineness, solidity and purity: and till you have settled that, you cannot measure, for you may be measuring vacuity under the idea that there is substance. You have still to get at the unit—i.e. the reality of pleasure. It was not Plato's view that pleasure was a separate and independent entity: that it was exactly as it was felt. Each pleasure is dependent for its pleasurable quality on the consciousness it belongs to, and has only a relative truth and reality. Bentham has written about computing the value of a "lot" of pleasures and pains. But Plato had his mind on an earlier and more fundamental problem, what is the truth and reality of pleasure; and his fullest but not his only essay towards determining the value or estimating the meaning of pleasure in the scale of being is that given in the Philebus.

This then is the knowledge which Greek philosophy meant: not mere intellect—though, of course, there is always a danger of theoretical inquiry degenerating into abstract and formal dogma. But of the meaning there can be no serious doubt. It is a knowledge, says Plato, to which the method of mathematical science—the most perfect he can find acknowledged—is only an ouverture, or perhaps, only the preliminary tuning of the strings. It is a knowledge not eternally hypothetical—a system of sequences which have no sure foundation. It is a knowledge which rests upon the conviction and belief of the "idea of good": a kind of knowledge which does not come by direct teaching, which is not mere theory, but implies a lively conviction, a personal apprehension, a crisis which is a kind of "conversion," or "inspiration." It is as it were the prize of a great contest, in which the sword that conquers is the sword of dialectic: a sword whereof the property is, like that of Ithuriel's spear, to lay bare all deceptions and illusions of life. Or, to vary the metaphor: the son of man is like the prince in the fairy tale who goes forth to win the true queen; but there are many false pretenders decked out to deceive his unwary eyes and foolish heart. Yet in himself there is a power of discernment: there is something kindred with the truth:—the witness of the Spirit—and all that education and discipline can do is to remove obstacles, especially the obstacles within the self which perturb the sight and mislead the judgment. Were not the soul originally possessed of and dominated by the idea of good, it could never discern it elsewhere. On this original kindred depends all the process of education; the influence of which therefore is primarily negative or auxiliary. Thus the process of history and experience,—which the work of education only reproduces in an accelerated tempo—serves but to bring out the implicit reason within into explicit conformity with the rationality of the world.

Knowledge, then, in this ethical sphere means the harmony of will, emotion, intellect: it means the clear light which has no illusions and no deceptions. And to those who feel that much of their life and of the common life is founded on prejudice and illusion, such white light will occasionally seem hard and steely. At its approach they fear the loss of the charm of that twilight hour ere the day has yet begun, or before the darkness has fully settled down. Thus the heart and feelings look upon the intellect as an enemy of sentiment. And Plato himself is not without anticipations of such an issue. Yet perhaps we may add that the danger is in part an imaginary one, and only arises because intelligence takes its task too lightly, and encroaches beyond its proper ground. Philosophy, in other words, mistakes its place when it sets itself up as a dogmatic system of life. Its function is to comprehend, and from comprehension to criticise, and through criticising to unify. It has no positive and additional teaching of its own: no addition to the burden of life and experience. And experience it must respect. Its work is to maintain the organic or super-organic interconnexion between all the spheres of life and all the forms of reality. It has to prevent stagnation and absorption of departments—to keep each in its proper place, but not more than its place, and yet to show how each is not independent of the others. And this is what the philosopher or ancient sage would be. If he is passionless, it is not that he has no passions, but that they no longer perturb and mislead. If his controlling spirit be reason, it is not the reason of the so-called "rationalist," but the reason which seeks in patience to comprehend, and to be at home in, a world it at first finds strange. And if he is critical of others, he is still more critical of himself: critical however not for criticism's sake (which is but a poor thing), but because through criticism the faith of reason may be more fully justified. To the last, if he is true to his mission and faithful to his loyalty to reality, he will have the simplicity of the child.

Whether therefore we agree or not with Plato's reduction of Right and Duty to self-actualisation, we may at least admit that in the idea of perfection or excellence, combined with the idea of knowledge or inward lucidity, he has got the fundamental ideas on which further ethical development must build. Self-control, self-knowledge, internal harmony, are good: and so are the development of our several faculties and of the totality of them to the fullest pitch of excellence. But their value does not lie entirely in themselves, or rather there is implicit in them a reference to something beyond themselves. They take for granted something which, because it is so taken, may also be ignored and neglected, just because it seems so obvious. And that implication is the social humanity in which they are the spirits of light and leading.

To lay the stress on ἀρετή or excellence tends to leave out of sight the force of duty; and to emphasise knowledge is allowed to disparage the heart and feelings. The mind—even of a philosopher—finds a difficulty in holding very different points of view in one, and where it is forced from one to another, tends to forget the earlier altogether. Thus when the ethical philosopher, presupposing as an absolute or unquestionable fact that man the individual was rooted in the community, proceeded to discuss the problem of the best and completest individual estate, he was easily led to lose sight of the fundamental and governing condition altogether. From the moment that Aristotle lays down the thesis that man is naturally social, to the moment when he asks how the bare ideal of excellence in character and life can become an actuality, the community in which man lives has retired out of sight away into the background. And it only comes in, as it first appears, as the paedagogue to bring us to morality. And Plato, though professedly he is speaking of the community, and is well aware that the individual can only be saved by the salvation of the community, is constantly falling back into another problem—the development of an individual soul. He feels the strength of the egoistic effort after perfection, and his essay in the end tends to lose sight altogether of its second theme. Instead of a man he gives us a mere philosopher, a man, that is, not living with his country's life, instinct with the heart and feeling of humanity, inspired by art and religion, but a being set apart and exalted above his fellows,—charged no doubt in theory with the duty of saving them, of acting vicariously as the mediator between them and the absolute truth—but really tending more and more to seclude himself on the edita templa of the world, on the high-towers of speculation.

And what Plato and Aristotle did, so to speak, against their express purpose and effort, yet did, because the force of contemporary tendency was irresistible—that the Stoa and Epicurus did more openly and professedly. With a difference in theory, it is true, owing to the difference in the surroundings. Virtue in the older day of the free and glorious commonwealth had meant physical and intellectual achievement, acts done in the public eye, and of course for the public good—a good with which the agent was identified at least in heart and soul, if not in his explicit consciousness. In later and worse days, when the political world, with the world divine, had withdrawn from actual identity with the central heart of the individual, and stood over-against him as a strange power and little better than a nuisance, virtue came to be counted as endurance, indifference, negative independence against a cold and a perplexing world. But even still, virtue is excellence: it is to rise above the ignoble level: to assert self-liberty against accident and circumstance—to attain self-controlled, self-satisfying independence— and to become God-like in its seclusion. Yet in two directions even it had to acknowledge something beyond the individual. The Epicurean—following out a suggestion of Aristotle—recognised the help which the free society of friends gave to the full development of the single seeker after a self-satisfying and complete life. The Stoic, not altogether refusing such help, tended rather to rest his single self on a fellowship of ideal sort, on the great city of gods and men, the civitas Dei. Thus, in separate halves, the two schools, into which Greek ethics was divided, gave expression to the sense that a new and higher community was needed—to the sense that the visible actual community no longer realised its latent idea. The Stoic emphasised the all-embracing necessity, the absolute comprehensiveness of the moral kingdom. The Epicurean saw more clearly that, if the everlasting city came from heaven, it could only visibly arise by initiation upon the earth. Christianity—in its best work—was a conjunction of the liberty with the necessity, of the human with the divine.

More interesting, perhaps, it is to note the misconception of reason and knowledge which grew up. Knowledge came more and more to be identified with the reflective and critical consciousness, which is outside reality and life, and judges it from a standpoint of its own. It came to be esteemed only in its formal and abstract shape, and at the expense of the heart and feelings. The antithesis of philosophy (or knowledge strictly so called) according to Plato was mere opinion, accidental and imperfect knowledge. The knowledge which is truly valuable is a knowledge which presupposes the full reality of life, and is the more and more completely articulated theory of it as a whole. It is—abstractly taken—a mere form of unity which has no value except in uniting: it is—taken concretely—the matter, we may say, in complete unity. It is ideal and perfect harmony of thought, appetite, and emotion: or putting it otherwise, the philosopher is one who is not merely a creature of appetite and production, not merely a creature of feeling and practical energy, but a creature, who to both of these superadds an intelligence which sets eyes in the blind forehead of these other powers, and thus, far from superseding them altogether, only raises them into completeness, and realises all that is worthy in their implicit natures. Always these two impulsive tendencies of our nature are guided by some sort of ideas and intelligence, by beliefs and opinions. But they, like their guides, are sporadically emergent, unconnected, and therefore apt to be contradictory. It is to such erratic and occasional ideas, half-truths and deceptions, that philosophy is opposed. Unfortunately for all parties, the antithesis is carried farther. Philosophy and the philosopher are further set in opposition to the faith of the heart, the intimacy and intensity of feeling, the depth of love and trust, which in practice often go along with imperfect ideas. The philosopher is made one who has emancipated himself from the heart and feelings,—a pure intelligence, who is set above all creeds, contemplating all, and holding none. Consistency and clearness become his idol, to be worshipped at any cost, save one sacrifice: and that one sacrifice is the sacrifice of his own self-conceit. For consistency generally means that all is made to harmonise with one assumed standpoint, and that whatever presents discrepancies with this alleged standard is ruthlessly thrown away. Such a philosophy mistakes its function, which is not, as Heine scoffs, to make an intelligible system by rejecting the discordant fragments of life, but to follow reverently, if slowly, in the wake of experience. Such a "perfect sage," with his parade of reasonableness, may often assume the post of a dictator.

And, above all, intelligence is only half itself when it is not also will. And both are more than mere consciousness. Plato—whom we refer to, because he is the coryphaeus of all the diverse host of Greek philosophy—seems to overestimate or rather to misconceive the place of knowledge. That it is the supreme and crowning grace of the soul, he sees. But he tends to identify it with the supreme or higher soul:—as Aristotle did after him, to be followed by the Stoics and Neo-Platonists. For them the supreme, or almost supreme reality is the intelligence or reason: the soul is only on a second grade of reality, on the borders of the natural or physical world. When Plato takes that line, he turns towards the path of asceticism, and treats the philosophic life as a preparation for that truer life when intelligence shall be all in all, for that better land where "divine dialogues" shall form the staple and substance of spiritual existence. Aristotle,—who less often treads these solitudes,—still extols the theoretic life, when the body and its needs trouble no more, when the activity of reason—the theory of theory—is attained at least as entirely as mortal conditions allow man to be deified. Of the "apathy" and the reasonable conformity of the Stoics, or of the purely negative character of Epicurean happiness (the excision of all that pained) we need not here speak. And in Plotinus and Proclus the deification of mere reason is at any rate the dominant note; whatever protests the larger Greek nature in the former may from time to time offer. The truth which philosophy should have taught was that Mind or intelligence was the element where the inner life culminated and expanded and flourished: the error which it often tended to spread was that intelligence was the higher life of which all other was a degenerate shortcoming, and something valuable on its own account.

It may be that thus to interpret Plato is to do him an injustice. It has been sometimes said that his division of parts or kinds of soul—or his distinction between its fighting horses—tends to destroy the unity of mental life. But perhaps this was exactly what he wanted to convey. There are—we may paraphrase his meaning—three kinds of human being, three types of human life. There is the man or the life of appetite and the flesh: there is the man of noble emotion and energetic depth of soul: there is the life of reasonable pursuits and organised principle. Or, we may take his meaning to be that there are three elements or provinces of mental life, which in all except a few are but imperfectly coherent and do not reach a true or complete unity. Some unity there always is: but in the life of mere appetite and impulse, even when these impulses are our nobler sentiments of love and hatred, the unity falls very far short. Or, as he puts the theme elsewhere, the soul has a passion for self-completion, a love of beauty, which in most is but a misleading lust. It is the business of the philosophic life to re-create or to foster this unity: or philosophy is the persistent search of the soul for its lost unity, the search to see that unity

43

which is always its animating principle, its inner faith. When the soul has reached this ideal—if it can be supposed to attain it (and of this the strong-souled ancient philosophers feel no doubt),—then a change must take place. The love of beauty is not suppressed; it is only made self-assured and its object freed from all imperfection. It is not that passion has ceased; but its nature is so transfigured, that it seems worthy of a nobler name, which yet we cannot give. To such a life, where battle and conflict are as such unknown, we cannot longer give the title of life: and we say that philosophy is in life a rehearsal of death[70]. And yet if there be no battle, there is not for that reason mere inaction. Hence, as the Republic concludes, the true philosopher is the complete man. He is the truth and reality which the appetitive and emotional man were seeking after and failed to realise. It is true they at first will not see this. But the whole long process of philosophy is the means to induce this conviction. And for Plato it remains clear that through experience, through wisdom, and through abstract deduction, the philosopher will justify his claim to him who hath ears to hear and heart to understand. If that be so, the asceticism of Plato is not a mere war upon flesh and sense as such, but upon flesh and sense as imperfect truth, fragmentary reality, which suppose themselves complete, though they are again and again confuted by experience, by wisdom, and by mere calculation,—a war against their blindness and shortsightedness.

Essay IV - Psycho-Genesis

"The key," says Carus, "for the ascertainment of the nature of the conscious psychical life lies in the region of the unconscious[71]." The view which these words take is at least as old as the days of Leibniz. It means that the mental world does not abruptly emerge a full-grown intelligence, but has a genesis, and follows a law of development: that its life may be described as the differentiation (with integration) of a simple or indifferentiated mass. The terms conscious and unconscious, indeed, with their lax popular uses, leave the door wide open for misconception. But they may serve to mark that the mind is to be understood only in a certain relation (partly of antithesis) to nature, and the soul only in reference to the body. The so-called "superior faculties"—specially characteristic of humanity—are founded upon, and do not abruptly supersede, the lower powers which are supposed to be specially obvious in the animals[72]. The individual and specific phenomena of consciousness, which the psychologist is generally supposed to study, rest upon a deeper, less explicated, more indefinite, life of sensibility, which in its turn fades away by immeasurable gradations into something irresponsive to the ordinary tests for sensation and life.

And yet the moment we attempt to leave the daylight of consciousness for the darker sides of sub-conscious life, the risks of misinterpretation multiply. The problem is to some extent the same as confronts the student of the ideas and principles of primitive races. There, the temptation of seeing things through the "spectacles of civilisation" is almost irresistible. So in psychology we are apt to import into the life of sensation and feeling the distinctions and relations of subsequent intellection. Nor is the difficulty lessened by Hegel's method which deals with soul, sentiency, and consciousness as grades or general characteristics in a developmental advance. He borrows his illustrations from many quarters, from morbid and anomalous states of consciousness,—less from the cases of savages, children and animals. These illustrations may be called a loose induction. But it requires a much more powerful instrument than mere induction to build up a scientific system; a framework of general principle or theory is the only basis on which to build theory by the allegation of facts, however numerous. Yet in philosophic science, which is systematised knowledge, all facts strictly so described will find their place and be estimated at their proper value.

(i.) Primitive Sensibility.

Psychology (with Hegel) takes up the work of science from biology. The mind comes before it as the supreme product of the natural world, the finest flower of organic life, the "truth" of the physical process. As such it is called by the time-honoured name of Soul. If we further go on to say that the soul is the principle of life, we must not understand this vital principle to be something over and above the life of which it is the principle. Such a locally-separable principle is an addition which is due to the analogy of mechanical movement, where a detached agent sets in motion and directs the machinery. But in the organism the principle is not thus detachable as a thing or agent. By calling Soul the principle of life we rather mean that in the vital organism, so far as it lives, all the real variety, separation, and discontinuity of parts must be reduced to unity and identity, or as Hegel would say, to ideality. To live is thus to keep all differences fluid and permeable in the fire of the life-process. Or to use a familiar term of logic, the Soul is the concept or intelligible unity of the organic body. But to call it a concept might suggest that it is only the conception through which we represent to ourselves the variety in unity of the organism. The soul, however, is more than a mere concept: and life is more than a mere mode of description for a group of movements forming an objective unity. It is a unity, subjective and objective. The organism is one life, controlling difference: and it is also one by our effort to comprehend it. The

Soul therefore is in Hegelian language described as the Idea rather than the concept of the organic body. Life is the generic title for this subject-object: but the life may be merely physical, or it may be intellectual and practical, or it may be absolute, i.e. will and know all that it is, and be all that it knows and wills.

Up to this point the world is what is called an external, which is here taken to mean (not a world external to the individual, but) a self-externalised world. That is to say, it is the observer who has hitherto by his interpretation of his perceptions supplied the "Spirit in Nature." In itself the external world has no inside, no centre: it is we who read into it the conception of a life-history. We are led to believe that a principle of unity is always at work throughout the physical world—even in the mathematical laws of natural operation. It is only intelligible and credible to us as a system, a continuous and regular development. But that system is only a hypothetical idea, though it is held to be a conclusion to which all the evidence seems unequivocally to point. And, even in organic life, the unity, though more perfect and palpable than in the mechanical and inorganic world, is only a perception, a vision,—a necessary mode of realising the unity of the facts. The phenomenon of life reveals as in a picture and an ocular demonstration the conformity of inward and outward, the identity of whole and parts, of power and utterance. But it is still outside the observer. In the function of sensibility and sentiency, however, we stand as it were on the border-line between biology and psychology. At one step we have been brought within the harmony, and are no longer mere observers and reflecters. The sentient not merely is, but is aware that it is. Hitherto as life, it only is the unity in diversity, and diversity in unity, for the outsider, i.e. only implicitly: now it is so for itself, or consciously. And in the first stage it does not know, but feels or is sentient. Here, for the first time, is created the distinction of inward and outward. Loosely indeed we may, like Mr. Spencer, speak of outward and inward in physiology: but strictly speaking, what Goethe says is true, Natur hat weder Kern noch Schaale[73]. Nature in the narrower sense knows no distinction of the inward and outward in its phenomena: it is a purely superficial order and succession of appearance and event. The Idea which has been visible to an intelligent percipient in the types and laws of the natural world, now is, actually is—is in and for itself—but at first in a minimum of content, a mere point of light, or rather the dawn which has yet to expand into the full day.

Spinoza has asserted that "all individual bodies are animate, though in different degrees[74]." Now it is to a great extent this diversity of degree on which the main interest turns. Yet it is well to remember that the abrupt and trenchant separations which popular practice loves are overridden to a deeper view by an essential unity of idea, reducing them to indifference. If, that is, we take seriously the Spinozist unity of Substance, and the continual correlation (to call it no more) of extension and consciousness therein, we cannot avoid the conclusion which even Bacon would admit of something describable as attraction and perception, something subduing diversity to unity. But whether it be well to name this soul or life is a different matter. It may indeed only be taken to mean that all true being must be looked on as a real unity and individuality, must, that is, be conceived as manifesting itself in organisation, must be referred to a self-centred and self-developing activity. But this—which is the fundamental thesis of idealism—is hardly all that is meant. Rather Spinoza would imply that all things which form a real unity must have life—must have inner principle and unifying reality: and what he teaches is closely akin to the Leibnitian doctrine that every substantial existence reposes upon a monad, a unity which is at once both a force and a cognition, a "representation" and an appetite or nisus to act. When Fechner in a series of works[75] expounds and defends the hypothesis that plants and planets are not destitute of soul, any more than man and animals, he only gives a more pronounced expression to this idealisation or spiritualisation of the natural world. But for the moment the point to be noted is that all of this idealistic doctrine is an inference, or a development which finds its point d'appui in the fact of sensation. And the problem of the Philosophy of Mind is just to trace the process whereby a mere shock of sensation has grown into a conception and a faith in the goodness, beauty and intelligence of the world.

Schopenhauer has put the point with his usual picturesqueness. Outward nature presents nothing but a play of forces. At first, however, this force shows merely the mechanical phenomena of pressure and impact, and its theory is sufficiently described by mathematical physics. But in the process of nature force assumes higher types, types where it loses a certain amount of its externality[76], till in the organic world it acquires a peculiar phase which Schopenhauer calls Will, meaning by that, however, an organising and controlling power, a tendency or nisus to be and live, which is persistent and potent, but without consciousness. This blind force, which however has a certain coherence and purposiveness, is in the animal organism endowed with a new character, in consequence of the emergence of a new organ. This organ, the brain and nervous system, causes the evolution into clear day of an element which has been growing more and more urgent. The gathering tendency of force to return into itself is now complete: the cycle of operation is formed: and the junction of the two currents issues in the spark of sensation. The blind force now becomes seeing.

But at first—and this is the point we have to emphasise—its powers of vision are limited. Sensibility is either a local and restricted phenomenon: or, in so far as it is not local, it is vague and indefinite, and hardly entitled to the name of sensibility. Either it is a dim, but far-reaching, sympathy with environing existence, and in that case only so-called blind will or feeling: or if it is clear, is locally confined, and at first within very narrow limits. Neither of these points must be lost sight of. On the one hand feeling has to be regarded as the dull and confused stirring of an almost infinite sympathy with the world—a pulse which has come from the far-distant movements of the universe, and bears with it, if but as a possibility, the wealth of an infinite message. On the other hand, feeling at first only becomes real, in this boundless ideality to which its possibilities extend, by restricting itself to one little point and from several points organising itself to a unity of bodily feeling, till it can go on from thence to embrace the universe in distinct and articulate comprehension.

Soul, says Hegel, is not a separate and additional something over and above the rest of nature: it is rather nature's "'universal immaterialism, and simple ideal life[77]." There were ancient philosophers who spoke of the soul as a self-adjusting number,—as a harmony, or equilibrium[78]—and the moderns have added considerably to the list of these analogical definitions. As definitions they obviously fall short. Yet these things give, as it were, by anticipation, an image of soul, as the "ideality," which reduces the manifold to unity. The adhesions and cohesions of matter, its gravitating attractions, its chemical affinities and electrical polarities, the intricate out-and-in of organic structure, are all preludes to the true incorporating unity which is the ever-immanent supersession of the endless self-externalism and successionalism of physical reality. But in sentiency, feeling, or sensibility, the unity which all of these imply without reaching, is explicitly present. It is implicitly an all-embracing unity: an infinite,—which has no doors and no windows, for the good reason that it needs none, because it has nothing outside it, because it "expresses" and "envelopes" (however confusedly at first) the whole universe. Thus, even if, with localising phraseology, we may describe mind, where it appears emerging in the natural world, as a mere feeble and incidental outburst,—a rebellion breaking out as in some petty province or isolated region against the great law of the physical realm—we are in so speaking taking only an external standpoint. But with the rise of mind in nature the bond of externalism is implicitly overcome. To it, and where it really is, there is nothing outside, nothing transcendent. Everything which is said to be outside mind is only outside a localised and limited mind—outside a mind which is imperfectly and abstractly realised—not outside mind absolutely. Mind is the absolute negation of externality: not a mere relative negative, as the organism may be biologically described as inner in respect of the environment. To accomplish this negation in actuality, to bring the multiplicity and externality of things into the unity and identity of one Idea, is the process of development of mind from animal sensibility to philosophic knowledge, from appetite to art,—the process of culture through the social state under the influence of religion.

Sentiency or psychic matter (mind-stuff), to begin with, is in some respects like the tabula rasa of the empiricists. It is the possibility—but the real possibility—of intelligence rather than intelligence itself. It is the monotonous undifferentiated inwardness—a faint self-awareness and self-realisation of the material world, but at first a mere vague psychical protoplasm and without defined nucleus, without perceptible organisation or separation of structures. If there is self-awareness, it is not yet discriminated into a distinct and unified self, not yet differentiated and integrated,—soul in the condition of a mere "Is," which, however, is nothing determinate. It is very much in the situation of Condillac's statue-man—une statue organisée intérieurement comme nous, et animée d'un esprit privé de toute espèce d'idées: alike at least so far that the rigid uniformity of the latter's envelope prevents all articulated organisation of its faculties. The foundation under all the diversity and individuality in the concrete intelligent and volitional life is a common feeling,—a sensus communis—a general and indeterminate susceptibility to influence, a sympathy responsive, but responsive vaguely and equivocally, to all the stimuli of the physical environment. There was once a time, according to primitive legend, when man understood the language of beast and bird, and even surprised the secret converse of trees and flowers. Such fancies are but the exaggeration of a solidarity of conscious life which seems to spread far in the sub-conscious realm, and to narrow the individual's soul into limited channels as it rises into clear self-perception,

> *"As thro' the frame that binds him in*
> *His isolation grows defined."*

It may be a mere dream that, as Goethe feigns of Makaria in his romance[79], there are men and women in sympathy with the vicissitudes of the starry regions: and hypotheses of lunar influence, or dogmas of astrological destiny, may count to the present guardians of the sciences as visionary superstitions. Yet science in these regions has no reason to be dogmatic; her function hitherto can only be critical; and even for that, her data are scanty and her principles extremely general. The influences on the mental mood and faculty, produced by climate and seasons, by local environment and national type, by individual peculiarities, by the differences of age and sex, and by the alternation of night and day, of sleep and waking, are less questionable. It is easy no doubt to ignore or forget them: easy to remark how indefinable and incalculable they are. But that does not lessen their radical and inevitable impress in the determination of the whole character. "The sum of our existence, divided by reason, never comes out exact, but always leaves a marvellous remainder[80]." Irrational this residue is, in the sense that it is inexplicable, and incommensurable with the well-known quantities of conscious and voluntarily organised life. But a scientific psychology, which is adequate to the real and concrete mind, should never lose sight of the fact that every one of its propositions in regard to the more advanced phases of intellectual development is thoroughly and in indefinable ways modified by these preconditions. When that is remembered, it will be obvious how complicated is the problem of adapting psychology for the application to education, and how dependent the solution of that problem is upon an experiential familiarity with the data of individual and national temperament and character.

The first stage in mental development is the establishment of regular and uniform relations between soul and body: it is the differentiation of organs and the integration of function: the balance between sensation and movement, between the afferent and efferent processes of sensitivity. Given a potential soul, the problem is to make it actual in an individual body. It is the business of a physical psychology to describe in detail the steps by which the body we are attached to is made inward as our idea through the several organs and their nervous appurtenances: whereas a psychical physiology would conversely explain the corresponding processes for the expression of the emotions and for the objectification of the volitions. Thus soul inwardises (erinnert) or envelops body: which body "expresses" or develops soul. The actual soul is the unity of both, is the percipient individual. The solidarity or "communion" of body and soul is here the dominant fact: the soul sentient of changes in its peripheral organs, and transmitting emotion and volition into physical effect. It is on this psychical unity,—the unity which is the soul of the diversity of body—that all the subsequent developments of mind rest. Sensation is thus the prius—or basis—of all mental life: the organisation of soul in body and of body in soul. It is the process which historically has been prepared in the evolution of animal life from those undifferentiated forms where specialised organs are yet unknown, and which each individual has further to realise and complete for himself, by learning to see and hear, and use his limbs. At first, moreover, it begins from many separate centres and only through much collision and mutual compliance arrives at comparative uniformity and centralisation. The common basis of united sensibility supplied by the one organism has to be made real and effective, and it is so at first by sporadic and comparatively independent developments. If self-hood means reference to self of what is prima facie not self, and projection of self therein, there is in primitive sensibility only the germ or possibility of self-hood. In the early phases of psychic development the centre is fluctuating and ill-defined, and it takes time and trouble to co-ordinate or unify the various starting-points of sensibility[81].

This consolidation of inward life may be looked at either formally or concretely. Under the first head, it means the growth of a central unity of apperception. In the second case, it means a peculiar aggregate of ideas and sentiments. There is growing up within him what we may call the individuality of the individual,—an irrational, i.e. not consciously intelligent, nether-self or inner soul, a firm aggregation of hopes and wishes, of views and feelings, or rather of tendencies and temperament, of character hereditary and acquired. It is the law of the natural will or character which from an inaccessible background dominates our action,—which, because it is not realised and formulated in consciousness, behaves like a guardian spirit, or genius, or destiny within us. This genius is the sub-conscious unity of the sensitive life—the manner of man which unknown to ourselves we are,—and which influences us against our nominal or formal purposes. So far as this predominates, our ends, rough hew them how we will, are given by a force which is not really, i.e. with full consciousness, ours: by a mass of ingrained prejudice and unreasoned sympathies, of instincts and passions, of fancies and feelings, which have condensed and organised themselves into a natural power. As the child in the mother's womb is responsive to her psychic influences, so the development of a man's psychic life is guided by feelings centred in objects and agents external to him, who form the genius presiding over his development. His soul, to that extent, is really in another: he himself is selfless, and when his stay is removed the principle of his life is gone[82]. He is but a bundle of impressions, held together by influences and ties which in years before consciousness proper began made him what he is. Such is the involuntary adaptation to example and environment, which establishes in the depths below personality a self which becomes hereafter the determinant of action. Early years, in which the human being is naturally susceptible, build up by imitation, by pliant obedience, an image, a system, reproducing the immediate surroundings. The soul, as yet selfless, and ready to accept any imprint, readily moulds itself into the likeness of an authoritative influence.

The step by which the universality or unity of the self is realised in the variety of its sensation is Habit. Habit gives us a definite standing-ground in the flux of single impressions: it is the identification of ourselves with what is most customary and familiar: an identification which takes place by practice and repetition. If it circumscribes us to one little province of being, it on the other frees us from the vague indeterminateness where we are at the mercy of every passing mood. It makes thus much of our potential selves our very own, our acquisition and permanent possession. It, above all, makes us free and at one with our bodily part, so that henceforth we start as a subjective unit of body and soul. We have now as the result of the anthropological process a self or ego, an individual consciousness able to reflect and compare, setting itself on one side (a soul in bodily organisation), and on the other setting an object of consciousness, or external world, a world of other things. All this presupposes that the soul has actualised itself by appropriating and acquiring as its expression and organ the physical sensibility which is its body. By restricting and establishing itself, it has gained a fixed standpoint. No doubt it has localised and confined itself, but it is no longer at the disposal of externals and accident: it has laid the foundation for higher developments.

(ii.) *Anomalies of Psychical Life.*

Psychology, as we have seen, goes for information regarding the earlier stages of mental growth to the child and the animal,—perhaps also to the savage. So too sociology founds certain conclusions upon the observations of savage customs and institutions, or on the earlier records of the race. In both cases with a limitation caused by the externality and fragmentariness of the facts and the need of interpreting them through our own conscious experiences. There is however another direction in which corresponding inquiries may be pursued; and where the danger of the conclusions arrived at, though not perhaps less real, is certainly of a different kind. In sociology we can observe—and almost experiment upon—the phenomena of the lapsed, degenerate and criminal classes. The advantage of such observation is that the object of study can be made to throw greater light on his own inner states. He is a little of the child and a little of the savage, but these aspects co-exist with other features which put him more on a level with the intelligent observer. Similar pathological regions are open to us in the case of psychology. There the anomalous and morbid conditions of mind co-exist with a certain amount of mature consciousness. So presented, they are thrown out into relief. They form the negative instances which serve to corroborate our positive inductions. The regularly concatenated and solid structure of normal mind is under abnormal and deranged conditions thrown into disorder, and its constituents are presented in their several isolation. Such phenomena are relapses into more rudimentary grades: but with the difference that they are set in the midst of a more advanced phase of intellectual life.

Even amongst candid and honest-minded students of psychology there is a certain reluctance to dabble in researches into the night-side of the mental range. Herbart is an instance of this shrinking. The region of the Unconscious seemed—and to many still seems—a region in which the charlatan and the dupe can and must play into each other's hands. Once in the whirl of spiritualist and crypto-psychical inquiry you could not tell how far you might be carried. The facts moreover were of a peculiar type. Dependent as they seemed to be on the frame of mind of observers and observed, they defied the ordinary criteria of detached and abstract observation. You can only observe them, it is urged, when you believe; scepticism destroys them. Now there is a widespread natural impatience against what Bacon has called "monodical" phenomena, phenomena i.e. which claim to come under a special law of their own, or to have a private and privileged sphere. And this impatience cuts the Gordian knot by a determination to treat all instances which oppose its hitherto ascertained laws as due to deception and fraud, or, at the best, to incompetent observation, confusions of memory, and superstitions of ignorance. Above all, great interests of religion and personality seemed to connect themselves with these revelations—interests, at any rate, to which our common humanity thrills; it seemed as if, in this region beyond the customary range of the conscious and the seen, one might learn something of the deeper realities which lie in the unseen. But to feel that so much was at stake was naturally unfavourable to purely dispassionate observation.

The philosophers were found—as might have been expected—amongst those most strongly attracted by these problems. Even Kant had been fascinated by the spiritualism of Swedenborg, though he finally turned away sceptical. At least as early as 1806 Schelling had been interested by Ritter's researches into the question of telepathy, or the power of the human will to produce without mechanical means of conveyance an effect at a distance. He was looking forward to the rise of a Physica coelestis, or New Celestial Physics, which should justify the old magic. About the same date his brother Karl published an essay on Animal Magnetism. The novel phenomena of galvanism and its congeners suggested vast possibilities in the range of the physical powers, especially of the physical powers of the human psyche as a natural agent. The divining-rod was revived. Clairvoyance and somnambulism were carefully studied, and the curative powers of animal magnetism found many advocates[83].

Interest in these questions went naturally with the new conception of the place of Man in Nature, and of Nature as the matrix of mind[84]. But it had been acutely stimulated by the performances and professions of Mesmer at Vienna and Paris in the last quarter of the eighteenth century. These—though by no means really novel—had forced the artificial world of science and fashion to discuss the claim advanced for a new force which, amongst other things, could cure ailments that baffled the ordinary practitioner. This new force—mainly because of the recent interest in the remarkable advances of magnetic and electrical research—was conceived as a fluid, and called Animal Magnetism. At one time indeed Mesmer actually employed a magnet in the manipulation by which he induced the peculiar condition in his patients. The accompaniments of his procedure were in many respects those of the quack-doctor; and with the quack indeed he was often classed. A French commission of inquiry appointed to examine into his performances reported in 1784 that, while there was no doubt as to the reality of many of the phenomena, and even of the cures, there was no evidence for the alleged new physical force, and declared the effects to be mainly attributable to the influence of imagination. And with the mention of this familiar phrase, further explanation was supposed to be rendered superfluous.

In France political excitement allowed the mesmeric theory and practice to drop out of notice till the fall of the first Empire. But in Germany there was a considerable amount of investigations and hypotheses into these mystical phenomena, though rarely by the ordinary routine workers in the scientific field. The phenomena where they were discussed were studied and interpreted in two directions. Some theorists, like Jung-Stilling, Eschenmayer, Schubert, and Kerner, took the more metaphysicist and spiritualistic view: they saw in them the witness to a higher truth, to the presence and operation in this lower world of a higher and spiritual matter, a so-called ether. Thus Animal Magnetism supplied a sort of physical theory of the other world and the other life. Jung-Stilling, e.g. in his "Theory of Spirit-lore." (1808), regarded the spiritualistic phenomena as a justification of—what he believed to be—the Kantian doctrine that in the truly real and persistent world space and time are no more. The other direction of inquiry kept more to the physical field. Ritter (whose researches interested both Schelling and Hegel) supposed he had detected the new force underlying mesmerism and the like, and gave to it the name of Siderism (1808); while Amoretti of Milan named the object of his experiments Animal Electrometry (1816). Kieser[85], again (1826) spoke of Tellurism, and connected animal magnetism with the play of general terrestrial forces in the human being.

At a later date (1857) Schindler, in his "Magical Spirit-life," expounded a theory of mental polarity. The psychical life has two poles or centres,—its day-pole, around which revolves our ordinary and superficial current of ideas, and its night-pole, round which gathers the sub-conscious and deeper group of beliefs and sentiments. Either life has a memory, a consciousness, a world of its own: and they flourish to a large extent inversely to each other. The day-world has for its organs of receiving information the ordinary senses. But the magical or night-world of the soul has its feelers also, which set men directly in telepathic rapport with influences, however distant, exerted by the whole world: and through this "inner sense" which serves to concentrate in itself all the telluric forces (—a sense which in its various aspects we name instinct, presentiment, conscience) is constructed the fabric of our sub-conscious system. Through it man is a sort of résumé of all the cosmic life, in secret affinity and sympathy with all natural processes; and by the will which stands in response therewith he can exercise a directly creative action on external nature. In normal and healthy conditions the two currents of psychic life run on harmonious but independent. But in the phenomena of somnambulism, clairvoyance, and delirium, the magic region becomes preponderant, and comes into collision with the other. The dark-world emerges into the realm of day as a portentous power: and there is the feeling of a double personality, or of an indwelling genius, familiar spirit, or demon.

To the ordinary physicist the so-called Actio in distans was a hopeless stumbling-block. If he did not comprehend the transmission (as it is called) of force where there was immediate contact, he was at least perfectly familiar with the outer aspect of it as a condition of his limited experience. It needed one beyond the mere hodman of science to say with Laplace: "We are so far from knowing all the agents of nature, that it would be very unphilosophical to deny the existence of phenomena solely because they are inexplicable in the present state of our knowledge." Accordingly mesmerism and its allied manifestations were generally abandoned to the bohemians of science, and to investigators with dogmatic bias. It was still employed as a treatment for certain ailments: and philosophers, as different as Fichte and Schopenhauer[86], watched its fate with attention. But the herd of professional scientists fought shy of it. The experiments of Braid at Manchester in 1841 gradually helped to give research into the subject a new character. Under the name of Hypnotism (or, rather at first Neuro-hypnotism) he described the phenomena of the magnetic sleep (induced through prolonged staring at a bright object), such as abnormal rigidity of body, perverted sensibility, and the remarkable obedience of the subject to the command or suggestions of the operator. Thirty years afterwards, the matter became an object of considerable experimental and theoretic work in France, at the rival schools of Paris and Nancy; and the question, mainly under the title of hypnotism, though the older name is still occasionally heard, has been for several years brought prominently under public notice.

It cannot be said that the net results of these observations and hypotheses are of a very definitive character. While a large amount of controversy has been waged on the comparative importance of the several methods and instruments by which the hypnotic or mesmeric trance may be induced, and a scarcely less wide range of divergence prevails with regard to the physiological and pathological conditions in connexion with which it has been most conspicuously manifested, there has been less anxiety shown to determine its precise psychical nature, or its significance in mental development. And yet the better understanding of these aspects may throw light on several points connected with primitive religion and the history of early civilisation, indeed over the whole range of what is called

Völkerpsychologie. Indeed this is one of the points which may be said to emerge out of the confusion of dispute. Phenomena at least analogous to those styled hypnotic have a wide range in the anthropological sphere[87]: and the proper characters which belong to them will only be caught by an observer who examines them in the widest variety of examples. Another feature which has been put in prominence is what has been called "psychological automatism." And in this name two points seem to deserve note. The first is the spontaneous and as it were mechanical consecution of mental states in the soul whence the interfering effect of voluntary consciousness has been removed. And the second is the unfailing or accurate regularity, so contrary to the hesitating and uncertain procedure of our conscious and reasoned action, which so often is seen in the unreflecting and unreasoned movements. To this invariable sequence of psychical movement the superior control and direction by the intelligent self has to adapt itself, just as it respects the order of physical laws.

But, perhaps, the chief conclusion to be derived from hypnotic experience is the value of suggestion or suggestibility. Even cool thinkers like Kant have recognised how much mere mental control has to do with bodily state,—how each of us, in this way, is often for good or for ill his own physician. An idea is a force, and is only inactive in so far as it is held in check by other ideas. "There is no such thing as hypnotism," says one: "there are only different degrees of suggestibility." This may be to exaggerate: yet it serves to impress the comparatively secondary character of many of the circumstances on which the specially mesmeric or hypnotic experimentalist is apt to lay exclusive stress. The methods may probably vary according to circumstances. But the essence of them all is to get the patient out of the general frame and system of ideas and perceptions in which his ordinary individuality is encased. Considering how for all of us the reality of concrete life is bound up with our visual perceptions, how largely our sanity depends upon the spatial idea, and how that depends on free ocular range, we can understand that darkness and temporary loss of vision are powerful auxiliaries in the hypnotic process, as in magical and superstitious rites. But a great deal short of this may serve to establish influence. The mind of the majority of human beings, but especially of the young, may be compared to a vacant seat waiting for some one to fill it.

In Hegel's view hypnotic phenomena produce a kind of temporary and artificial atavism. Mechanical or chemical means, or morbid conditions of body, may cause even for the intelligent adult a relapse into states of mind closely resembling those exhibited by the primitive or the infantile sensibility. The intelligent personality, where powers are bound up with limitations and operate through a chain of means and ends, is reduced to its primitively undifferentiated condition. Not that it is restored to its infantile simplicity; but that all subsequent acquirements operate only as a concentrated individuality, or mass of will and character, released from the control of the self-possessed mind, and invested (by the latter's withdrawal) with a new quasi-personality of their own. With the loss of the world of outward things, there may go, it is supposed, a clearer perception of the inward and particularly of the organic life. The Soul contains the form of unity which other experiences had impressed upon it: but this form avails in its subterranean existence where it creates a sort of inner self. And this inner self is no longer, like the embodied self of ordinary consciousness, an intelligence served by organs, and proceeding by induction and inference. Its knowledge is not mediated or carried along specific channels: it does not build up, piecemeal, by successive steps of synthesis and analysis, by gradual idealisation, the organised totality of its intellectual world. The somnambulist and the clairvoyant see without eyes, and carry their vision directly into regions where the waking consciousness of orderly intelligence cannot enter. But that region is not the world of our higher ideas,—of art, religion, and philosophy. It is still the sensitivity—that realm of sensitivity which is ordinarily covered by unconsciousness. Such sensitive clairvoyants may, as it were, hear themselves growing; they may discern the hidden quivers and pulses of blood and tissue, the seats of secret pain and all the unrevealed workings in the dark chambers of the flesh. But always their vision seems confined to that region, and will fall short of the world of light and ideal truth. It is towards the nature-bond of sensitive solidarity with earth, and flowers, and trees, the life that "rolls through all things," not towards the spiritual unity which broods over the world and "impels all thinking things," that these immersions in the selfless universe lead us.

What Hegel chiefly sees in these phenomena is their indication, even on the natural side of man, of that ideality of the material, which it is the work of intelligence to produce in the more spiritual life, in the fully-developed mind. The latter is the supreme over-soul, that Absolute Mind which in our highest moods, aesthetic and religious, we approximate to. But mind, as it tends towards the higher end to "merge itself in light," to identify itself yet not wholly lost, but retained, in the fullness of undivided intellectual being, so at the lower end it springs from a natural and underlying unity, the immense solidarity of nether-soul, the great Soul of Nature—the "Substance" which is to be raised into the "Subject" which is true divinity. Between these two unities, the nature-given nether-soul and the spirit-won over-soul, lies the conscious life of man: a process of differentiation which narrows and of redintegration which enlarges,—which alternately builds up an isolated personality and dissolves it in a common intelligence and sympathy. It is because mental or tacit "suggestion"[88] (i.e. will-influence exercised without word or sign, or other sensible mode of connexion), thought-transference, or thought-reading (which is more than dexterous apprehension of delicate muscular signs), exteriorisation or transposition of sensibility into objects primarily non-sensitive, clairvoyance (i.e. the power of describing, as if from direct perception, objects or events removed in space beyond the recognised limits of sensation), and somnambulism, so far as it implies lucid vision with sealed eyes,—it is because these things seem to show the essential ideality of matter, that Hegel is interested in them. The ordinary conditions of consciousness and even of practical life in society are a derivative and secondary state; a product of processes of individualism, which however are never completed, and leave a large margin for idealising intelligence to fulfil. From a state which is not yet personality to a state which is more than can be described as personality—lies the mental movement. So Fichte, too, had regarded the power of the somnambulist as laying open a world underlying the development of egoity and self-consciousness[89]: "the merely sensuous man is still in somnambulism," only a somnambulism of waking hours: "the true waking is the life in God, to be free in him, all else is sleep and dream." "Egoity," he adds, "is a merely formal principle, utterly, and never qualitative (i.e. the essence and universal force)." For Schopenhauer, too, the experiences of animal magnetism had seemed to prove the absolute supernatural power of the radical will in its superiority to the intellectual categories of space, time, and causal sequence: to prove the reality of the metaphysical which is at the basis of all conscious divisions.

(iii.) *The Development of Inner Freedom.*

The result of the first range in the process of psycho-genesis was to make the body a sign and utterance of the Soul, with a fixed and determinate type. The "anthropological process" has defined and settled the mere general sentiency of soul into an individualised shape, a localised and limited self, a bundle of habits. It has made the soul an Ego or self: a power which looks out upon the world as a spectator, lifted above immanence in the general tide of being, but only so lifted because it has made itself one in the world of objects, a thing among things. The Mind has reached the point of view of reflection. Instead of a general identifiability with all nature, it has encased itself in a limited range, from which it looks forth on what is now other than itself. If previously it was mere inward sensibility, it is now sense, perceptive of an object here and now, of an external world. The step has involved some price: and that price is, that it has attained independence and self-hood at the cost of surrendering the content it had hitherto held in one with itself. It is now a blank receptivity, open to the impressions of an outside world: and the changes which take place in its process of apprehension seem to it to be given from outside. The world it perceives is a world of isolated and independent objects: and it takes them as they are given. But a closer insistance on the perception develops the implicit intelligence, which makes it possible. The percipient mind is no mere recipiency or susceptibility with its forms of time and space: it is spontaneously active, it is the source of categories, or is an apperceptive power,—an understanding. Consciousness, thus discovered to be a creative or constructive faculty, is strictly speaking self-consciousness[90].

Self-consciousness appears at first in the selfish or narrowly egoistic form of appetite and impulse. The intelligence which claims to mould and construe the world of objects—which, in Kant's phrase, professes to give us nature—is implicitly the lord of that world. And that supremacy it carries out as appetite—as destruction. The self is but a bundle of wants—its supremacy over things is really subjection to them: the satisfaction of appetite is baffled by a new desire which leaves it as it was before. The development of self-consciousness to a more adequate shape is represented by Hegel as taking place through the social struggle for existence. Human beings, too, are in the first instance to the uninstructed appetite or the primitive self-consciousness (which is simply a succession of individual desires for satisfaction of natural want) only things,—adjectival to that self's individual existence. To them, too, his primary relation is to appropriate and master them. Might precedes right. But the social struggle for existence forces him to recognise something other which is kindred to himself,—a limiting principle, another self which has to form an element in his calculations, not to be neglected. And gradually, we may suppose, the result is the division of humanity into two levels, a ruling lordly class, and a class of slaves,—a state of inequality in which each knows that his appetite is in some measure checked by a more or less permanent other. Lastly, perhaps soonest in the inferior order, there is fashioned the perception that its self-seeking in its isolated appetites is subject to an abiding authority, a continuing consciousness. There grows up a social self—a sense of general humanity and solidarity with other beings—a larger self with which each identifies himself, a common ground. Understanding was selfish intelligence: practical in the egoistic sense. In the altruistic or universal sense practical, a principle social and unifying character, intelligence is Reason.

Thus, Man, beginning as a percipient consciousness, apprehending single objects in space and time, and as an appetitive self bent upon single gratifications, has ended as a rational being,—a consciousness purged of its selfishness and isolation, looking forward openly and impartially on the universe of things and beings. He has ceased to be a mere animal, swallowed up in the moment and the individual, using his intelligence only in selfish satisfactions. He is no longer bound down by the struggle for existence, looking on everything as a mere thing, a mere means. He has erected himself above himself and above his environment, but that because he occupies a point of view at which he and his environment are no longer purely antithetical and exclusive[91]. He has reached what is really the moral standpoint: the point i.e. at which he is inspired by a universal self-consciousness, and lives in that peaceful world where the antitheses of individualities and of outward and inward have ceased to trouble. "The natural man," says Hegel[92], "sees in the woman flesh of his flesh: the moral and spiritual man sees spirit of his spirit in the moral and spiritual being and by its means." Hitherto we have been dealing with something falling below the full truth of mind: the region of immediate sensibility with its thorough immersion of mind in body, first of all, and secondly its gradual progress to a general standpoint. It is only in the third part of Subjective mind that we are dealing with the psychology of a being who in the human sense knows and wills, i.e. apprehends general truth, and carries out ideal purposes.

Thus, for the third time, but now on a higher plane, that of intelligence and rationality, is traced the process of development or realisation by which reason becomes reasoned knowledge and rational will, a free or autonomous intelligence. And, as before, the starting-point, alike in theoretical and practical mind, is feeling—or immediate knowledge and immediate sense of Ought. The basis of thought is an immediate perception—a sensuous affection or given something, and the basis of the idea of a general satisfaction is the natural claim to determine the outward existence conformably to individual feeling. In intelligent perception or intuition the important factor is attention, which raises it above mere passive acceptance and awareness of a given fact. Attention thus involves on one hand the externality of its object, and on the other affirms its dependence on the act of the subject: it sets the objects before and out of itself, in space and time, but yet in so doing it shows itself master of the objects. If perception presuppose attention, in short, they cease to be wholly outward: we make them ours, and the space and time they fill are projected by us. So attended to, they are appropriated, inwardised and recollected: they take their place in a mental place and mental time: they receive a general or de-individualised character in the memory-image. These are retained as mental property, but retained actually only in so far they are revivable and revived. Such revival is the work of imagination working by the so-called laws of association. But the possession of its ideas thus inwardised and recollected by the mind is largely a matter of chance. The mind is not really fully master of them until it has been able to give them a certain objectivity, by replacing the mental image by a vocal, i.e. a sensible sign. By means of words, intelligence turns its ideas or representations into quasi-realities: it creates a sort of superior sense-world, the world of language, where ideas live a potential, which is also an actual, life. Words are sensibles, but they are sensibles which completely lose themselves in their meaning. As sensibles, they render possible that verbal memory which is the handmaid of thought: but which also as merely mechanical can leave thought altogether out of account. It is through words that thought is made possible: for it alone permits the movement through ideas without being distracted through a multitude of associations. In them thought has an instrument completely at its own level, but still only a machine, and in memory the working of that machine. We think in names, not in general images, but in terms which only serve as vehicles for mental synthesis and analysis.

It is as such a thinking being—a being who can use language, and manipulate general concepts or take comprehensive views, that man is a rational will. A concept of something to be done—a feeling even of some end more or less comprehensive in its quality, is the implication of what can be called will. At first indeed its material may be found as immediately given and all its volitionality may lie in the circumstance that the intelligent being sets this forward as a governing and controlling Ought. Its vehicle, in short, may be mere impulse, or inclination, and even passion: but it is the choice and the purposive adoption of means to the given end. Gradually it attains to the idea of a general satisfaction, or of happiness. And this end seems positive and definite. It soon turns out however to be little but a prudent and self-denying superiority to particular passions and inclinations in the interest of a comprehensive ideal. The free will or intelligence has so far only a negative and formal value: it is the perfection of an autonomous and freely self-developing mind. Such a mind, which in language has acquired the means of realising an intellectual system of things superior to the restrictions of sense, and which has emancipated reason from the position of slave to inclination, is endued with the formal conditions of moral conduct. Such a mind will transform its own primarily physical dependence into an image of the law of reason and create the ethical life: and in the strength of that establishment will go forth to conquer the world into a more and more adequate realisation of the eternal Idea.

Essay V - Ethics And Politics

"In dealing," says Hegel, "with the Idea of the State, we must not have before our eyes a particular state, or a particular institution: we must rather study the Idea, this actual God, on his own account. Every State, however bad we may find it according to our principles, however defective we may discover this or that feature to be, still contains, particularly if it belongs to the mature states of our time, all the essential factors of its existence. But as it is easier to discover faults than to comprehend the affirmative, people easily fall into the mistake of letting individual aspects obscure the intrinsic organism of the State itself. The State is no ideal work of art: it stands in the everyday world, in the sphere, that is, of arbitrary act, accident, and error, and a variety of faults may mar the regularity of its traits. But the ugliest man, the criminal, a sick man and a cripple, is after all a living man; the affirmative, Life, subsists in spite of the defect: and this affirmative is here the theme[93]." "It is the theme of philosophy," he adds, "to ascertain the substance which is immanent in the show of the temporal and transient, and the eternal which is present."

(i.) *Hegel as a Political Critic.*

But if this is true, it is also to be remembered that the philosopher is, like other men, the son of his age, and estimates the value of reality from preconceptions and aspirations due to his generation. The historical circumstances of his nation as well as the personal experiences of his life help to determine his horizon, even in the effort to discover the hidden pulse and movement of the social organism. This is specially obvious in political philosophy. The conception of ethics and politics which is presented in the Encyclopaedia was in 1820 produced with more detail as the Grundlinien der Philosophie des Rechts. Appearing, as it did, two years after his appointment to a professorship at Berlin, and in the midst of a political struggle between the various revolutionary and conservative powers and parties of Germany, the book became, and long remained, a target for embittered criticism. The so-called War of Liberation or national movement to shake off the French yoke was due to a coalition of parties, and had naturally been in part supported by tendencies and aims which went far beyond the ostensive purpose either of leaders or of combatants. Aspirations after a freer state were entwined with radical and socialistic designs to reform the political hierarchy of the Fatherland: high ideals and low vulgarities were closely intermixed: and the noble enthusiasm of youth was occasionally played on by criminal and anarchic intriguers. In a strong and wise and united Germany some of these schemes might have been tolerated. But strength, wisdom, and unity were absent. In the existing tension between Austria and Prussia for the leadership, in the ill-adapted and effete constitutions of the several principalities which were yet expected to realise the advance which had taken place in society and ideas during the last thirty years, the outlook on every hand seemed darker and more threatening than it might have otherwise done. Governments, which had lost touch with their peoples, suspected conspiracy and treason: and a party in the nation credited their rulers with gratuitous designs against private liberty and rights. There was a vast but ill-defined enthusiasm in the breasts of the younger world, and it was shared by many of their teachers. It seemed to their immense aspirations that the war of liberation had failed of its true object and left things much as they were. The volunteers had not fought for the political systems of Austria or Prussia, or for the three-and-thirty princes of Germany: but for ideas, vague, beautiful, stimulating. To such a mood the continuance of the old system was felt as a cruel deception and a reaction. The governments on their part had not realised the full importance of the spirit that had been aroused, and could not at a moment's notice set their house in order, even had there been a clearer outlook for reform than was offered. They too had suffered, and had realised their insecurity: and were hardly in a mood to open their gates to the enemy.

Coming on such a situation of affairs, Hegel's book would have been likely in any case to provoke criticism. For it took up a line of political theory which was little in accord with the temper of the age. The conception of the state which it expounded is not far removed in essentials from the conception which now dominates the political life of the chief European nations. But in his own time it came upon ears which were naturally disposed to misconceive it. It was unacceptable to the adherents of the ancien régime, as much as to the liberals. It was declared by one party to be a glorification of the Prussian state: by another to rationalise the sanctities of authority. It was pointed out that the new professor was a favourite of the leading minister, that his influence was dominant in scholastic appointments, and that occasional gratuities from the crown proved his acceptability. A contemporary professor, Fries, remarked that Hegel's theory of the state had grown "not in the gardens of science but on the dung-hill of servility." Hegel himself was aware that he had planted a blow in the face of a "shallow and pretentious sect," and that his book had "given great offence to the demagogic folk." Alike in religious and political life he was impatient of sentimentalism, of rhetorical feeling, of wordy enthusiasm. A positive storm of scorn burst from him at much-promising and little-containing declamation that appealed to the pathos of ideas, without sense of the complex work of construction and the system of principles which were needed to give them reality. His impatience of demagogic gush led him (in the preface) into a tactless attack on Fries, who was at the moment in disgrace for his participation in the demonstration at the Wartburg. It led him to an attack on the bumptiousness of those who held that conscientious conviction was ample justification for any proceeding:—an attack which opponents were not unwilling to represent as directed against the principle of conscience itself.

Yet Hegel's views on the nature of political unity were not new. Their nucleus had been formed nearly twenty years before. In the years that immediately followed the French revolution he had gone through the usual anarchic stage of intelligent youth. He had wondered whether humanity might not have had a nobler destiny, had fate given supremacy to some heresy rather than the orthodox creed of Christendom. He had seen religion in the past "teaching what despotism wished,—contempt of the human race, its incapacity for anything good[94]." But his earliest reflections on political power belong to a later date, and are inspired, not so much by the vague ideals of humanitarianism, as by the spirit of national patriotism. They are found in a "Criticism of the German Constitution" apparently dating from the year 1802[95]. It is written after the peace of Lunéville had sealed for Germany the loss of her provinces west of the Rhine, and subsequent to the disasters of the German arms at Hohenlinden and Marengo. It is almost contemporaneous with the measures of 1803 and 1804, which affirmed the dissolution of the "Holy Roman Empire" of German name. The writer of this unpublished pamphlet sees his country in a situation almost identical with that which Macchiavelli saw around him in Italy. It is abused by petty despots, distracted by mean particularist ambitions, at the mercy of every foreign power. It was such a scene which, as Hegel recalls, had prompted and justified the drastic measures proposed in the Prince,—measures which have been ill-judged by the closet moralist, but evince the high statesmanship of the Florentine. In the Prince, an intelligent reader can see "the enthusiasm of patriotism underlying the cold and dispassionate doctrines." Macchiavelli dared to declare that Italy must become a state, and to assert that "there is no higher duty for a state than to maintain itself, and to punish relentlessly every author of anarchy,—the supreme, and perhaps sole political crime." And like teaching, Hegel adds, is needed for Germany. Only, he concludes, no mere demonstration of the insanity of utter separation of the particular from his kin will ever succeed in converting the particularists from their conviction of the absoluteness of personal and private rights. "Insight and intelligence always excite so much distrust that force alone avails to justify them; then man yields them obedience[96]."

"The German political edifice," says the writer, "is nothing else but the sum of the rights which the single parts have withdrawn from the whole; and this justice, which is ever on the watch to prevent the state having any power left, is the essence of the constitution." The Peace of Westphalia had but served to constitute or stereotype anarchy: the German empire had by that instrument divested itself of all rights of political unity, and thrown itself on the goodwill of its members. What then, it may be asked, is, in Hegel's view, the indispensable minimum essential to a state? And the answer will be, organised strength,—a central and united force. "The strength of a country lies neither in the multitude of its inhabitants and fighting men, nor in its fertility, nor in its size, but solely in the way its parts are by reasonable combination made a single political force enabling everything to be used for the common defence." Hegel speaks scornfully of "the philanthropists and moralists who decry politics as an endeavour and an art to seek private utility at the cost of right": he tells them that "it is foolish to oppose the interest or (as it is expressed by the more morally-obnoxious word) the utility of the state to its right": that the "rights of a state are the utility of the state as established and recognised by compacts": and that "war" (which they would fain abolish or moralise) "has to decide not which of the rights asserted by either party is the true right (—for both parties have a true right), but which right has to give way to the other."

It is evident from these propositions that Hegel takes that view of political supremacy which has been associated with the name of Hobbes. But his views also reproduce the Platonic king of men, "who can rule and dare not lie." "All states," he declares, "are founded by the sublime force of great men, not by physical strength. The great man has something in his features which others would gladly call their lord. They obey him against their will. Their immediate will is his will, but their conscious will is otherwise.... This is the prerogative of the great man to ascertain and to express the absolute will. All gather round his banner. He is their God." "The state," he says again, "is the self-certain absolute mind which recognises no definite authority but its own: which acknowledges no abstract rules of good and bad, shameful and mean, craft and deception." So also Hobbes describes the prerogatives of the sovereign Leviathan. But the Hegelian God immanent in the state is a higher power than Hobbes knows: he is no mortal, but in his truth an immortal God. He speaks by (what in this early essay is called) the Absolute Government[97]: the government of the Law—the true impersonal sovereign,—distinct alike from the single ruler and the multitude of the ruled. "It is absolutely only universality as against particular. As this absolute, ideal, universal, compared to which everything else is a particular, it is the phenomenon of God. Its words are his decision, and it can appear and exist under no other form.... The Absolute government is divine, self-sanctioned and not made[98]." The real strength—the real connecting-mean which gives life to sovereign and to subject—is intelligence free and entire, independent both of what individuals feel and believe and of the quality of the ruler. "The spiritual bond," he says in a lower form of speech, "is public opinion: it is the true legislative body, national assembly, declaration of the universal will which lives in the execution of all commands." This still small voice of public opinion is the true and real parliament: not literally making laws, but revealing them. If we ask, where does this public opinion appear and how does it disengage itself from the masses of partisan judgment? Hegel answers,—and to the surprise of those who have not entered into the spirit of his age[99]—it is embodied in the Aged and the Priests. Both of these have ceased to live in the real world: they are by nature and function disengaged from the struggles of particular existence, have risen above the divergencies of social classes. They breathe the ether of pure contemplation. "The sunset of life gives them mystical lore," or at least removes from old age the distraction of selfishness: while the priest is by function set apart from the divisions of human interest. Understood in a large sense, Hegel's view is that the real voice of experience is elicited through those who have attained indifference to the distorting influence of human parties, and who see life steadily and whole.

If this utterance shows the little belief Hegel had in the ordinary methods of legislation through "representative" bodies, and hints that the real substance of political life is deeper than the overt machinery of political operation, it is evident that this theory of "divine right" is of a different stamp from what used to go under that name. And, again, though the power of the central state is indispensable, he is far from agreeing with the so-called bureaucratic view that "a state is a machine with a single spring which sets in motion all the rest of the machinery." "Everything," he says, "which is not directly required to organise and maintain the force for giving security without and within must be left by the central government to the freedom of the citizens. Nothing ought to be so sacred in the eyes of a government as to leave alone and to protect, without regard to utilities, the free action of the citizens in such matters as do not affect its fundamental aim: for this freedom is itself sacred[100]." He is no friend of paternal bureaucracy. "The pedantic craving to settle every detail, the mean jealousy against estates and corporations administrating and directing their own affairs, the base fault-finding with all independent action on the part of the citizens, even when it has no immediate bearing on the main political interest, has been decked out with reasons to show that no penny of public expenditure, made for a country of twenty or thirty millions' population, can be laid out, without first being, not permitted, but commanded, controlled and revised by the supreme government." You can see, he remarks, in the first village after you enter Prussian territory the lifeless and wooden routine which prevails. The whole country suffers also from the way religion has been mixed up with political rights, and a particular creed pronounced by law indispensable both for sovereign and full-privileged subject. In a word, the unity and vigour of the state is quite compatible with considerable latitude and divergence in laws and judicature, in the imposition and levying of taxes, in language, manners, civilisation and religion. Equality in all these points is desirable for social unity: but it is not indispensable for political strength.

This decided preference for the unity of the state against the system of checks and counterchecks, which sometimes goes by the name of a constitution, came out clearly in Hegel's attitude in discussing the dispute between the Würtembergers and their sovereign in 1815-16. Würtemberg, with its complicated aggregation of local laws, had always been a paradise of lawyers, and the feudal rights or privileges of the local oligarchies—the so-called "good old law"—were the boast of the country. All this had however been aggravated by the increase of territory received in 1805: and the king, following the examples set by France and even by Bavaria, promulgated of his own grace a "constitution" remodelling the electoral system of the country. Immediately an outcry burst out against the attempt to destroy the ancient liberties. Uhland tuned his lyre to the popular cry: Rückert sang on the king's side. To Hegel the contest presented itself as a struggle between the attachment to traditional rights, merely because they are old, and the resolution to carry out reasonable reform whether it be agreeable to the reformed or not: or rather he saw in it resistance of particularism, of separation, clinging to use and wont, and basing itself on formal pettifogging objections, against the spirit of organisation. Anything more he declined to see. And probably he was right in ascribing a large part of the opposition to inertia, to vanity and self-interest, combined with the want of political perception of the needs of Würtemberg and Germany. But on the other hand, he failed to remember the insecurity and danger of such "gifts of the Danai": he forgot the sense of free-born men that a constitution is not something to be granted (octroyé) as a grace, but something that must come by the spontaneous act of the innermost self of the community. He dealt rather with the formal arguments which were used to refuse progress, than with the underlying spirit which prompted the opposition[101].

The philosopher lives (as Plato has well reminded us) too exclusively within the ideal. Bent on the essential nucleus of institutions, he attaches but slight importance to the variety of externals, and fails to realise the practice of the law-courts. He forgets that what weighs lightly in logic, may turn the scale in real life and experience. For feeling and sentiment he has but scant respect: he is brusque and uncompromising: and cannot realise all the difficulties and dangers that beset the Idea in the mazes of the world, and may ultimately quite alter a plan which at first seemed independent of petty details.

Better than other men perhaps he recognises in theory how the mere universal only exists complete in an individual shape: but more than other men he forgets these truths of insight, when the business of life calls for action or for judgment. He cannot at a moment's notice remember that he is, if not, as Cicero says, in faece Romuli, the member of a degenerate commonwealth, at least living in a world where good and evil are not, as logic presupposes, sharply divided but intricately intertwined.

(ii.) The Ethics and Religion of the State.

        This idealism of political theory is illustrated by the sketch of the Ethical Life which he drew up about 1802. Under the name of "Ethical System" it presents in concentrated or undeveloped shape the doctrine which subsequently swelled into the "Philosophy of Mind." At a later date he worked out more carefully as introduction the psychological genesis of moral and intelligent man, and he separated out more distinctly as a sequel the universal powers which give to social life its higher characters. In the earlier sketch the Ethical Part stands by itself, with the consequence that Ethics bears a meaning far exceeding all that had been lately called moral. The word "moral" itself he avoids[102]. It savours of excessive subjectivity, of struggle, of duty and conscience. It has an ascetic ring about it—an aspect of negation, which seeks for abstract holiness, and turns its back on human nature. Kant's words opposing duty to inclination, and implying that moral goodness involves a struggle, an antagonism, a victory, seem to him (and to his time) one-sided. That aspect of negation accordingly which Kant certainly began with, and which Schopenhauer magnified until it became the all-in-all of Ethics, Hegel entirely subordinates. Equally little does he like the emphasis on the supremacy of insight, intention, conscience: they lead, he thinks, to a view which holds the mere fact of conviction to be all-important, as if it mattered not what we thought and believed and did, so long as we were sincere in our belief. All this emphasis on the good-will, on the imperative of duty, on the rights of conscience, has, he admits, its justification in certain circumstances, as against mere legality, or mere natural instinctive goodness; but it has been overdone. Above all, it errs by an excess of individualism. It springs from an attitude of reflection,—in which the individual, isolated in his conscious and superficial individuality, yet tries—but probably tries in vain—to get somewhat in touch with a universal which he has allowed to slip outside him, forgetting that it is the heart and substance of his life. Kant, indeed, hardly falls under this condemnation. For he aims at showing that the rational will inevitably creates as rational a law or universal; that the individual act becomes self-regulative, and takes its part in constituting a system or realm of duty.

        Still, on the whole, "morality" in this narrower sense belongs to an age of reflection, and is formal or nominal goodness rather than the genuine and full reality. It is the protest against mere instinctive or customary virtue, which is but compliance with traditional authority, and compliance with it as if it were a sort of quasi-natural law. Moralising reflection is the awakening of subjectivity and of a deeper personality. The age which thus precedes morality is not an age in which kindness, or love, or generosity is unknown. And if Hegel says that "Morality," strictly so called, began with Socrates, he does not thereby accuse the pre-Socratic Greeks of inhumanity. But what he does say is that such ethical life as existed was in the main a thing of custom and law: of law, moreover, which was not set objectively forward, but left still in the stage of uncontradicted usage, a custom which was a second nature, part of the essential and quasi-physical ordinance of life. The individual had not yet learned to set his self-consciousness against these usages and ask for their justification. These are like the so-called law of the Medes and Persians which alters not: customs of immemorial antiquity and unquestionable sway. They are part of a system of things with which for good or evil the individual is utterly identified, bound as it were hand and foot. These are, as a traveller says[103], "oral and unwritten traditions which teach that certain rules of conduct are to be observed under certain penalties; and without the aid of fixed records, or the intervention of a succession of authorised depositaries and expounders, these laws have been transmitted to father and son, through unknown generations, and are fixed in the minds of the people as sacred and unalterable."

        The antithesis then in Hegel, as in Kant, is between Law and Morality, or rather Legality and Morality,—two abstractions to which human development is alternately prone to attach supreme importance. The first stage in the objectivation of intelligence or in the evolution of personality is the constitution of mere, abstract, or strict right. It is the creation of institutions and uniformities, i.e. of laws, or rights, which express definite and stereotyped modes of behaviour. Or, if we look at it from the individual's standpoint, we may say his consciousness awakes to find the world parcelled out under certain rules and divisions, which have objective validity, and govern him with the same absolute authority as do the circumstances of physical nature. Under their influence every rank and individual is alike forced to bow: to each his place and function is assigned by an order or system which claims an inviolable and eternal supremacy. It is not the same place and function for each: but for each the position and duties are predetermined in this metaphysically-physical order. The situation and its duties have been created by super-human and natural ordinance. As the Platonic myth puts it, each order in the social hierarchy has been framed underground by powers that turned out men of gold, and silver, and baser metal: or as the Norse legend tells, they are the successive offspring of the white God, Heimdal, in his dealings with womankind.

The central idea of the earlier social world is the supremacy of rights—but not of right. The sum (for it cannot be properly called a system) of rights is a self-subsistent world, to which man is but a servant; and a second peculiarity of it is its inequality. If all are equal before the laws, this only means here that the laws, with their absolute and thorough inequality, are indifferent to the real and personal diversities of individuals. Even the so-called equality of primitive law is of the "Eye-for-eye, Tooth-for-tooth" kind; it takes no note of special circumstances; it looks abstractly and rudely at facts, and maintains a hard and fast uniformity, which seems the height of unfairness. Rule stands by rule, usage beside usage,—a mere aggregate or multitude of petty tyrants, reduced to no unity or system, and each pressing with all the weight of an absolute mandate. The pettiest bit of ceremonial law is here of equal dignity with the most far-reaching principle of political obligation.

In the essay already referred to, Hegel has designated something analogous to this as Natural or Physical Ethics, or as Ethics in its relative or comparative stage. Here Man first shows his superiority to nature, or enters on his properly ethical function, by transforming the physical world into his possession. He makes himself the lord of natural objects—stamping them as his, and not their own, making them his permanent property, his tools, his instruments of exchange and production. The fundamental ethical act is appropriation by labour, and the first ethical world is the creation of an economic system, the institution of property. For property, or at least possession and appropriation, is the dominant idea, with its collateral and sequent principles. And at first, even human beings are treated on the same method as other things: as objects in a world of objects or aggregate of things: as things to be used and acquired, as means and instruments,—not in any sense as ends in themselves. It is a world in which the relation of master and slave is dominant,—where owner and employer is set in antithesis against his tools and chattels. But the Nemesis of his act issues in making the individual the servant of his so-called property. He has become an objective power by submitting himself to objectivity: he has literally put himself into the object he has wrought, and is now a thing among things: for what he owns, what he has appropriated, determines what he is. The real powers in the world thus established are the laws of possession-holding: the laws dominate man: and he is only freed from dependence on casual externals, by making himself thoroughly the servant of his possessions.

The only salvation, and it is but imperfect, that can be reached on this stage is by the family union. The sexual tie, is at first entirely on a level with the other arrangements of the sphere. The man or woman is but a chattel and a tool; a casual appropriation which gradually is transformed into a permanent possession and a permanent bond[104]. But, as the family constituted itself, it helped to afford a promise of better things. An ideal interest—the religion of the household—extending beyond the individual, and beyond the moment,—binding past and present, and parents to offspring, gave a new character to the relation of property. Parents and children form a unity, which overrides and essentially permeates their "difference" from each other: there is no exchange, no contract, nor, in the stricter sense, property between the members. In the property-idea they are lifted out of their isolation, and in the continuity of family life there is a certain analogue of immortality. But, says Hegel, "though the family be the highest totality of which Nature is capable, the absolute identity is in it inward, and is not instituted in absolute form; and hence, too, the reproduction of the totality is an appearance, the appearance of the children[105]." "The power and the intelligence, the 'difference' of the parents, stands in inverse proportion to the youth and vigour of the child: and these two sides of life flee from and are sequent on each other, and are reciprocally external[106]." Or, as we may put it, the god of the family is a departed ancestor, a ghost in the land of the dead: it has not really a continuous and unified life. In such a state of society—a state of nature—and in its supreme form, the family, there is no adequate principle which though real shall still give ideality and unity to the self-isolating aspects of life. There is wanted something which shall give expression to its "indifference," which shall control the tendency of this partial moralisation to sink at every moment into individuality, and lift it from its immersion in nature. Family life and economic groups (—for these two, which Hegel subsequently separates, are here kept close together) need an ampler and wider life to keep them from stagnating in their several selfishnesses.

This freshening and corrective influence they get in the first instance from deeds of violence and crime. Here is the "negative unsettling" of the narrow fixities, of the determinate conditions or relationships into which the preceding processes of labour and acquisition have tended to stereotype life. The harsh restriction brings about its own undoing. Man may subject natural objects to his formative power, but the wild rage of senseless devastation again and again bursts forth to restore the original formlessness. He may build up his own pile of wealth, store up his private goods, but the thief and the robber with the instincts of barbarian socialism tread on his steps: and every stage of appropriation has for its sequel a crop of acts of dispossession. He may secure by accumulation his future life; but the murderer for gain's sake cuts it short. And out of all this as a necessary consequence stands avenging justice. And in the natural world of ethics—where true moral life has not yet arisen—this is mere retaliation or the *lex talionis*;—the beginning of an endless series of vengeance and counter-vengeance, the blood-feud. Punishment, in the stricter sense of the term,—which looks both to antecedents and effects in character—cannot yet come into existence; for to punish there must be something superior to individualities, an ethical idea embodied in an institution, to which the injurer and the injured alike belong. But as yet punishment is only vengeance, the personal and natural equivalent, the physical reaction against injury, perhaps regulated and formulated by custom and usage, but not essentially altered from its purely retaliatory character. These crimes—or transgressions—are thus by Hegel quaintly conceived as storms which clear the air—which shake the individualist out of his slumber. The scene in which transgression thus acts is that of the so-called state of nature, where particularism was rampant: where moral right was not, but only the right of nature, of pre-occupation, of the stronger, of the first maker and discoverer. Crime is thus the "dialectic" which shakes the fixity of practical arrangements, and calls for something in which the idea of a higher unity, a permanent substance of life, shall find realisation.

The "positive supersession[107]" of individualism and naturalism in ethics is by Hegel called "Absolute Ethics." Under this title he describes the ethics and religion of the state—a religion which is immanent in the community, and an ethics which rises superior to particularity. The picture he draws is a romance fashioned upon the model of the Greek commonwealth as that had been idealised by Greek literature and by the longings of later ages for a freer life. It is but one of the many modes in which Helena—to quote Goethe—has fascinated the German Faust. He dreams himself away from the prosaic worldliness of a German municipality to the unfading splendour of the Greek city with its imagined coincidence of individual will with universal purpose. There is in such a commonwealth no pain of surrender and of sacrifice, and no subsequent compensation: for, at the very moment of resigning self-will to common aims, he enjoys it retained with the added zest of self-expansion. He is not so left to himself as to feel from beyond the restraint of a law which controls—even if it wisely and well controls—individual effort. There is for his happy circumstances no possibility of doing otherwise. Or, it may be, Hegel has reminiscences from the ideals of other nations than the Greek. He recalls the Israelite depicted by the Law-adoring psalmist, whose delight is to do the will of the Lord, whom the zeal of God's house has consumed, whose whole being runs on in one pellucid stream with the universal and eternal stream of divine commandment. Such a frame of spirit, where the empirical consciousness with all its soul and strength and mind identifies its mission into conformity with the absolute order, is the mood of absolute Ethics. It is what some have spoken of as the True life, as the Eternal life; in it, says Hegel, the individual exists *auf ewige Weise*[108], as it were sub specie aeternitatis: his life is hid with his fellows in the common life of his people. His every act, and thought, and will, get their being and significance from a reality which is established in him as a permanent spirit. It is there that he, in the fuller sense, attains αὐτάρκεια, or finds himself no longer a mere part, but an ideal totality. This totality is realised under the particular form of a Nation (Volk), which in the visible sphere represents (or rather is, as a particular) the absolute and infinite. Such a unity is neither the mere sum of isolated individuals, nor a mere majority ruling by numbers: but the fraternal and organic commonwealth which brings all classes and all rights from their particularistic independence into an ideal identity and indifference[109]. Here all are not merely equal before the laws: but the law itself is a living and organic unity, self-correcting, subordinating and organising, and no longer merely defining individual privileges and so-called liberties. "In such conjunction of the universal with the particularity lies the divinity of a nation: or, if we give this universal a separate place in our ideas, it is the God of the nation." But in this complete accordance between concept and intuition, between visible and invisible, where symbol and significate are one, religion and ethics are indistinguishable. It is the old conception (and in its highest sense) of Theocracy[110]. God is the national head and the national life: and in him all individuals have their "difference" rendered "indifferent." "Such an ethical life is absolute truth, for untruth is only in the fixture of a single mode: but in the everlasting being of the nation all singleness is superseded. It is absolute culture; for in the eternal is the real and empirical annihilation and prescription of all limited modality. It is absolute disinterestedness: for in the eternal there is nothing private and personal. It, and each of its movements, is the highest beauty: for beauty is but the eternal made actual and given concrete shape. It is without pain, and blessed: for in it all difference and all pain is superseded. It is the divine, absolute, real, existing and being, under no veil; nor need one first raise it up into the ideality of divinity, and extract it from the appearance and empirical intuition; but it is, and immediately, absolute intuition[111]."

If we compare this language with the statement of the Encyclopaedia we can see how for the moment Hegel's eye is engrossed with the glory of the ideal nation. In it, the moral life embraces and is co-extensive with religion, art and science: practice and theory are at one: life in the idea knows none of those differences which, in the un-ideal world, make art and morality often antithetical, and set religion at variance with science. It is, as we have said, a memory of Greek and perhaps Hebrew ideals. Or rather it is by the help of such memories the affirmation of the essential unity of life—the true, complete, many-sided life—which is the presupposition and idea that culture and morals rest upon and from which they get their supreme sanction, i.e. their constitutive principle and unity. Even in the Encyclopaedia[112] Hegel endeavours to guard against the severance of morality and art and philosophy which may be rashly inferred in consequence of his serial order of treatment. "Religion," he remarks, "is the very substance of the moral life itself and of the state.... The ethical life is the divine spirit indwelling in consciousness, as it is actually present in a nation and its individual members." Yet, as we see, there is a distinction. The process of history carries out a judgment on nation after nation, and reveals the divine as not only immanent in the ethical life but as ever expanding the limited national spirit till it become a spirit of universal humanity. Still—and this is perhaps for each time always the more important—the national unity—not indeed as a multitude, nor as a majority—is the supreme real appearance of the Eternal and Absolute.

Having thus described the nation as an organic totality, he goes on to point out that the political constitution shows this character by forming a triplicity of political orders. In one of these there is but a silent, practical identity, in faith and trust, with the totality: in the second there is a thorough disruption of interest into particularity: and in the third, there is a living and intellectual identity or indifference, which combines the widest range of individual development with the completest unity of political loyalty. This last order is that which lives in conscious identification of private with public duty: all that it does has a universal and public function. Such a body is the ideal Nobility—the nobility which is the servus servorum Dei, the supreme servant of humanity. Its function is to maintain general interests, to give the other orders (peasantry and industrials) security,—receiving in return from these others the means of subsistence. Noblesse oblige gives the death-blow to particular interests, and imposes the duty of exhibiting, in the clearest form, the supreme reality of absolute morality, and of being to the rest an unperturbed ideal of aesthetic, ethical, religious, and philosophical completeness.

It is here alone, in this estate which is absolutely disinterested, that the virtues appear in their true light. To the ordinary moralising standpoint they seem severally to be, in their separation, charged with independent value. But from the higher point of view the existence, and still more the accentuation of single virtues, is a mark of incompleteness. Even quality, it has been said, involves its defects: it can only shine by eclipsing or reflecting something else. The completely moral is not the sum of the several virtues, but the reduction of them to indifference. It is thus that when Plato tries to get at the unity of virtue, their aspect of difference tends to be subordinated. "The movement of absolute morality runs through all the virtues, but settles fixedly in none." It is more than love to fatherland, and nation, and laws:—that still implies a relation to something and involves a difference. For love—the mortal passion, where "self is not annulled"—is the process of approximation, while unity is not yet attained, but wished and aimed at: and when it is complete—and become "such love as spirits know[113]"—it gives place to a calmer rest and an active immanence. The absolute morality is life in the fatherland and for the nation. In the individual however it is the process upward and inward that we see, not the consummation. Then the identity appears as an ideal, as a tendency not yet accomplished to its end, a possibility not yet made fully actual. At bottom—in the divine substance in which the individual inheres—the identity is present: but in the appearance, we have only the passage from possible to actual, a passage which has the aspect of a struggle. Hence the moral act appears as a virtue, with merit or desert. It is accordingly the very characteristic of virtue to signalise its own incompleteness: it emerges into actuality only through antagonism, and with a taint of imperfection clinging to it. Thus, in the field of absolute morality, if the virtues appear, it is only in their transiency. If they were undisputedly real in morality, they would not separately show. To feel that you have done well implies that you have not done wholly well: self-gratulation in meritorious deed is the re-action from the shudder at feeling that the self was not wholly good.

The essential unity of virtue—its negative character as regards all the empirical variety of virtues—is seen in the excellences required by the needs of war. These military requirements demonstrate the mere relativity and therefore non-virtuousness of the special virtues. They equally protest against the common beliefs in the supreme dignity of labour and its utilities. But if bravery or soldierlike virtue be essentially a virtue of virtues, it is only a negative virtue after all. It is the blast of the universal sweeping away all the habitations and fixed structures of particularist life. If it is a unity of virtue, it is only a negative unity—an indifference. If it avoid the parcelling of virtue into a number of imperfect and sometimes contradictory parts, it does so only to present a bare negation. The soldier, therefore, if in potentiality the unity of all the virtues, may tend in practice to represent the ability to do without any of them[114].

The home of these "relative" virtues—of morality in the ordinary sense—is the life of the second order in the commonwealth: the order of industry and commerce. In this sphere the idea of the universal is gradually lost to view: it becomes, says Hegel, only a thought or a creature of the mind, which does not affect practice. The materialistic worker of civilisation does not see further than the empirical existence of individuals: his horizon is limited by the family, and his final ideal is a competency of comfort in possessions and revenues. The supreme universal to which he attains as the climax of his evolution is only money. But it is only with the vaster development of commerce that this terrible consequence ensues. At first as a mere individual, he has higher aims, though not the highest. He has a limited ideal determined by his special sphere of work. To win respect—the character for a limited truthfulness and honesty and skilful work—is his ambition. He lives in a conceit of his performance—his utility—the esteem of his special circle. To his commercial soul the military order is a scarecrow and a nuisance: military honour is but trash. Yet if his range of idea is narrow and engrossing in details, his aim is to get worship, to be recognised as the best in his little sphere. But with the growth of the trading spirit his character changes: he becomes the mere capitalist, is denationalised, has no definite work and can claim no individualised function. Money now measures all things: it is the sole ultimate reality. It transforms everything into a relation of contract: even vengeance is equated in terms of money. Its motto is, The Exchanges must be honoured, though honour and morality may go to the dogs. So far as it is concerned, there is no nation, but a federation of shopkeepers. Such an one is the bourgeois (the Bürger, as distinct from the peasant or Bauer and the Adel). As an artisan—i.e. a mere industrial, he knows no country, but at best the reputation and interest of his own guild-union with its partial object. He is narrow, but honest and respectable. As a mere commercial agent, he knows no country: his field is the world, but the world not in its concreteness and variety, but in the abstract aspect of a money-bag and an exchange. The larger totality is indeed not altogether out of sight. But if he contribute to the needy, either his sacrifice is lifeless in proportion as it becomes general, or loses generality as it becomes lively. As regards his general services to the great life of his national state[115], they are unintelligently and perhaps grudgingly rendered.

Of the peasant order Hegel has less to say. On one side the "country" as opposed to the "town" has a closer natural sympathy with the common and general interest: and the peasantry is the undifferentiated, solid and sound, basis of the national life. It forms the submerged mass, out of which the best soldiers are made, and which out of the depths of earth brings forward nourishment as well as all the materials of elementary necessity. Faithfulness and loyalty are its virtues: but it is personal allegiance to a commanding superior,—not to a law or a general view—for the peasant is weak in comprehensive intelligence, though shrewd in detailed observation.

Of the purely political function of the state Hegel in this sketch says almost nothing. But under the head of the general government of the state he deals with its social functions. For a moment he refers to the well-known distinction of the legislative, judicial and executive powers. But it is only to remark that "in every governmental act all three are conjoined. They are abstractions, none of which can get a reality of its own,—which, in other words, cannot be constituted and organised as powers. Legislation, judicature, and executive are something completely formal, empty, and contentless.... Whether the others are or are not bare abstractions, empty activities, depends entirely on the executive power; and this is absolutely the government[116]." Treating government as the organic movement by which the universal and the particular in the commonwealth come into relations, he finds that it presents three forms, or gives rise to three systems. The highest and last of these is the "educational" system. By this he understands all that activity by which the intelligence of the state tries directly to mould and guide the character and fortunes of its members: all the means of culture and discipline, whether in general or for individuals, all training to public function, to truthfulness, to good manners. Under the same head come conquest and colonisation as state agencies. The second system is the judicial, which instead of, like the former, aiming at the formation or reformation of its members is satisfied by subjecting individual transgression to a process of rectification by the general principle. With regard to the system of judicature, Hegel argues for a variety of procedure to suit different ranks, and for a corresponding modification of penalties. "Formal rigid equality is just what does not spare the character. The same penalty which in one estate brings no infamy causes in another a deep and irremediable hurt." And with regard to the after life of the transgressor who has borne his penalty: "Punishment is the reconciliation of the law with itself. No further reproach for his crime can be addressed to the person who has undergone his punishment. He is restored to membership of his estate[117]."

In the first of the three systems, the economic system, or "System of wants," the state seems at first hardly to appear in its universal and controlling function at all. Here the individual depends for the satisfaction of his physical needs on a blind, unconscious destiny, on the obscure and incalculable properties of supply and demand in the whole interconnexion of commodities. But even this is not all. With the accumulation of wealth in inequality, and the growth of vast capitals, there is substituted for the dependence of the individual on the general resultant of a vast number of agencies a dependence on one enormously rich individual, who can control the physical destinies of a nation. But a nation, truly speaking, is there no more. The industrial order has parted into a mere abstract workman on one hand, and the grande richesse on the other. "It has lost its capacity of an organic absolute intuition and of respect for the divine—external though its divinity be: and there sets in the bestiality of contempt for all that is noble. The mere wisdomless universal, the mass of wealth, is the essential: and the ethical principle, the absolute bond of the nation, is vanished; and the nation is dissolved[118]."

It would be a long and complicated task to sift, in these ill-digested but profound suggestions, the real meaning from the formal statement. They are, like Utopia, beyond the range of practical politics.

The modern reader, whose political conceptions are limited by contemporary circumstance, may find them archaic, medieval, quixotic. But for those who behind the words and forms can see the substance and the idea, they will perhaps come nearer the conception of ideal commonwealth than many reforming programmes. Compared with the maturer statements of the Philosophy of Law, they have the faults of the Romantic age to which their inception belongs. Yet even in that later exposition there is upheld the doctrine of the supremacy of the eternal State against everything particular, class-like, and temporary; a doctrine which has made Hegel—as it made Fichte—a voice in that "professorial socialism" which is at least as old as Plato.

INTRODUCTION

§ 377. The knowledge of Mind is the highest and hardest, just because it is the most "concrete" of sciences. The significance of that "absolute" commandment, Know thyself—whether we look at it in itself or under the historical circumstances of its first utterance—is not to promote mere self-knowledge in respect of the particular capacities, character, propensities, and foibles of the single self. The knowledge it commands means that of man's genuine reality—of what is essentially and ultimately true and real—of mind as the true and essential being. Equally little is it the purport of mental philosophy to teach what is called knowledge of men—the knowledge whose aim is to detect the peculiarities, passions, and foibles of other men, and lay bare what are called the recesses of the human heart. Information of this kind is, for one thing, meaningless, unless on the assumption that we know the universal—man as man, and, that always must be, as mind. And for another, being only engaged with casual, insignificant and untrue aspects of mental life, it fails to reach the underlying essence of them all—the mind itself.

§ 378. Pneumatology, or, as it was also called, Rational Psychology, has been already alluded to in the Introduction to the Logic as an abstract and generalising metaphysic of the subject. Empirical (or inductive) psychology, on the other hand, deals with the "concrete" mind: and, after the revival of the sciences, when observation and experience had been made the distinctive methods for the study of concrete reality, such psychology was worked on the same lines as other sciences. In this way it came about that the metaphysical theory was kept outside the inductive science, and so prevented from getting any concrete embodiment or detail: whilst at the same time the inductive science clung to the conventional common-sense metaphysic, with its analysis into forces, various activities, &c., and rejected any attempt at a "speculative" treatment.

The books of Aristotle on the Soul, along with his discussions on its special aspects and states, are for this reason still by far the most admirable, perhaps even the sole, work of philosophical value on this topic. The main aim of a philosophy of mind can only be to re-introduce unity of idea and principle into the theory of mind, and so re-interpret the lesson of those Aristotelian books.

§ 379. Even our own sense of the mind's living unity naturally protests against any attempt to break it up into different faculties, forces, or, what comes to the same thing, activities, conceived as independent of each other. But the craving for a comprehension of the unity is still further stimulated, as we soon come across distinctions between mental freedom and mental determinism, antitheses between free psychic agency and the corporeity that lies external to it, whilst we equally note the intimate interdependence of the one upon the other. In modern times especially the phenomena of animal magnetism have given, even in experience, a lively and visible confirmation of the underlying unity of soul, and of the power of its "ideality." Before these facts, the rigid distinctions of practical common sense were struck with confusion; and the necessity of a "speculative" examination with a view to the removal of difficulties was more directly forced upon the student.

§ 380. The "concrete" nature of mind involves for the observer the peculiar difficulty that the several grades and special types which develop its intelligible unity in detail are not left standing as so many separate existences confronting its more advanced aspects. It is otherwise in external nature. There, matter and movement, for example, have a manifestation all their own—it is the solar system; and similarly the differentiae of sense-perception have a sort of earlier existence in the properties of bodies, and still more independently in the four elements. The species and grades of mental evolution, on the contrary, lose their separate existence and become factors, states and features in the higher grades of development. As a consequence of this, a lower and more abstract aspect of mind betrays the presence in it, even to experience, of a higher grade. Under the guise of sensation, e.g., we may find the very highest mental life as its modification or its embodiment. And so sensation, which is but a mere form and vehicle, may to the superficial glance seem to be the proper seat and, as it were, the source of those moral and religious principles with which it is charged; and the moral and religious principles thus modified may seem to call for treatment as species of sensation. But at the same time, when lower grades of mental life are under examination, it becomes necessary, if we desire to point to actual cases of them in experience, to direct attention to more advanced grades for which they are mere forms. In this way subjects will be treated of by anticipation which properly belong to later stages of development (e.g. in dealing with natural awaking from sleep we speak by anticipation of consciousness, or in dealing with mental derangement we must speak of intellect).

What Mind (or Spirit) is

§ 381. From our point of view Mind has for its presupposition Nature, of which it is the truth, and for that reason its absolute prius. In this its truth Nature is vanished, and mind has resulted as the "Idea" entered on possession of itself. Here the subject and object of the Idea are one—either is the intelligent unity, the notion. This identity is absolute negativity—for whereas in Nature the intelligent unity has its objectivity perfect but externalised, this self-externalisation has been nullified and the unity in that way been made one and the same with itself. Thus at the same time it is this identity only so far as it is a return out of nature.

§ 382. For this reason the essential, but formally essential, feature of mind is Liberty: i.e. it is the notion's absolute negativity or self-identity. Considered as this formal aspect, it may withdraw itself from everything external and from its own externality, its very existence; it can thus submit to infinite pain, the negation of its individual immediacy: in other words, it can keep itself affirmative in this negativity and possess its own identity. All this is possible so long as it is considered in its abstract self-contained universality.

§ 383. This universality is also its determinate sphere of being. Having a being of its own, the universal is self-particularising, whilst it still remains self-identical. Hence the special mode of mental being is "manifestation." The spirit is not some one mode or meaning which finds utterance or externality only in a form distinct from itself: it does not manifest or reveal something, but its very mode and meaning is this revelation. And thus in its mere possibility Mind is at the same moment an infinite, "absolute," actuality.

§ 384. Revelation, taken to mean the revelation of the abstract Idea, is an unmediated transition to Nature which comes to be. As Mind is free, its manifestation is to set forth Nature as its world; but because it is reflection, it, in thus setting forth its world, at the same time presupposes the world as a nature independently existing. In the intellectual sphere to reveal is thus to create a world as its being—a being in which the mind procures the affirmation and truth of its freedom.

The Absolute is Mind (Spirit)—this is the supreme definition of the Absolute. To find this definition and to grasp its meaning and burthen was, we may say, the ultimate purpose of all education and all philosophy: it was the point to which turned the impulse of all religion and science: and it is this impulse that must explain the history of the world. The word "Mind" (Spirit)—and some glimpse of its meaning—was found at an early period: and the spirituality of God is the lesson of Christianity. It remains for philosophy in its own element of intelligible unity to get hold of what was thus given as a mental image, and what implicitly is the ultimate reality: and that problem is not genuinely, and by rational methods, solved so long as liberty and intelligible unity is not the theme and the soul of philosophy.

Subdivision

§ 385. The development of Mind (Spirit) is in three stages:—

[1] In the form of self-relation: within it it has the ideal totality of the Idea—i.e. it has before it all that its notion contains: its being is to be self-contained and free. This is Mind Subjective.

[2] In the form of reality: realised, i.e. in a world produced and to be produced by it: in this world freedom presents itself under the shape of necessity. This is Mind Objective.

[3] In that unity of mind as objectivity and, of mind as ideality and concept, which essentially and actually is and for ever produces itself, mind in its absolute truth. This is Mind Absolute.

§ 386. The two first parts of the doctrine of Mind embrace the finite mind. Mind is the infinite Idea; thus finitude here means the disproportion between the concept and the reality—but with the qualification that it is a shadow cast by the mind's own light—a show or illusion which the mind implicitly imposes as a barrier to itself, in order, by its removal, actually to realise and become conscious of freedom as its very being, i.e. to be fully manifested. The several steps of this activity, on each of which, with their semblance of being, it is the function of the finite mind to linger, and through which it has to pass, are steps in its liberation. In the full truth of that liberation is given the identification of the three stages—finding a world presupposed before us, generating a world as our own creation, and gaining freedom from it and in it. To the infinite form of this truth the show purifies itself till it becomes a consciousness of it.

A rigid application of the category of finitude by the abstract logician is chiefly seen in dealing with Mind and reason: it is held not a mere matter of strict logic, but treated also as a moral and religious concern, to adhere to the point of view of finitude, and the wish to go further is reckoned a mark of audacity, if not of insanity, of thought. Whereas in fact such a modesty of thought, as treats the finite as something altogether fixed and absolute, is the worst of virtues; and to stick to a post which has no sound ground in itself is the most unsound sort of theory. The category of finitude was at a much earlier period elucidated and explained at its place in the Logic: an elucidation which, as in logic for the more specific though still simple thought-forms of finitude, so in the rest of philosophy for the concrete forms, has merely to show that the finite is not, i.e. is not the truth, but merely a transition and an emergence to something higher. This finitude of the spheres so far examined is the dialectic that makes a thing have its cessation by another and in another: but Spirit, the intelligent unity and the implicit Eternal, is itself just the consummation of that internal act by which nullity is nullified and vanity is made vain. And so, the modesty alluded to is a retention of this vanity—the finite—in opposition to the true: it is itself therefore vanity. In the course of the mind's development we shall see this vanity appear as wickedness at that turning-point at which mind has reached its extreme immersion in its subjectivity and its most central contradiction.

SECTION I - MIND SUBJECTIVE

§ 387. Mind, on the ideal stage of its development, is mind as cognitive: Cognition, however, being taken here not as a merely logical category of the Idea (§ 223), but in the sense appropriate to the concrete mind.

Subjective mind is:—

(A) Immediate or implicit: a soul—the Spirit in Nature—the object treated by Anthropology.

(B) Mediate or explicit: still as identical reflection into itself and into other things: mind in correlation or particularisation: consciousness—the object treated by the Phenomenology of Mind.

(C) Mind defining itself in itself, as an independent subject—the object treated by Psychology.

In the Soul is the awaking of Consciousness: Consciousness sets itself up as Reason, awaking at one bound to the sense of its rationality: and this Reason by its activity emancipates itself to objectivity and the consciousness of its intelligent unity.

For an intelligible unity or principle of comprehension each modification it presents is an advance of development: and so in mind every character under which it appears is a stage in a process of specification and development, a step forward towards its goal, in order to make itself into, and to realise in itself, what it implicitly is. Each step, again, is itself such a process, and its product is that what the mind was implicitly at the beginning (and so for the observer) it is for itself—for the special form, viz. which the mind has in that step. The ordinary method of psychology is to narrate what the mind or soul is, what happens to it, what it does. The soul is presupposed as a ready-made agent, which displays such features as its acts and utterances, from which we can learn what it is, what sort of faculties and powers it possesses—all without being aware that the act and utterance of what the soul is really invests it with that character in our conception and makes it reach a higher stage of being than it explicitly had before.

We must, however, distinguish and keep apart from the progress here studied what we call education and instruction. The sphere of education is the individual's only: and its aim is to bring the universal mind to exist in them. But in the philosophic theory of mind, mind is studied as self-instruction and self-education in very essence; and its acts and utterances are stages in the process which brings it forward to itself, links it in unity with itself, and so makes it actual mind.

Sub-Section A - Anthropology. The Soul.

§ 388. Spirit (Mind) came into being as the truth of Nature. But not merely is it, as such a result, to be held the true and real first of what went before: this becoming or transition bears in the sphere of the notion the special meaning of "free judgment." Mind, thus come into being, means therefore that Nature in its own self realises its untruth and sets itself aside: it means that Mind presupposes itself no longer as the universality which in corporal individuality is always self-externalised, but as a universality which in its concretion and totality is one and simple. At such a stage it is not yet mind, but soul.

§ 389. The soul is no separate immaterial entity. Wherever there is Nature, the soul is its universal immaterialism, its simple "ideal" life. Soul is the substance or "absolute" basis of all the particularising and individualising of mind: it is in the soul that mind finds the material on which its character is wrought, and the soul remains the pervading, identical ideality of it all. But as it is still conceived thus abstractly, the soul is only the sleep of mind—the passive νοῦς of Aristotle, which is potentially all things.

The question of the immateriality of the soul has no interest, except where, on the one hand, matter is regarded as something true, and mind conceived as a thing, on the other. But in modern times even the physicists have found matters grow thinner in their hands: they have come upon imponderable matters, like heat, light, &c., to which they might perhaps add space and time. These "imponderables," which have lost the property (peculiar to matter) of gravity and, in a sense, even the capacity of offering resistance, have still, however, a sensible existence and outness of part to part; whereas the "vital" matter, which may also be found enumerated among them, not merely lacks gravity, but even every other aspect of existence which might lead us to treat it as material. The fact is that in the Idea of Life the self-externalism of nature is implicitly at an end: subjectivity is the very substance and conception of life—with this proviso, however, that its existence or objectivity is still at the same time forfeited to the sway of self-externalism. It is otherwise with Mind. There, in the intelligible unity which exists as freedom, as absolute negativity, and not as the immediate or natural individual, the object or the reality of the intelligible unity is the unity itself; and so the self-externalism, which is the fundamental feature of matter, has been completely dissipated and transmuted into universality, or the subjective ideality of the conceptual unity. Mind is the existent truth of matter—the truth that matter itself has no truth.

A cognate question is that of the community of soul and body. This community (interdependence) was assumed as a fact, and the only problem was how to comprehend it. The usual answer, perhaps, was to call it an incomprehensible mystery; and, indeed, if we take them to be absolutely antithetical and absolutely independent, they are as impenetrable to each other as one piece of matter to another, each being supposed to be found only in the pores of the other, i.e. where the other is not: whence Epicurus, when attributing to the gods a residence in the pores, was consistent in not imposing on them any connexion with the world. A somewhat different answer has been given by all philosophers since this relation came to be expressly discussed. Descartes, Malebranche, Spinoza, and Leibnitz have all indicated God as this nexus. They meant that the finitude of soul and matter were only ideal and unreal distinctions; and, so holding, these philosophers took God, not, as so often is done, merely as another word for the incomprehensible, but rather as the sole true identity of finite mind and matter. But either this identity, as in the case of Spinoza, is too abstract, or, as in the case of Leibnitz, though his Monad of monads brings things into being, it does so only by an act of judgment or choice. Hence, with Leibnitz, the result is a distinction between soul and the corporeal (or material), and the identity is only like the copula of a judgment, and does not rise or develop into system, into the absolute syllogism.

§ 390. The Soul is at first—

(a) In its immediate natural mode—the natural soul, which only is.

(b) Secondly, it is a soul which feels, as individualised, enters into correlation with its immediate being, and, in the modes of that being, retains an abstract independence.

(c) Thirdly, its immediate being—or corporeity—is moulded into it, and with that corporeity it exists as actual soul.

(a) *The Physical Soul*[119].

§ 391. The soul universal, described, it may be, as an anima mundi, a world-soul, must not be fixed on that account as a single subject; it is rather the universal substance which has its actual truth only in individuals and single subjects. Thus, when it presents itself as a single soul, it is a single soul which is merely: its only modes are modes of natural life. These have, so to speak, behind its ideality a free existence: i.e. they are natural objects for consciousness, but objects to which the soul as such does not behave as to something external. These features rather are physical qualities of which it finds itself possessed.

(α) Physical Qualities[120].

§ 392. While still a "substance" (i.e. a physical soul) the mind [1] takes part in the general planetary life, feels the difference of climates, the changes of the seasons and the periods of the day, &c. This life of nature for the main shows itself only in occasional strain or disturbance of mental tone.

In recent times a good deal has been said of the cosmical, sidereal, and telluric life of man. In such a sympathy with nature the animals essentially live: their specific characters and their particular phases of growth depend, in many cases completely, and always more or less, upon it. In the case of man these points of dependence lose importance, just in proportion to his civilisation, and the more his whole frame of soul is based upon a substructure of mental freedom. The history of the world is not bound up with revolutions in the solar system, any more than the destinies of individuals with the positions of the planets.

The difference of climate has a more solid and vigorous influence. But the response to the changes of the seasons and hours of the day is found only in faint changes of mood, which come expressly to the fore only in morbid states (including insanity) and at periods when the self-conscious life suffers depression.

In nations less intellectually emancipated, which therefore live more in harmony with nature, we find amid their superstitions and aberrations of imbecility a few real cases of such sympathy, and on that foundation what seems to be marvellous prophetic vision of coming conditions and of events arising therefrom. But as mental freedom gets a deeper hold, even these few and slight susceptibilities, based upon participation in the common life of nature, disappear. Animals and plants, on the contrary, remain for ever subject to such influences.

§ 393. [2] According to the concrete differences of the terrestrial globe, the general planetary life of the nature-governed mind specialises itself and breaks up into the several nature-governed minds which, on the whole, give expression to the nature of the geographical continents and constitute the diversities of race.

The contrast between the earth's poles, the land towards the north pole being more aggregated and preponderant over sea, whereas in the southern hemisphere it runs out in sharp points, widely distant from each other, introduces into the differences of continents a further modification which Treviranus (Biology, Part II) has exhibited in the case of the flora and fauna.

§ 394. This diversity descends into specialities, that may be termed local minds—shown in the outward modes of life and occupation, bodily structure and disposition, but still more in the inner tendency and capacity of the intellectual and moral character of the several peoples.

Back to the very beginnings of national history we see the several nations each possessing a persistent type of its own.

§ 395. [3] The soul is further de-universalised into the individualised subject. But this subjectivity is here only considered as a differentiation and singling out of the modes which nature gives; we find it as the special temperament, talent, character, physiognomy, or other disposition and idiosyncrasy, of families or single individuals.

(β) *Physical Alterations.*

§ 396. Taking the soul as an individual, we find its diversities, as alterations in it, the one permanent subject, and as stages in its development. As they are at once physical and mental diversities, a more concrete definition or description of them would require us to anticipate an acquaintance with the formed and matured mind.

The [1] first of these is the natural lapse of the ages in man's life. He begins with Childhood—mind wrapt up in itself. His next step is the fully-developed antithesis, the strain and struggle of a universality which is still subjective (as seen in ideals, fancies, hopes, ambitions) against his immediate individuality. And that individuality marks both the world which, as it exists, fails to meet his ideal requirements, and the position of the individual himself, who is still short of independence and not fully equipped for the part he has to play (Youth). Thirdly, we see man in his true relation to his environment, recognising the objective necessity and reasonableness of the world as he finds it,—a world no longer incomplete, but able in the work which it collectively achieves to afford the individual a place and a security for his performance. By his share in this collective work he first is really somebody, gaining an effective existence and an objective value (Manhood). Last of all comes the finishing touch to this unity with objectivity: a unity which, while on its realist side it passes into the inertia of deadening habit, on its idealist side gains freedom from the limited interests and entanglements of the outward present (Old Age).

§ 397. [2] Next we find the individual subject to a real antithesis, leading it to seek and find itself in another individual. This—the sexual relation—on a physical basis, shows, on its one side, subjectivity remaining in an instinctive and emotional harmony of moral life and love, and not pushing these tendencies to an extreme universal phase, in purposes political, scientific or artistic; and on the other, shows an active half, where the individual is the vehicle of a struggle of universal and objective interests with the given conditions (both of his own existence and of that of the external world), carrying out these universal principles into a unity with the world which is his own work. The sexual tie acquires its moral and spiritual significance and function in the family.

§ 398. [3] When the individuality, or self-centralised being, distinguishes itself from its mere being, this immediate judgment is the waking of the soul, which confronts its self-absorbed natural life, in the first instance, as one natural quality and state confronts another state, viz. sleep.—The waking is not merely for the observer, or externally distinct from the sleep: it is itself the judgment (primary partition) of the individual soul—which is self-existing only as it relates its self-existence to its mere existence, distinguishing itself from its still undifferentiated universality. The waking state includes generally all self-conscious and rational activity in which the mind realises its own distinct self.—Sleep is an invigoration of this activity—not as a merely negative rest from it, but as a return back from the world of specialisation, from dispersion into phases where it has grown hard and stiff,—a return into the general nature of subjectivity, which is the substance of those specialised energies and their absolute master.

The distinction between sleep and waking is one of those posers, as they may be called, which are often addressed to philosophy:—Napoleon, e.g., on a visit to the University of Pavia, put this question to the class of ideology. The characterisation given in the section is abstract; it primarily treats waking merely as a natural fact, containing the mental element implicite but not yet as invested with a special being of its own. If we are to speak more concretely of this distinction (in fundamentals it remains the same), we must take the self-existence of the individual soul in its higher aspects as the Ego of consciousness and as intelligent mind. The difficulty raised anent the distinction of the two states properly arises, only when we also take into account the dreams in sleep and describe these dreams, as well as the mental representations in the sober waking consciousness, under one and the same title of mental representations. Thus superficially classified as states of mental representation the two coincide, because we have lost sight of the difference; and in the case of any assignable distinction of waking consciousness, we can always return to the trivial remark that all this is nothing more than mental idea. But the concrete theory of the waking soul in its realised being views it as consciousness and intellect: and the world of intelligent consciousness is something quite different from a picture of mere ideas and images. The latter are in the main only externally conjoined, in an unintelligent way, by the laws of the so-called Association of Ideas; though here and there of course logical principles may also be operative. But in the waking state man behaves essentially as a concrete ego, an intelligence: and because of this intelligence his sense-perception stands before him as a concrete totality of features in which each member, each point, takes up its place as at the same time determined through and with all the rest. Thus the facts embodied in his sensation are authenticated, not by his mere subjective representation and distinction of the facts as something external from the person, but by virtue of the concrete interconnexion in which each part stands with all parts of this complex. The waking state is the concrete consciousness of this mutual corroboration of each single factor of its content by all the others in the picture as perceived. The consciousness of this interdependence need not be explicit and distinct. Still this general setting to all sensations is implicitly present in the concrete feeling of self.—In order to see the difference of dreaming and waking we need only keep in view the Kantian distinction between subjectivity and objectivity of mental representation (the latter depending upon determination through categories): remembering, as already noted, that what is actually present in mind need not be therefore explicitly realised in consciousness, just as little as the exaltation of the intellectual sense to God need stand before consciousness in the shape of proofs of God's existence, although, as before explained, these proofs only serve to express the net worth and content of that feeling.

(γ) *Sensibility*[121].

§ 399. Sleep and waking are, primarily, it is true, not mere alterations, but alternating conditions (a progression in infinitum). This is their formal and negative relationship: but in it the affirmative relationship is also involved. In the self-certified existence of waking soul its mere existence is implicit as an "ideal" factor: the features which make up its sleeping nature, where they are implicitly as in their substance, are found by the waking soul, in its own self, and, be it noted, for itself. The fact that these particulars, though as a mode of mind they are distinguished from the self-identity of our self-centred being, are yet simply contained in its simplicity, is what we call sensibility.

§ 400. Sensibility (feeling) is the form of the dull stirring, the inarticulate breathing, of the spirit through its unconscious and unintelligent individuality, where every definite feature is still "immediate,"—neither specially developed in its content nor set in distinction as objective to subject, but treated as belonging to its most special, its natural peculiarity. The content of sensation is thus limited and transient, belonging as it does to natural, immediate being,—to what is therefore qualitative and finite.

Everything is in sensation (feeling): if you will, everything that emerges in conscious intelligence and in reason has its source and origin in sensation; for source and origin just means the first immediate manner in which a thing appears. Let it not be enough to have principles and religion only in the head: they must also be in the heart, in the feeling. What we merely have in the head is in consciousness, in a general way: the facts of it are objective—set over against consciousness, so that as it is put in me (my abstract ego) it can also be kept away and apart from me (from my concrete subjectivity). But if put in the feeling, the fact is a mode of my individuality, however crude that individuality be in such a form: it is thus treated as my very own. My own is something inseparate from the actual concrete self: and this immediate unity of the soul with its underlying self in all its definite content is just this inseparability; which however yet falls short of the ego of developed consciousness, and still more of the freedom of rational mind-life. It is with a quite different intensity and permanency that the will, the conscience, and the character, are our very own, than can ever be true of feeling and of the group of feelings (the heart): and this we need no philosophy to tell us. No doubt it is correct to say that above everything the heart must be good. But feeling and heart is not the form by which anything is legitimated as religious, moral, true, just, &c., and an appeal to heart and feeling either means nothing or means something bad. This should hardly need enforcing. Can any experience be more trite than that feelings and hearts are also bad, evil, godless, mean, &c.? That the heart is the source only of such feelings is stated in the words: "From the heart proceed evil thoughts, murder, adultery, fornication, blasphemy, &c." In such times when "scientific" theology and philosophy make the heart and feeling the criterion of what is good, moral, and religious, it is necessary to remind them of these trite experiences; just as it is nowadays necessary to repeat that thinking is the characteristic property by which man is distinguished from the beasts, and that he has feeling in common with them.

§ 401. What the sentient soul finds within it is, on one hand, the naturally immediate, as "ideally" in it and made its own. On the other hand and conversely, what originally belongs to the central individuality (which as further deepened and enlarged is the conscious ego and free mind) get the features of the natural corporeity, and is so felt. In this way we have two spheres of feeling. One, where what at first is a corporeal affection (e.g. of the eye or of any bodily part whatever) is made feeling (sensation) by being driven inward, memorised in the soul's self-centred part. Another, where affections originating in the mind and belonging to it, are in order to be felt, and to be as if found, invested with corporeity. Thus the mode or affection gets a place in the subject: it is felt in the soul. The detailed specification of the former branch of sensibility is seen in the system of the senses. But the other or inwardly originated modes of feeling no less necessarily systematise themselves; and their corporisation, as put in the living and concretely developed natural being, works itself out, following the special character of the mental mode, in a special system of bodily organs.

Sensibility in general is the healthy fellowship of the individual mind in the life of its bodily part. The senses form the simple system of corporeity specified. (a) The "ideal" side of physical things breaks up into two—because in it, as immediate and not yet subjective ideality, distinction appears as mere variety—the senses of definite light, § 287—and of sound, § 300. The "real" aspect similarly is with its difference double: (b) the senses of smell and taste, §§ 321, 322; (c) the sense of solid reality, of heavy matter, of heat and shape. Around the centre of the sentient individuality these specifications arrange themselves more simply than when they are developed in the natural corporeity.

The system by which the internal sensation comes to give itself specific bodily forms would deserve to be treated in detail in a peculiar science—a psychical physiology. Somewhat pointing to such a system is implied in the feeling of the appropriateness or inappropriateness of an immediate sensation to the persistent tone of internal sensibility (the pleasant and unpleasant): as also in the distinct parallelism which underlies the symbolical employment of sensations, e.g. of colours, tones, smells. But the most interesting side of a psychical physiology would lie in studying not the mere sympathy, but more definitely the bodily form adopted by certain mental modifications, especially the passions or emotions. We should have, e.g., to explain the line of connexion by which anger and courage are felt in the breast, the blood, the "irritable" system, just as thinking and mental occupation are felt in the head, the centre of the 'sensible' system. We should want a more satisfactory explanation than hitherto of the most familiar connexions by which tears, and voice in general, with its varieties of language, laughter, sighs, with many other specialisations lying in the line of pathognomy and physiognomy, are formed from their mental source. In physiology the viscera and the organs are treated merely as parts subservient to the animal organism; but they form at the same time a physical system for the expression of mental states, and in this way they get quite another interpretation.

§ 402. Sensations, just because they are immediate and are found existing, are single and transient aspects of psychic life,—alterations in the substantiality of the soul, set in its self-centred life, with which that substance is one. But this self-centred being is not merely a formal factor of sensation: the soul is virtually a reflected totality of sensations—it feels in itself the total substantiality which it virtually is—it is a soul which feels.

In the usage of ordinary language, sensation and feeling are not clearly distinguished: still we do not speak of the sensation,—but of the feeling (sense) of right, of self; sentimentality (sensibility) is connected with sensation: we may therefore say sensation emphasises rather the side of passivity—the fact that we find ourselves feeling, i.e. the immediacy of mode in feeling—whereas feeling at the same time rather notes the fact that it is we ourselves who feel.

(b) *The Feeling Soul.—(Soul as Sentiency.)*[122]

§ 403. The feeling or sentient individual is the simple "ideality" or subjective side of sensation. What it has to do, therefore, is to raise its substantiality, its merely virtual filling-up, to the character of subjectivity, to take possession of it, to realise its mastery over its own. As sentient, the soul is no longer a mere natural, but an inward, individuality: the individuality which in the merely substantial totality was only formal to it has to be liberated and made independent.

Nowhere so much as in the case of the soul (and still more of the mind) if we are to understand it, must that feature of "ideality" be kept in view, which represents it as the negation of the real, but a negation, where the real is put past, virtually retained, although it does not exist. The feature is one with which we are familiar in regard to our mental ideas or to memory. Every individual is an infinite treasury of sensations, ideas, acquired lore, thoughts, &c.; and yet the ego is one and uncompounded, a deep featureless characterless mine, in which all this is stored up, without existing. It is only when I call to mind an idea, that I bring it out of that interior to existence before consciousness. Sometimes, in sickness, ideas and information, supposed to have been forgotten years ago, because for so long they had not been brought into consciousness, once more come to light. They were not in our possession, nor by such reproduction as occurs in sickness do they for the future come into our possession; and yet they were in us and continue to be in us still. Thus a person can never know how much of things he once learned he really has in him, should he have once forgotten them: they belong not to his actuality or subjectivity as such, but only to his implicit self. And under all the superstructure of specialised and instrumental consciousness that may subsequently be added to it, the individuality always remains this single-souled inner life. At the present stage this singleness is, primarily, to be defined as one of feeling—as embracing the corporeal in itself: thus denying the view that this body is something material, with parts outside parts and outside the soul. Just as the number and variety of mental representations is no argument for an extended and real multeity in the ego; so the "real" outness of parts in the body has no truth for the sentient soul. As sentient, the soul is characterised as immediate, and so as natural and corporeal: but the outness of parts and sensible multiplicity of this corporeal counts for the soul (as it counts for the intelligible unity) not as anything real, and therefore not as a barrier: the soul is this intelligible unity in existence,—the existent speculative principle. Thus in the body it is one simple, omnipresent unity. As to the representative faculty the body is but one representation, and the infinite variety of its material structure and organisation is reduced to the simplicity of one definite conception: so in the sentient soul, the corporeity, and all that outness of parts to parts which belongs to it, is reduced to ideality (the truth of the natural multiplicity). The soul is virtually the totality of nature: as an individual soul it is a monad: it is itself the explicitly put totality of its particular world,—that world being included in it and filling it up; and to that world it stands but as to itself.

§ 404. As individual, the soul is exclusive and always exclusive: any difference there is, it brings within itself. What is differentiated from it is as yet no external object (as in consciousness), but only the aspects of its own sentient totality, &c. In this partition (judgment) of itself it is always subject: its object is its substance, which is at the same time its predicate. This substance is still the content of its natural life, but turned into the content of the individual sensation-laden soul; yet as the soul is in that content still particular, the content is its particular world, so far as that is, in an implicit mode, included in the ideality of the subject.

By itself, this stage of mind is the stage of its darkness: its features are not developed to conscious and intelligent content: so far it is formal and only formal. It acquires a peculiar interest in cases where it is as a form and appears as a special state of mind (§ 350), to which the soul, which has already advanced to consciousness and intelligence, may again sink down. But when a truer phase of mind thus exists in a more subordinate and abstract one, it implies a want of adaptation, which is disease. In the present stage we must treat, first, of the abstract psychical modifications by themselves, secondly, as morbid states of mind: the latter being only explicable by means of the former.

(α) The Feeling Soul in its Immediacy.

§ 405. (αα) Though the sensitive individuality is undoubtedly a monadic individual, it is because immediate, not yet as its self not a true subject reflected into itself, and is therefore passive. Hence the individuality of its true self is a different subject from it—a subject which may even exist as another individual. By the self-hood of the latter it—a substance, which is only a non-independent predicate—is then set in vibration and controlled without the least resistance on its part. This other subject by which it is so controlled may be called its genius.

In the ordinary course of nature this is the condition of the child in its mother's womb:—a condition neither merely bodily nor merely mental, but psychical—a correlation of soul to soul. Here are two individuals, yet in undivided psychic unity: the one as yet no self, as yet nothing impenetrable, incapable of resistance: the other is its actuating subject, the single self of the two. The mother is the genius of the child; for by genius we commonly mean the total mental self-hood, as it has existence of its own, and constitutes the subjective substantiality of some one else who is only externally treated as an individual and has only a nominal independence. The underlying essence of the genius is the sum total of existence, of life, and of character, not as a mere possibility, or capacity, or virtuality, but as efficiency and realised activity, as concrete subjectivity.

If we look only to the spatial and material aspects of the child's existence as an embryo in its special integuments, and as connected with the mother by means of umbilical cord, placenta, &c., all that is presented to the senses and reflection are certain anatomical and physiological facts— externalities and instrumentalities in the sensible and material which are insignificant as regards the main point, the psychical relationship. What ought to be noted as regards this psychical tie are not merely the striking effects communicated to and stamped upon the child by violent emotions, injuries, &c. of the mother, but the whole psychical judgment (partition) of the underlying nature, by which the female (like the monocotyledons among vegetables) can suffer disruption in twain, so that the child has not merely got communicated to it, but has originally received morbid dispositions as well as other pre-dispositions of shape, temper, character, talent, idiosyncrasies, &c.

Sporadic examples and traces of this magic tie appear elsewhere in the range of self-possessed conscious life, say between friends, especially female friends with delicate nerves (a tie which may go so far as to show "magnetic" phenomena), between husband and wife and between members of the same family.

The total sensitivity has its self here in a separate subjectivity, which, in the case cited of this sentient life in the ordinary course of nature, is visibly present as another and a different individual. But this sensitive totality is meant to elevate its self-hood out of itself to subjectivity in one and the same individual: which is then its indwelling consciousness, self-possessed, intelligent, and reasonable. For such a consciousness the merely sentient life serves as an underlying and only implicitly existent material; and the self-possessed subjectivity is the rational, self-conscious, controlling genius thereof. But this sensitive nucleus includes not merely the purely unconscious, congenital disposition and temperament, but within its enveloping simplicity it acquires and retains also (in habit, as to which see later) all further ties and essential relationships, fortunes, principles—everything in short belonging to the character, and in whose elaboration self-conscious activity has most effectively participated. The sensitivity is thus a soul in which the whole mental life is condensed. The total individual under this concentrated aspect is distinct from the existing and actual play of his consciousness, his secular ideas, developed interests, inclinations, &c. As contrasted with this looser aggregate of means and methods the more intensive form of individuality is termed the genius, whose decision is ultimate whatever may be the show of reasons, intentions, means, of which the more public consciousness is so liberal. This concentrated individuality also reveals itself under the aspect of what is called the heart and soul of feeling. A man is said to be heartless and unfeeling when he looks at things with self-possession and acts according to his permanent purposes, be they great substantial aims or petty and unjust interests: a good-hearted man, on the other hand, means rather one who is at the mercy of his individual sentiment, even when it is of narrow range and is wholly made up of particularities. Of such good nature or goodness of heart it may be said that it is less the genius itself than the indulgere genio.

§ 406. (ββ) The sensitive life, when it becomes a form or state of the self-conscious, educated, self-possessed human being is a disease. The individual in such a morbid state stands in direct contact with the concrete contents of his own self, whilst he keeps his self-possessed consciousness of self and of the causal order of things apart as a distinct state of mind. This morbid condition is seen in magnetic somnambulism and cognate states.

In this summary encyclopaedic account it is impossible to supply a demonstration of what the paragraph states as the nature of the remarkable condition produced chiefly by animal magnetism—to show, in other words, that it is in harmony with the facts. To that end the phenomena, so complex in their nature and so very different one from another, would have first of all to be brought under their general points of view. The facts, it might seem, first of all call for verification. But such a verification would, it must be added, be superfluous for those on whose account it was called for: for they facilitate the inquiry for themselves by declaring the narratives—infinitely numerous though they be and accredited by the education and character of the witnesses—to be mere deception and imposture. The a priori conceptions of these inquirers are so rooted that no testimony can avail against them, and they have even denied what they had seen with their own eyes. In order to believe in this department even what one sees with these eyes, and still more to understand it, the first requisite is not to be in bondage to the hard and fast categories of the practical intellect. The chief points on which the discussion turns may here be given:

(α) To the concrete existence of the individual belongs the aggregate of his fundamental interests, both the essential and the particular empirical ties which connect him with other men and the world at large. This totality forms his actuality, in the sense that it lies in fact immanent in him; it has already been called his genius. This genius is not the free mind which wills and thinks: the form of sensitivity, in which the individual here appears immersed, is, on the contrary, a surrender of his self-possessed intelligent existence. The first conclusion to which these considerations lead, with reference to the contents of consciousness in the somnambulist stage, is that it is only the range of his individually moulded world (of his private interests and narrow relationships) which appear there. Scientific theories and philosophic conceptions or general truths require a different soil,—require an intelligence which has risen out of the inarticulate mass of mere sensitivity to free consciousness. It is foolish therefore to expect revelations about the higher ideas from the somnambulist state.

(β) Where a human being's senses and intellect are sound, he is fully and intelligently alive to that reality of his which gives concrete filling to his individuality: but he is awake to it in the form of interconnexion between himself and the features of that reality conceived as an external and a separate world, and he is aware that this world is in itself also a complex of interconnexions of a practically intelligible kind. In his subjective ideas and plans he has also before him this causally connected scheme of things he calls his world and the series of means which bring his ideas and his purposes into adjustment with the objective existences, which are also means and ends to each other. At the same time, this world which is outside him has its threads in him to such a degree that it is these threads which make him what he really is: he too would become extinct if these externalities were to disappear, unless by the aid of religion, subjective reason, and character, he is in a remarkable degree self-supporting and independent of them. But, then, in the latter case he is less susceptible of the psychical state here spoken of.—As an illustration of that identity with the surroundings may be noted the effect produced by the death of beloved relatives, friends, &c. on those left behind, so that the one dies or pines away with the loss of the other. (Thus Cato, after the downfall of the Roman republic, could live no longer: his inner reality was neither wider than higher than it.) Compare home-sickness, and the like.

(γ) But when all that occupies the waking consciousness, the world outside it and its relationship to that world is under a veil, and the soul is thus sunk in sleep (in magnetic sleep, in catalepsy, and other diseases, e.g. those connected with female development, or at the approach of death, &c.), then that immanent actuality of the individual remains the same substantial total as before, but now as a purely sensitive life with an inward vision and an inward consciousness. And because it is the adult, formed, and developed consciousness which is degraded into this state of sensitivity, it retains along with its content a certain nominal self-hood, a formal vision and awareness, which however does not go so far as the conscious judgment or discernment by which its contents, when it is healthy and awake, exist for it as an outward objectivity. The individual is thus a monad which is inwardly aware of its actuality—a genius which beholds itself. The characteristic point in such knowledge is that the very same facts (which for the healthy consciousness are an objective practical reality, and to know which, in its sober moods, it needs the intelligent chain of means and conditions in all their real expansion) are now immediately known and perceived in this immanence. This perception is a sort of clairvoyance; for it is a consciousness living in the undivided substantiality of the genius, and finding itself in the very heart of the interconnexion, and so can dispense with the series of conditions, external one to another, which lead up to the result,—conditions which cool reflection has in succession to traverse and in so doing feels the limits of its own individual externality. But such clairvoyance—just because its dim and turbid vision does not present the facts in a rational interconnexion—is for that very reason at the mercy of every private contingency of feeling and fancy, &c.—not to mention that foreign suggestions (see later) intrude into its vision. It is thus impossible to make out whether what the clairvoyants really see preponderates over what they deceive themselves in.—But it is absurd to treat this visionary state as a sublime mental phase and as a truer state, capable of conveying general truths[123].

(δ) An essential feature of this sensitivity, with its absence of intelligent and volitional personality, is this, that it is a state of passivity, like that of the child in the womb. The patient in this condition is accordingly made, and continues to be, subject to the power of another person, the magnetiser; so that when the two are thus in psychical rapport, the selfless individual, not really a "person," has for his subjective consciousness the consciousness of the other. This latter self-possessed individual is thus the effective subjective soul of the former, and the genius which may even supply him with a train of ideas. That the somnambulist perceives in himself tastes and smells which are present in the person with whom he stands en rapport, and that he is aware of the other inner ideas and present perceptions of the latter as if they were his own, shows the substantial identity which the soul (which even in its concreteness is also truly immaterial) is capable of holding with another. When the substance of both is thus made one, there is only one subjectivity of consciousness: the patient has a sort of individuality, but it is empty, not on the spot, not actual: and this nominal self accordingly derives its whole stock of ideas from the sensations and ideas of the other, in whom it sees, smells, tastes, reads, and hears. It is further to be noted on this point that the somnambulist is thus brought into rapport with two genii and a twofold set of ideas, his own and that of the magnetiser. But it is impossible to say precisely which sensations and which visions he, in this nominal perception, receives, beholds and brings to knowledge from his own inward self, and which from the suggestions of the person with whom he stands in relation. This uncertainty may be the source of many deceptions, and accounts among other things for the diversity that inevitably shows itself among somnambulists from different countries and under rapport with persons of different education, as regards their views on morbid states and the methods of cure, or medicines for them, as well as on scientific and intellectual topics.

(ε) As in this sensitive substantiality there is no contrast to external objectivity, so within itself the subject is so entirely one that all varieties of sensation have disappeared, and hence, when the activity of the sense-organs is asleep, the "common sense," or "general feeling" specifies itself to several functions; one sees and hears with the fingers, and especially with the pit of the stomach, &c.

To comprehend a thing means in the language of practical intelligence to be able to trace the series of means intervening between a phenomenon and some other existence on which it depends,—to discover what is called the ordinary course of nature, in compliance with the laws and relations of the intellect, e.g. causality, reasons, &c. The purely sensitive life, on the contrary, even when it retains that mere nominal consciousness, as in the morbid state alluded to, is just this form of immediacy, without any distinctions between subjective and objective, between intelligent personality and objective world, and without the aforementioned finite ties between them. Hence to understand this intimate conjunction, which, though all-embracing, is without any definite points of attachment, is impossible, so long as we assume independent personalities, independent one of another and of the objective world which is their content—so long as we assume the absolute spatial and material externality of one part of being to another.

(β) *Self-feeling (Sense of Self)*[124].

§ 407. (αα) The sensitive totality is, in its capacity of individual, essentially the tendency to distinguish itself in itself, and to wake up to the judgment in itself, in virtue of which it has particular feelings and stands as a subject in respect of these aspects of itself. The subject as such gives these feelings a place as its own in itself. In these private and personal sensations it is immersed, and at the same time, because of the "ideality" of the particulars, it combines itself in them with itself as a subjective unit. In this way it is self-feeling, and is so at the same time only in the particular feeling.

§ 408. (ββ) In consequence of the immediacy, which still marks the self-feeling, i.e. in consequence of the element of corporeality which is still undetached from the mental life, and as the feeling too is itself particular and bound up with a special corporeal form, it follows that although the subject has been brought to acquire intelligent consciousness, it is still susceptible of disease, so far as to remain fast in a special phase of its self-feeling, unable to refine it to "ideality" and get the better of it. The fully-furnished self of intelligent consciousness is a conscious subject, which is consistent in itself according to an order and behaviour which follows from its individual position and its connexion with the external world, which is no less a world of law. But when it is engrossed with a single phase of feeling, it fails to assign that phase its proper place and due subordination in the individual system of the world which a conscious subject is. In this way the subject finds itself in contradiction between the totality systematised in its consciousness, and the single phase or fixed idea which is not reduced to its proper place and rank. This is Insanity or mental Derangement.

In considering insanity we must, as in other cases, anticipate the full-grown and intelligent conscious subject, which is at the same time the natural self of self-feeling. In such a phase the self can be liable to the contradiction between its own free subjectivity and a particularity which, instead of being "idealised" in the former, remains as a fixed element in self-feeling. Mind as such is free, and therefore not susceptible of this malady. But in older metaphysics mind was treated as a soul, as a thing; and it is only as a thing, i.e. as something natural and existent, that it is liable to insanity—the settled fixture of some finite element in it. Insanity is therefore a psychical disease, i.e. a disease of body and mind alike: the commencement may appear to start from one more than other, and so also may the cure.

The self-possessed and healthy subject has an active and present consciousness of the ordered whole of his individual world, into the system of which he subsumes each special content of sensation, idea, desire, inclination, &c., as it arises, so as to insert them in their proper place. He is the dominant genius over these particularities. Between this and insanity the difference is like that between waking and dreaming: only that in insanity the dream falls within the waking limits, and so makes part of the actual self-feeling. Error and that sort of thing is a proposition consistently admitted to a place in the objective interconnexion of things. In the concrete, however, it is often difficult to say where it begins to become derangement. A violent, but groundless and senseless outburst of hatred, &c., may, in contrast to a presupposed higher self-possession and stability of character, make its victim seem to be beside himself with frenzy. But the main point in derangement is the contradiction which a feeling with a fixed corporeal embodiment sets up against the whole mass of adjustments forming the concrete consciousness. The mind which is in a condition of mere being, and where such being is not rendered fluid in its consciousness, is diseased. The contents which are set free in this reversion to mere nature are the self-seeking affections of the heart, such as vanity, pride, and the rest of the passions—fancies and hopes—merely personal love and hatred. When the influence of self-possession and of general principles, moral and theoretical, is relaxed, and ceases to keep the natural temper under lock and key, the earthly elements are set free—that evil which is always latent in the heart, because the heart as immediate is natural and selfish. It is the evil genius of man which gains the upper hand in insanity, but in distinction from and contrast to the better and more intelligent part, which is there also. Hence this state is mental derangement and distress. The right psychical treatment therefore keeps in view the truth that insanity is not an abstract loss of reason (neither in the point of intelligence nor of will and its responsibility), but only derangement, only a contradiction in a still subsisting reason;—just as physical disease is not an abstract, i.e. mere and total, loss of health (if it were that, it would be death), but a contradiction in it. This humane treatment, no less benevolent than reasonable (the services of Pinel towards which deserve the highest acknowledgment), presupposes the patient's rationality, and in that assumption has the sound basis for dealing with him on this side—just as in the case of bodily disease the physician bases his treatment on the vitality which as such still contains health.

(γ) *Habit*[125].

§ 409. Self-feeling, immersed in the detail of the feelings (in simple sensations, and also desires, instincts, passions, and their gratification), is undistinguished from them. But in the self there is latent a simple self-relation of ideality, a nominal universality (which is the truth of these details): and as so universal, the self is to be stamped upon, and made appear in, this life of feeling, yet so as to distinguish itself from the particular details, and be a realised universality. But this universality is not the full and sterling truth of the specific feelings and desires; what they specifically contain is as yet left out of account. And so too the particularity is, as now regarded, equally formal; it counts only as the particular being or immediacy of the soul in opposition to its equally formal and abstract realisation. This particular being of the soul is the factor of its corporeity; here we have it breaking with this corporeity, distinguishing it from itself,—itself a simple being,—and becoming the "ideal," subjective substantiality of it,—just as in its latent notion (§ 359) it was the substance, and the mere substance, of it.

But this abstract realisation of the soul in its corporeal vehicle is not yet the self—not the existence of the universal which is for the universal. It is the corporeity reduced to its mere ideality; and so far only does corporeity belong to the soul as such. That is to say, as space and time—the abstract one-outside-another, as, in short, empty space and empty time—are only subjective form—pure act of intuition; so that pure being (which through the supersession in it of the particularity of the corporeity, or of the immediate corporeity as such has realised itself) is mere intuition and no more, lacking consciousness, but the basis of consciousness. And consciousness it becomes, when the corporeity, of which it is the subjective substance, and which still continues to exist, and that as a barrier for it, has been absorbed by it, and it has been invested with the character of self-centred subject.

§ 410. The soul's making itself an abstract universal being, and reducing the particulars of feelings (and of consciousness) to a mere feature of its being is Habit. In this manner the soul has the contents in possession, and contains them in such manner that in these features it is not as sentient, nor does it stand in relationship with them as distinguishing itself from them, nor is absorbed in them, but has them and moves in them, without feeling or consciousness of the fact. The soul is freed from them, so far as it is not interested in or occupied with them: and whilst existing in these forms as its possession, it is at the same time open to be otherwise occupied and engaged—say with feeling and with mental consciousness in general.

This process of building up the particular and corporeal expressions of feeling into the being of the soul appears as a repetition of them, and the generation of habit as practice. For, this being of the soul, if in respect of the natural particular phase it be called an abstract universality to which the former is transmuted, is a reflexive universality (§ 175); i.e. one and the same, that recurs in a series of units of sensation, is reduced to unity, and this abstract unity expressly stated.

Habit, like memory, is a difficult point in mental organisation: habit is the mechanism of self-feeling, as memory is the mechanism of intelligence. The natural qualities and alterations of age, sleep and waking, are "immediately" natural: habit, on the contrary, is the mode of feeling (as well as intelligence, will, &c., so far as they belong to self-feeling) made into a natural and mechanical existence. Habit is rightly called a second nature; nature, because it is an immediate being of the soul; a second nature, because it is an immediacy created by the soul, impressing and moulding the corporeality which enters into the modes of feeling as such and into the representations and volitions so far as they have taken corporeal form (§ 401).

In habit the human being's mode of existence is "natural," and for that reason not free; but still free, so far as the merely natural phase of feeling is by habit reduced to a mere being of his, and he is no longer involuntarily attracted or repelled by it, and so no longer interested, occupied, or dependent in regard to it. The want of freedom in habit is partly merely formal, as habit merely attaches to the being of the soul; partly only relative, so far as it strictly speaking arises only in the case of bad habits, or so far as a habit is opposed by another purpose: whereas the habit of right and goodness is an embodiment of liberty. The main point about Habit is that by its means man gets emancipated from the feelings, even in being affected by them. The different forms of this may be described as follows: (α) The immediate feeling is negated and treated as indifferent. One who gets inured against external sensations (frost, heat, weariness of the limbs, &c., sweet tastes, &c.), and who hardens the heart against misfortune, acquires a strength which consists in this, that although the frost, &c.—or the misfortune—is felt, the affection is deposed to a mere externality and immediacy; the universal psychical life keeps its own abstract independence in it, and the self-feeling as such, consciousness, reflection, and any other purposes and activity, are no longer bothered with it. (β) There is indifference towards the satisfaction: the desires and impulses are by the habit of their satisfaction deadened. This is the rational liberation from them; whereas monastic renunciation and forcible interference do not free from them, nor are they in conception rational. Of course in all this it is assumed that the impulses are kept as the finite modes they naturally are, and that they, like their satisfaction, are subordinated as partial factors to the reasonable will. (γ) In habit regarded as aptitude, or skill, not merely has the abstract psychical life to be kept intact per se, but it has to be imposed as a subjective aim, to be made a power in the bodily part, which is

74

rendered subject and thoroughly pervious to it. Conceived as having the inward purpose of the subjective soul thus imposed upon it, the body is treated as an immediate externality and a barrier. Thus comes out the more decided rupture between the soul as simple self-concentration, and its earlier naturalness and immediacy; it has lost its original and immediate identity with the bodily nature, and as external has first to be reduced to that position. Specific feelings can only get bodily shape in a perfectly specific way (§ 401); and the immediate portion of body is a particular possibility for a specific aim (a particular aspect of its differentiated structure, a particular organ of its organic system). To mould such an aim in the organic body is to bring out and express the "ideality" which is implicit in matter always, and especially so in the specific bodily part, and thus to enable the soul, under its volitional and conceptual characters, to exist as substance in its corporeity. In this way an aptitude shows the corporeity rendered completely pervious, made into an instrument, so that when the conception (e.g. a series of musical notes) is in me, then without resistance and with ease the body gives them correct utterance.

The form of habit applies to all kinds and grades of mental action. The most external of them, i.e. the spatial direction of an individual, viz. his upright posture, has been by will made a habit—a position taken without adjustment and without consciousness—which continues to be an affair of his persistent will; for the man stands only because and in so far as he wills to stand, and only so long as he wills it without consciousness. Similarly our eyesight is the concrete habit which, without an express adjustment, combines in a single act the several modifications of sensation, consciousness, intuition, intelligence, &c., which make it up. Thinking, too, however free and active in its own pure element it becomes, no less requires habit and familiarity (this impromptuity or form of immediacy), by which it is the property of my single self where I can freely and in all directions range. It is through this habit that I come to realise my existence as a thinking being. Even here, in this spontaneity of self-centred thought, there is a partnership of soul and body (hence, want of habit and too-long-continued thinking cause headache); habit diminishes this feeling, by making the natural function an immediacy of the soul. Habit on an ampler scale, and carried out in the strictly intellectual range, is recollection and memory, whereof we shall speak later.

Habit is often spoken of disparagingly and called lifeless, casual and particular. And it is true that the form of habit, like any other, is open to anything we chance to put into it; and it is habit of living which brings on death, or, if quite abstract, is death itself: and yet habit is indispensable for the existence of all intellectual life in the individual, enabling the subject to be a concrete immediacy, an "ideality" of soul—enabling the matter of consciousness, religious, moral, &c., to be his as this self, this soul, and no other, and be neither a mere latent possibility, nor a transient emotion or idea, nor an abstract inwardness, cut off from action and reality, but part and parcel of his being. In scientific studies of the soul and the mind, habit is usually passed over—either as something contemptible—or rather for the further reason that it is one of the most difficult questions of psychology.

(c) *The Actual Soul.*[126]

§ 411. The Soul, when its corporeity has been moulded and made thoroughly its own, finds itself there a single subject; and the corporeity is an externality which stands as a predicate, in being related to which, it is related to itself. This externality, in other words, represents not itself, but the soul, of which it is the sign. In this identity of interior and exterior, the latter subject to the former, the soul is actual: in its corporeity it has its free shape, in which it feels itself and makes itself felt, and which as the Soul's work of art has human pathognomic and physiognomic expression.

Under the head of human expression are included, e.g., the upright figure in general, and the formation of the limbs, especially the hand, as the absolute instrument, of the mouth—laughter, weeping, &c., and the note of mentality diffused over the whole, which at once announces the body at the externality of a higher nature. This note is so slight, indefinite, and inexpressible a modification, because the figure in its externality is something immediate and natural, and can therefore only be an indefinite and quite imperfect sign for the mind, unable to represent it in its actual universality. Seen from the animal world, the human figure is the supreme phase in which mind makes an appearance. But for the mind it is only its first appearance, while language is its perfect expression. And the human figure, though its proximate phase of existence, is at the same time in its physiognomic and pathognomic quality something contingent to it. To try to raise physiognomy and above all cranioscopy (phrenology) to the rank of sciences, was therefore one of the vainest fancies, still vainer than a signatura rerum, which supposed the shape of a plant to afford indication of its medicinal virtue.

§ 412. Implicitly the soul shows the untruth and unreality of matter; for the soul, in its concentrated self, cuts itself off from its immediate being, placing the latter over against it as a corporeity incapable of offering resistance to its moulding influence. The soul, thus setting in opposition its being to its (conscious) self, absorbing it, and making it its own, has lost the meaning of mere soul, or the "immediacy" of mind. The actual soul with its sensation and its concrete self-feeling turned into habit, has implicitly realised the 'ideality' of its qualities; in this externality it has recollected and inwardised itself, and is infinite self-relation. This free universality thus made explicit shows the soul awaking to the higher stage of the ego, or abstract universality in so far as it is for the abstract universality. In this way it gains the position of thinker and subject—specially a subject of the judgment in which the ego excludes from itself the sum total of its merely natural features as an object, a world external to it,—but with such respect to that object that in it it is immediately reflected into itself. Thus soul rises to become Consciousness.

Sub-Section B - Phenomenology Of Mind. Consciousness.

§ 413. Consciousness constitutes the reflected or correlational grade of mind: the grade of mind as appearance. Ego is infinite self-relation of mind, but as subjective or as self-certainty. The immediate identity of the natural soul has been raised to this pure "ideal" self-identity; and what the former contained is for this self-subsistent reflection set forth as an object. The pure abstract freedom of mind lets go from it its specific qualities,—the soul's natural life—to an equal freedom as an independent object. It is of this latter, as external to it, that the ego is in the first instance aware (conscious), and as such it is Consciousness. Ego, as this absolute negativity, is implicitly the identity in the otherness: the ego is itself that other and stretches over the object (as if that object were implicitly cancelled)—it is one side of the relationship and the whole relationship—the light, which manifests itself and something else too.

§ 414. The self-identity of the mind, thus first made explicit as the Ego, is only its abstract formal identity. As soul it was under the phase of substantial universality; now, as subjective reflection in itself, it is referred to this substantiality as to its negative, something dark and beyond it. Hence consciousness, like reciprocal dependence in general, is the contradiction between the independence of the two sides and their identity in which they are merged into one. The mind as ego is essence; but since reality, in the sphere of essence, is represented as in immediate being and at the same time as "ideal," it is as consciousness only the appearance (phenomenon) of mind.

§ 415. As the ego is by itself only a formal identity, the dialectical movement of its intelligible unity, i.e. the successive steps in further specification of consciousness, does not to it seem to be its own activity, but is implicit, and to the ego it seems an alteration of the object. Consciousness consequently appears differently modified according to the difference of the given object; and the gradual specification of consciousness appears as a variation in the characteristics of its objects. Ego, the subject of consciousness, is thinking: the logical process of modifying the object is what is identical in subject and object, their absolute interdependence, what makes the object the subject's own.

The Kantian philosophy may be most accurately described as having viewed the mind as consciousness, and as containing the propositions only of a phenomenology (not of a philosophy) of mind. The Ego Kant regards as reference to something away and beyond (which in its abstract description is termed the thing-at-itself); and it is only from this finite point of view that he treats both intellect and will. Though in the notion of a power of reflective judgment he touches upon the Idea of mind—a subject-objectivity, an intuitive intellect, &c., and even the Idea of Nature, still this Idea is again deposed to an appearance, i.e. to a subjective maxim (§ 58). Reinhold may therefore be said to have correctly appreciated Kantism when he treated it as a theory of consciousness (under the name of "faculty of ideation"). Fichte kept to the same point of view: his non-ego is only something set over against the ego, only defined as in consciousness: it is made no more than an infinite "shock," i.e. a thing-in-itself. Both systems therefore have clearly not reached the intelligible unity or the mind as it actually and essentially is, but only as it is in reference to something else.

As against Spinozism, again, it is to be noted that the mind in the judgment by which it "constitutes" itself an ego (a free subject contrasted with its qualitative affection) has emerged from substance, and that the philosophy, which gives this judgment as the absolute characteristic of mind, has emerged from Spinozism.

§ 416. The aim of conscious mind is to make its appearance identical with its essence, to raise its self-certainty to truth. The existence of mind in the stage of consciousness is finite, because it is merely a nominal self-relation, or mere certainty. The object is only abstractly characterised as its; in other words, in the object it is only as an abstract ego that the mind is reflected into itself: hence its existence there has still a content, which is not as its own.

§ 417. The grades of this elevation of certainty to truth are three in number: first (a) consciousness in general, with an object set against it; (b) self-consciousness, for which ego is the object; (c) unity of consciousness and self-consciousness, where the mind sees itself embodied in the object and sees itself as implicitly and explicitly determinate, as Reason, the notion of mind.

(a) *Consciousness Proper*[127].

(α) *Sensuous consciousness.*

§ 418. Consciousness is, first, immediate consciousness, and its reference to the object accordingly the simple and underived certainty of it. The object similarly, being immediate, an existent, reflected in itself, is further characterised as immediately singular. This is sense-consciousness.

Consciousness—as a case of correlation—comprises only the categories belonging to the abstract ego or formal thinking; and these it treats as features of the object (§ 415). Sense-consciousness therefore is aware of the object as an existent, a something, an existing thing, a singular, and so on. It appears as wealthiest in matter, but as poorest in thought. That wealth of matter is made out of sensations: they are the material of consciousness (§ 414), the substantial and qualitative, what the soul in its anthropological sphere is and finds in itself. This material the ego (the reflection of the soul in itself) separates from itself, and puts it first under the category of being. Spatial and temporal Singularness, here and now (the terms by which in the Phenomenology of the Mind (W. II. p. 73), I described the object of sense-consciousness) strictly belongs to intuition. At present the object is at first to be viewed only in its correlation to consciousness, i.e. a something external to it, and not yet as external on its own part, or as being beside and out of itself.

§ 419. The sensible as somewhat becomes an other: the reflection in itself of this somewhat, the thing, has many properties; and as a single (thing) in its immediacy has several predicates. The muchness of the sense-singular thus becomes a breadth—a variety of relations, reflectional attributes, and universalities. These are logical terms introduced by the thinking principle, i.e. in this case by the Ego, to describe the sensible. But the Ego as itself apparent sees in all this characterisation a change in the object; and self-consciousness, so construing the object, is sense-perception.

(β) *Sense-perception*[128].

§ 420. Consciousness, having passed beyond the sensibility, wants to take the object in its truth, not as merely immediate, but as mediated, reflected in itself, and universal. Such an object is a combination of sense qualities with attributes of wider range by which thought defines concrete relations and connexions. Hence the identity of consciousness with the object passes from the abstract identity of "I am sure" to the definite identity of "I know, and am aware."

The particular grade of consciousness on which Kantism conceives the mind is perception: which is also the general point of view taken by ordinary consciousness, and more or less by the sciences. The sensuous certitudes of single apperceptions or observations form the starting-point: these are supposed to be elevated to truth, by being regarded in their bearings, reflected upon, and on the lines of definite categories turned at the same time into something necessary and universal, viz. experiences.

§ 421. This conjunction of individual and universal is admixture—the individual remains at the bottom hard and unaffected by the universal, to which however it is related. It is therefore a tissue of contradictions—between the single things of sense apperception, which form the alleged ground of general experience, and the universality which has a higher claim to be the essence and ground— between the individuality of a thing which, taken in its concrete content, constitutes its independence and the various properties which, free from this negative link and from one another, are independent universal matters (§ 123). This contradiction of the finite which runs through all forms of the logical spheres turns out most concrete, when the somewhat is defined as object (§ 194 seqq.).

(γ) *The Intellect*[129].

§ 422. The proximate truth of perception is that it is the object which is an appearance, and that the object's reflection in self is on the contrary a self-subsistent inward and universal. The consciousness of such an object is intellect. This inward, as we called it, of the thing is on one hand the suppression of the multiplicity of the sensible, and, in that manner, an abstract identity: on the other hand, however, it also for that reason contains the multiplicity, but as an interior "simple" difference, which remains self-identical in the vicissitudes of appearance. This simple difference is the realm of the laws of the phenomena—a copy of the phenomenon, but brought to rest and universality.

§ 423. The law, at first stating the mutual dependence of universal, permanent terms, has, in so far as its distinction is the inward one, its necessity on its own part; the one of the terms, as not externally different from the other, lies immediately in the other. But in this manner the interior distinction is, what it is in truth, the distinction on its own part, or the distinction which is none. With this new form-characteristic, on the whole, consciousness implicitly vanishes: for consciousness as such implies the reciprocal independence of subject and object. The ego in its judgment has an object which is not distinct from it,—it has itself. Consciousness has passed into self-consciousness.

(b) *Self-consciousness*[130].

§ 424. Self-consciousness is the truth of consciousness: the latter is a consequence of the former, all consciousness of an other object being as a matter of fact also self-consciousness. The object is my idea: I am aware of the object as mine; and thus in it I am aware of me. The formula of self-consciousness is I = I:—abstract freedom, pure "ideality." In so far it lacks "reality": for as it is its own object, there is strictly speaking no object, because there is no distinction between it and the object.

§ 425. Abstract self-consciousness is the first negation of consciousness, and for that reason it is burdened with an external object, or, nominally, with the negation of it. Thus it is at the same time the antecedent stage, consciousness: it is the contradiction of itself as self-consciousness and as consciousness. But the latter aspect and the negation in general is in I = I potentially suppressed; and hence as this certitude of self against the object it is the impulse to realise its implicit nature, by giving its abstract self-awareness content and objectivity, and in the other direction to free itself from its sensuousness, to set aside the given objectivity and identify it with itself. The two processes are one and the same, the identification of its consciousness and self-consciousness.

(α) *Appetite or Instinctive Desire*[131].

§ 426. Self-consciousness, in its immediacy, is a singular, and a desire (appetite),—the contradiction implied in its abstraction which should yet be objective,—or in its immediacy which has the shape of an external object and should be subjective. The certitude of one's self, which issues from the suppression of mere consciousness, pronounces the object null: and the outlook of self-consciousness towards the object equally qualifies the abstract ideality of such self-consciousness as null.

§ 427. Self-consciousness, therefore, knows itself implicit in the object, which in this outlook is conformable to the appetite. In the negation of the two one-sided moments by the ego's own activity, this identity comes to be for the ego. To this activity the object, which implicitly and for self-consciousness is self-less, can make no resistance: the dialectic, implicit in it, towards self-suppression exists in this case as that activity of the ego. Thus while the given object is rendered subjective, the subjectivity divests itself of its one-sidedness and becomes objective to itself.

§ 428. The product of this process is the fast conjunction of the ego with itself, its satisfaction realised, and itself made actual. On the external side it continues, in this return upon itself, primarily describable as an individual, and maintains itself as such; because its bearing upon the self-less object is purely negative, the latter, therefore, being merely consumed. Thus appetite in its satisfaction is always destructive, and in its content selfish: and as the satisfaction has only happened in the individual (and that is transient) the appetite is again generated in the very act of satisfaction.

§ 429. But on the inner side, or implicitly, the sense of self which the ego gets in the satisfaction does not remain in abstract self-concentration or in mere individuality; on the contrary,—as negation of immediacy and individuality the result involves a character of universality and of the identity of self-consciousness with its object. The judgment or diremption of this self-consciousness is the consciousness of a "free" object, in which ego is aware of itself as an ego, which however is also still outside it.

(β) *Self-consciousness Recognitive*[132].

§ 430. Here there is a self-consciousness for a self-consciousness, at first immediately as one of two things for another. In that other as ego I behold myself, and yet also an immediately existing object, another ego absolutely independent of me and opposed to me. (The suppression of the singleness of self-consciousness was only a first step in the suppression, and it merely led to the characterisation of it as particular.) This contradiction gives either self-consciousness the impulse to show itself as a free self, and to exist as such for the other:—the process of recognition.

§ 431. The process is a battle. I cannot be aware of me as myself in another individual, so long as I see in that other an other and an immediate existence: and I am consequently bent upon the suppression of this immediacy of his. But in like measure I cannot be recognised as immediate, except so far as I overcome the mere immediacy on my own part, and thus give existence to my freedom. But this immediacy is at the same time the corporeity of self-consciousness, in which as in its sign and tool the latter has its own sense of self, and its being for others, and the means for entering into relation with them.

§ 432. The fight of recognition is a life and death struggle: either self-consciousness imperils the other's like, and incurs a like peril for its own—but only peril, for either is no less bent on maintaining his life, as the existence of its freedom. Thus the death of one, though by the abstract, therefore rude, negation of immediacy, it, from one point of view, solves the contradiction, is yet, from the essential point of view (i.e. the outward and visible recognition), a new contradiction (for that recognition is at the same time undone by the other's death) and a greater than the other.

§ 433. But because life is as requisite as liberty to the solution, the fight ends in the first instance as a one-sided negation with inequality. While the one combatant prefers life, retains his single self-consciousness, but surrenders his claim for recognition, the other holds fast to his self-assertion and is recognised by the former as his superior. Thus arises the status of master and slave.

In the battle for recognition and the subjugation under a master, we see, on their phenomenal side, the emergence of man's social life and the commencement of political union. Force, which is the basis of this phenomenon, is not on that account a basis of right, but only the necessary and legitimate factor in the passage from the state of self-consciousness sunk in appetite and selfish isolation into the state of universal self-consciousness. Force, then, is the external or phenomenal commencement of states, not their underlying and essential principle.

§ 434. This status, in the first place, implies common wants and common concern for their satisfaction,—for the means of mastery, the slave, must likewise be kept in life. In place of the rude destruction of the immediate object there ensues acquisition, preservation, and formation of it, as the instrumentality in which the two extremes of independence and non-independence are welded together. The form of universality thus arising in satisfying the want, creates a permanent means and a provision which takes care for and secures the future.

§ 435. But secondly, when we look to the distinction of the two, the master beholds in the slave and his servitude the supremacy of his single self-hood, and that by the suppression of immediate self-hood, a suppression, however, which falls on another. This other, the slave, however, in the service of the master, works off his individualist self-will, overcomes the inner immediacy of appetite, and in this divestment of self and in "the fear of his lord" makes "the beginning of wisdom"—the passage to universal self-consciousness.

(γ) *Universal Self-consciousness.*

§ 436. Universal self-consciousness is the affirmative awareness of self in an other self: each self as a free individuality has his own "absolute" independence, yet in virtue of the negation of its immediacy or appetite without distinguishing itself from that other. Each is thus universal self-conscious and objective; each has "real" universality in the shape of reciprocity, so far as each knows itself recognised in the other freeman, and is aware of this in so far as it recognises the other and knows him to be free.

This universal re-appearance of self-consciousness—the notion which is aware of itself in its objectivity as a subjectivity identical with itself and for that reason universal—is the form of consciousness which lies at the root of all true mental or spiritual life—in family, fatherland, state, and of all virtues, love, friendship, valour, honour, fame. But this appearance of the underlying essence may be severed from that essential, and be maintained apart in worthless honour, idle fame, &c.

§ 437. This unity of consciousness and self-consciousness implies in the first instance the individuals mutually throwing light upon each other. But the difference between those who are thus identified is mere vague diversity—or rather it is a difference which is none. Hence its truth is the fully and really existent universality and objectivity of self-consciousness,—which is Reason.

Reason, as the Idea (§ 213) as it here appears, is to be taken as meaning that the distinction between notion and reality which it unifies has the special aspect of a distinction between the self-concentrated notion or consciousness, and the object subsisting external and opposed to it.

(c) *Reason*[133].

§ 438. The essential and actual truth which reason is, lies in the simple identity of the subjectivity of the notion, with its objectivity and universality. The universality of reason, therefore, whilst it signifies that the object, which was only given in consciousness quâ consciousness, is now itself universal, permeating and encompassing the ego, also signifies that the pure ego is the pure form which overlaps the object, and encompasses it without it.

§ 439. Self-consciousness, thus certified that its determinations are no less objective, or determinations of the very being of things, than they are its own thoughts, is Reason, which as such an identity is not only the absolute substance, but the truth that knows it. For truth here has, as its peculiar mode and immanent form, the self-centred pure notion, ego, the certitude of self as infinite universality. Truth, aware of what it is, is mind (spirit).

Sub-Section C - Psychology. Mind[134].

§ 440. Mind has defined itself as the truth of soul and consciousness,—the former a simple immediate totality, the latter now an infinite form which is not, like consciousness, restricted by that content, and does not stand in mere correlation to it as to its object, but is an awareness of this substantial totality, neither subjective nor objective. Mind, therefore, starts only from its own being and is in correlation only with its own features.

Psychology accordingly studies the faculties or general modes of mental activity quâ mental— mental vision, ideation, remembering, &c., desires, &c.—apart both from the content, which on the phenomenal side is found in empirical ideation, in thinking also and in desire and will, and from the two forms in which these modes exist, viz. in the soul as a physical mode, and in consciousness itself as a separately existent object of that consciousness. This, however, is not an arbitrary abstraction by the psychologist. Mind is just this elevation above nature and physical modes, and above the complication with an external object—in one word, above the material, as its concept has just shown. All it has now to do is to realise this notion of its freedom, and get rid of the form of immediacy with which it once more begins. The content which is elevated to intuitions is its sensations: it is its intuitions also which are transmuted into representations, and its representations which are transmuted again into thoughts, &c.

§ 441. The soul is finite, so far as its features are immediate or con-natural. Consciousness is finite, in so far as it has an object. Mind is finite, in so far as, though it no longer has an object, it has a mode in its knowledge; i.e., it is finite by means of its immediacy, or, what is the same thing, by being subjective or only a notion. And it is a matter of no consequence, which is defined as its notion, and which as the reality of that notion. Say that its notion is the utterly infinite objective reason, then its reality is knowledge or intelligence: say that knowledge is its notion, then its reality is that reason, and the realisation of knowledge consists in appropriating reason. Hence the finitude of mind is to be placed in the (temporary) failure of knowledge to get hold of the full reality of its reason, or, equally, in the (temporary) failure of reason to attain full manifestation in knowledge. Reason at the same time is only infinite so far as it is "absolute" freedom; so far, that is, as presupposing itself for its knowledge to work upon, it thereby reduces itself to finitude, and appears as everlasting movement of superseding this immediacy, of comprehending itself, and being a rational knowledge.

§ 442. The progress of mind is development, in so far as its existent phase, viz. knowledge, involves as its intrinsic purpose and burden that utter and complete autonomy which is rationality; in which case the action of translating this purpose into reality is strictly only a nominal passage over into manifestation, and is even there a return into itself. So far as knowledge which has not shaken off its original quality of mere knowledge is only abstract or formal, the goal of mind is to give it objective fulfilment, and thus at the same time produce its freedom.

The development here meant is not that of the individual (which has a certain anthropological character), where faculties and forces are regarded as successively emerging and presenting themselves in external existence—a series of steps, on the ascertainment on which there was for a long time great stress laid (by the system of Condillac), as if a conjectural natural emergence could exhibit the origin of these faculties and explain them. In Condillac's method there is an unmistakable intention to show how the several modes of mental activity could be made intelligible without losing sight of mental unity, and to exhibit their necessary interconnexion. But the categories employed in doing so are of a wretched sort. Their ruling principle is that the sensible is taken (and with justice) as the prius or the initial basis, but that the later phases that follow this starting-point present themselves as emerging in a solely affirmative manner, and the negative aspect of mental activity, by which this material is transmuted into mind and destroyed as a sensible, is misconceived and overlooked. As the theory of Condillac states it, the sensible is not merely the empirical first, but is left as if it were the true and essential foundation.

Similarly, if the activities of mind are treated as mere manifestations, forces, perhaps in terms stating their utility or suitability for some other interest of head or heart, there is no indication of the true final aim of the whole business. That can only be the intelligible unity of mind, and its activity can only have itself as aim; i.e. its aim can only be to get rid of the form of immediacy or subjectivity, to reach and get hold of itself, and to liberate itself to itself. In this way the so-called faculties of mind as thus distinguished are only to be treated as steps of this liberation. And this is the only rational mode of studying the mind and its various activities.

§ 443. As consciousness has for its object the stage which preceded it, viz. the natural soul (§ 413), so mind has or rather makes consciousness its object: i.e. whereas consciousness is only the virtual identity of the ego with its other (§ 415), the mind realises that identity as the concrete unity which it and it only knows. Its productions are governed by the principle of all reason that the contents are at once potentially existent, and are the mind's own, in freedom. Thus, if we consider the initial aspect of mind, that aspect is twofold—as being and as its own: by the one, the mind finds in itself something which is, by the other it affirms it to be only its own. The way of mind is therefore

(a) to be theoretical: it has to do with the rational as its immediate affection which it must render its own: or it has to free knowledge from its pre-supposedness and therefore from its abstractness, and make the affection subjective. When the affection has been rendered its own, and the knowledge consequently characterised as free intelligence, i.e. as having its full and free characterisation in itself, it is

(b) Will: practical mind, which in the first place is likewise formal—i.e. its content is at first only its own, and is immediately willed; and it proceeds next to liberate its volition from its subjectivity, which is the one-sided form of its contents, so that it

(c) confronts itself as free mind and thus gets rid of both its defects of one-sidedness.

§ 444. The theoretical as well as the practical mind still fall under the general range of Mind Subjective. They are not to be distinguished as active and passive. Subjective mind is productive: but it is a merely nominal productivity. Inwards, the theoretical mind produces only its "ideal" world, and gains abstract autonomy within; while the practical, while it has to do with autonomous products, with a material which is its own, has a material which is only nominally such, and therefore a restricted content, for which it gains the form of universality. Outwards, the subjective mind (which as a unity of soul and consciousness, is thus also a reality,—a reality at once anthropological and conformable to consciousness) has for its products, in the theoretical range, the word, and in the practical (not yet deed and action, but) enjoyment.

Psychology, like logic, is one of those sciences which in modern times have yet derived least profit from the more general mental culture and the deeper conception of reason. It is still extremely ill off. The turn which the Kantian philosophy has taken has given it greater importance: it has, and that in its empirical condition, been claimed as the basis of metaphysics, which is to consist of nothing but the empirical apprehension and the analysis of the facts of human consciousness, merely as facts, just as they are given. This position of psychology, mixing it up with forms belonging to the range of consciousness and with anthropology, has led to no improvement in its own condition: but it has had the further effect that, both for the mind as such, and for metaphysics and philosophy generally, all attempts have been abandoned to ascertain the necessity of essential and actual reality, to get at the notion and the truth.

(a) *Theoretical mind.*

§ 445. Intelligence[135] finds itself determined: this is its apparent aspect from which in its immediacy it starts. But as knowledge, intelligence consists in treating what is found as its own. Its activity has to do with the empty form—the pretence of finding reason: and its aim is to realise its concept or to be reason actual, along with which the content is realised as rational. This activity is cognition. The nominal knowledge, which is only certitude, elevates itself, as reason is concrete, to definite and conceptual knowledge. The course of this elevation is itself rational, and consists in a necessary passage (governed by the concept) of one grade or term of intelligent activity (a so-called faculty of mind) into another. The refutation which such cognition gives of the semblance that the rational is found, starts from the certitude or the faith of intelligence in its capability of rational knowledge, and in the possibility of being able to appropriate the reason, which it and the content virtually is.

The distinction of Intelligence from Will is often incorrectly taken to mean that each has a fixed and separate existence of its own, as if volition could be without intelligence, or the activity of intelligence could be without will. The possibility of a culture of the intellect which leaves the heart untouched, as it is said, and of the heart without the intellect—of hearts which in one-sided way want intellect, and heartless intellects—only proves at most that bad and radically untrue existences occur. But it is not philosophy which should take such untruths of existence and of mere imagining for truth—take the worthless for the essential nature. A host of other phrases used of intelligence, e.g. that it receives and accepts impressions from outside, that ideas arise through the causal operations of external things upon it, &c., belong to a point of view utterly alien to the mental level or to the position of philosophic study.

A favourite reflectional form is that of powers and faculties of soul, intelligence, or mind. Faculty, like power or force, is the fixed quality of any object of thought, conceived as reflected into self. Force (§ 136) is no doubt the infinity of form—of the inward and the outward: but its essential finitude involves the indifference of content to form (ib. note). In this lies the want of organic unity which by this reflectional form, treating mind as a "lot" of forces, is brought into mind, as it is by the same method brought into nature. Any aspect which can be distinguished in mental action is stereotyped as an independent entity, and the mind thus made a skeleton-like mechanical collection. It makes absolutely no difference if we substitute the expression "activities" for powers and faculties. Isolate the activities and you similarly make the mind a mere aggregate, and treat their essential correlation as an external incident.

The action of intelligence as theoretical mind has been called cognition (knowledge). Yet this does not mean intelligence inter alia knows,—besides which it also intuites, conceives, remembers, imagines, &c. To take up such a position is in the first instance part and parcel of that isolating of mental activity just censured; but it is also in addition connected with the great question of modern times, as to whether true knowledge or the knowledge of truth is possible,—which, if answered in the negative, must lead to abandoning the effort. The numerous aspects and reasons and modes of phrase with which external reflection swells the bulk of this question are cleared up in their place: the more external the attitude of understanding in the question, the more diffuse it makes a simple object. At the present place the simple concept of cognition is what confronts the quite general assumption taken up by the question, viz. the assumption that the possibility of true knowledge in general is in dispute, and the assumption that it is possible for us at our will either to prosecute or to abandon cognition. The concept or possibility of cognition has come out as intelligence itself, as the certitude of reason: the act of cognition itself is therefore the actuality of intelligence. It follows from this that it is absurd to speak of intelligence and yet at the same time of the possibility or choice of knowing or not. But cognition is genuine, just so far as it realises itself, or makes the concept its own. This nominal description has its concrete meaning exactly where cognition has it. The stages of its realising activity are intuition, conception, memory, &c.: these activities have no other immanent meaning: their aim is solely the concept of cognition (§ 445 note). If they are isolated, however, then an impression is implied that they are useful for something else than cognition, or that they severally procure a cognitive satisfaction of their own; and that leads to a glorification of the delights of intuition, remembrance, imagination. It is true that even as isolated (i.e. as non-intelligent), intuition, imagination, &c. can afford a certain satisfaction: what physical nature succeeds in doing by its fundamental quality—its out-of-selfness,—exhibiting the elements or factors of immanent reason external to each other,—that the intelligence can do by voluntary act, but the same result may happen where the intelligence is itself only natural and untrained. But the true satisfaction, it is admitted, is only afforded by an intuition permeated by intellect and mind, by rational conception, by products of imagination which are permeated by reason and exhibit ideas—in a word, by cognitive intuition, cognitive conception, &c. The truth ascribed to such satisfaction lies in this, that intuition, conception, &c. are not isolated, and exist only as "moments" in the totality of cognition itself.

(α) *Intuition (Intelligent Perception)*[136].

§ 446. The mind which as soul is physically conditioned,—which as consciousness stands to this condition on the same terms as to an outward object,—but which as intelligence finds itself so characterised—is [1] an inarticulate embryonic life, in which it is to itself as it were palpable and has the whole material of its knowledge. In consequence of the immediacy in which it is thus originally, it is in this stage only as an individual and possesses a vulgar subjectivity. It thus appears as mind in the guise of feeling.

If feeling formerly turned up (§ 399) as a mode of the soul's existence, the finding of it or its immediacy was in that case essentially to be conceived as a congenital or corporeal condition; whereas at present it is only to be taken abstractly in the general sense of immediacy.

§ 447. The characteristic form of feeling is that though it is a mode of some "affection," this mode is simple. Hence feeling, even should its import be most sterling and true, has the form of casual particularity,—not to mention that its import may also be the most scanty and most untrue.

It is commonly enough assumed that mind has in its feeling the material of its ideas, but the statement is more usually understood in a sense the opposite of that which it has here. In contrast with the simplicity of feeling it is usual rather to assume that the primary mental phase is judgment generally, or the distinction of consciousness into subject and object; and the special quality of sensation is derived from an independent object, external or internal. With us, in the truth of mind, the mere consciousness point of view, as opposed to true mental "idealism," is swallowed up, and the matter of feeling has rather been supposed already as immanent in the mind.—It is commonly taken for granted that as regards content there is more in feeling than in thought: this being specially affirmed of moral and religious feelings. Now the material, which the mind as it feels is to itself, is here the result and the mature result of a fully organised reason: hence under the head of feeling is comprised all rational and indeed all spiritual content whatever. But the form of selfish singleness to which feeling reduces the mind is the lowest and worst vehicle it can have—one in which it is not found as a free and infinitely universal principle, but rather as subjective and private, in content and value entirely contingent. Trained and sterling feeling is the feeling of an educated mind which has acquired the consciousness of the true differences of things, of their essential relationships and real characters; and it is with such a mind that this rectified material enters into its feeling and receives this form. Feeling is the immediate, as it were the closest, contact in which the thinking subject can stand to a given content. Against that content the subject re-acts first of all with its particular self-feeling, which though it may be of more sterling value and of wider range than a onesided intellectual standpoint, may just as likely be narrow and poor; and in any case is the form of the particular and subjective. If a man on any topic appeals not to the nature and notion of the thing, or at least to reasons—to the generalities of common sense—but to his feeling, the only thing to do is to let him alone, because by his behaviour he refuses to have any lot or part in common rationality, and shuts himself up in his own isolated subjectivity—his private and particular self.

§ 448. [2] As this immediate finding is broken up into elements, we have the one factor in Attention—the abstract identical direction of mind (in feeling, as also in all other more advanced developments of it)—an active self-collection—the factor of fixing it as our own, but with an as yet only nominal autonomy of intelligence. Apart from such attention there is nothing for the mind. The other factor is to invest the special quality of feeling, as contrasted with this inwardness of mind, with the character of something existent, but as a negative or as the abstract otherness of itself. Intelligence thus defines the content of sensation as something that is out of itself, projects it into time and space, which are the forms in which it is intuitive. To the view of consciousness the material is only an object of consciousness, a relative other: from mind it receives the rational characteristic of being its very other (§§ 147, 254).

§ 449. [3] When intelligence reaches a concrete unity of the two factors, that is to say, when it is at once self-collected in this externally existing material, and yet in this self-collectedness sunk in the out-of-selfness, it is Intuition or Mental Vision.

§ 450. At and towards this its own out-of-selfness, intelligence no less essentially directs its attention. In this its immediacy it is an awaking to itself, a recollection of itself. Thus intuition becomes a concretion of the material with the intelligence, which makes it its own, so that it no longer needs this immediacy, no longer needs to find the content.

(β) *Representation (or Mental Idea)*[137].

§ 451. Representation is this recollected or inwardised intuition, and as such is the middle between that stage of intelligence where it finds itself immediately subject to modification and that where intelligence is in its freedom, or, as thought. The representation is the property of intelligence; with a preponderating subjectivity, however, as its right of property is still conditioned by contrast with the immediacy, and the representation cannot as it stands be said to be. The path of intelligence in representations is to render the immediacy inward, to invest itself with intuitive action in itself, and at the same time to get rid of the subjectivity of the inwardness, and inwardly divest itself of it; so as to be in itself in an externality of its own. But as representation begins from intuition and the ready-found material of intuition, the intuitional contrast still continues to affect its activity, and makes its concrete products still "syntheses," which do not grow to the concrete immanence of the notion till they reach the stage of thought.

(αα) *Recollection*[138].

§ 452. Intelligence, as it at first recollects the intuition, places the content of feeling in its own inwardness—in a space and a time of its own. In this way that content is [1] an image or picture, liberated from its original immediacy and abstract singleness amongst other things, and received into the universality of the ego. The image loses the full complement of features proper to intuition, and is arbitrary or contingent, isolated, we may say, from the external place, time, and immediate context in which the intuition stood.

§ 453. [2] The image is of itself transient, and intelligence itself is as attention its time and also its place, its when and where. But intelligence is not only consciousness and actual existence, but quâ intelligence is the subject and the potentiality of its own specialisations. The image when thus kept in mind is no longer existent, but stored up out of consciousness.

To grasp intelligence as this night-like mine or pit in which is stored a world of infinitely many images and representations, yet without being in consciousness, is from the one point of view the universal postulate which bids us treat the notion as concrete, in the way we treat e.g. the germ as affirmatively containing, in virtual possibility, all the qualities that come into existence in the subsequent development of the tree. Inability to grasp a universal like this, which, though intrinsically concrete, still continues simple, is what has led people to talk about special fibres and areas as receptacles of particular ideas. It was felt that what was diverse should in the nature of things have a local habitation peculiar to itself. But whereas the reversion of the germ from its existing specialisations to its simplicity in a purely potential existence takes place only in another germ,—the germ of the fruit; intelligence quâ intelligence shows the potential coming to free existence in its development, and yet at the same time collecting itself in its inwardness. Hence from the other point of view intelligence is to be conceived as this sub-conscious mine, i.e. as the existent universal in which the different has not yet been realised in its separations. And it is indeed this potentiality which is the first form of universality offered in mental representation.

§ 454. [3] An image thus abstractly treasured up needs, if it is to exist, an actual intuition: and what is strictly called Remembrance is the reference of the image to an intuition,—and that as a subsumption of the immediate single intuition (impression) under what is in point of form universal, under the representation (idea) with the same content. Thus intelligence recognises the specific sensation and the intuition of it as what is already its own,—in them it is still within itself: at the same time it is aware that what is only its (primarily) internal image is also an immediate object of intuition, by which it is authenticated. The image, which in the mine of intelligence was only its property, now that it has been endued with externality, comes actually into its possession. And so the image is at once rendered distinguishable from the intuition and separable from the blank night in which it was originally submerged. Intelligence is thus the force which can give forth its property, and dispense with external intuition for its existence in it. This "synthesis" of the internal image with the recollected existence is representation proper: by this synthesis the internal now has the qualification of being able to be presented before intelligence and to have its existence in it.

(ββ) *Imagination*[139].

§ 455. [1] The intelligence which is active in this possession is the reproductive imagination, where the images issue from the inward world belonging to the ego, which is now the power over them. The images are in the first instance referred to this external, immediate time and space which is treasured up along with them. But it is solely in the conscious subject, where it is treasured up, that the image has the individuality in which the features composing it are conjoined: whereas their original concretion, i.e. at first only in space and time, as a unit of intuition, has been broken up. The content reproduced, belonging as it does to the self-identical unity of intelligence, and an out-put from its universal mine, has a general idea (representation) to supply the link of association for the images which according to circumstances are more abstract or more concrete ideas.

The so-called laws of the association of ideas were objects of great interest, especially during that outburst of empirical psychology which was contemporaneous with the decline of philosophy. In the first place, it is not Ideas (properly so called) which are associated. Secondly, these modes of relation are not laws, just for the reason that there are so many laws about the same thing, as to suggest a caprice and a contingency opposed to the very nature of law. It is a matter of chance whether the link of association is something pictorial, or an intellectual category, such as likeness and contrast, reason and consequence. The train of images and representations suggested by association is the sport of vacant-minded ideation, where, though intelligence shows itself by a certain formal universality, the matter is entirely pictorial.—Image and idea, if we leave out of account the more precise definition of those forms given above, present also a distinction in content. The former is the more consciously-concrete idea, whereas the idea (representation), whatever be its content (from image, notion, or idea), has always the peculiarity, though belonging to intelligence, of being in respect of its content given and immediate. It is still true of this idea or representation, as of all intelligence, that it finds its material, as a matter of fact, to be so and so; and the universality which the aforesaid material receives by ideation is still abstract. Mental representation is the mean in the syllogism of the elevation of intelligence, the link between the two significations of self-relatedness—viz. being and universality, which in consciousness receive the title of object and subject. Intelligence complements what is merely found by the attribution of universality, and the internal and its own by the attribution of being, but a being of its own institution. (On the distinction of representations and thoughts, see Introd. to the Logic, § 20 note.)

Abstraction, which occurs in the ideational activity by which general ideas are produced (and ideas quâ ideas virtually have the form of generality), is frequently explained as the incidence of many similar images one upon another and is supposed to be thus made intelligible. If this super-imposing is to be no mere accident and without principle, a force of attraction in like images must be assumed, or something of the sort, which at the same time would have the negative power of rubbing off the dissimilar elements against each other. This force is really intelligence itself,—the self-identical ego which by its internalising recollection gives the images ipso facto generality, and subsumes the single intuition under the already internalised image (§ 453).

§ 456. Thus even the association of ideas is to be treated as a subsumption of the individual under the universal, which forms their connecting link. But here intelligence is more than merely a general form: its inwardness is an internally definite, concrete subjectivity with a substance and value of its own, derived from some interest, some latent concept or Ideal principle, so far as we may by anticipation speak of such. Intelligence is the power which wields the stores of images and ideas belonging to it, and which thus [2] freely combines and subsumes these stores in obedience to its peculiar tenor. Such is creative imagination[140]—symbolic, allegoric, or poetical imagination—where the intelligence gets a definite embodiment in this store of ideas and informs them with its general tone. These more or less concrete, individualised creations are still "syntheses": for the material, in which the subjective principles and ideas get a mentally pictorial existence, is derived from the data of intuition.

§ 457. In creative imagination intelligence has been so far perfected as to need no helps for intuition. Its self-sprung ideas have pictorial existence. This pictorial creation of its intuitive spontaneity is subjective—still lacks the side of existence. But as the creation unites the internal idea with the vehicle of materialisation, intelligence has therein implicitly returned both to identical self-relation and to immediacy. As reason, its first start was to appropriate the immediate datum in itself (§§ 445, 455), i.e. to universalise it; and now its action as reason (§ 458) is from the present point directed towards giving the character of an existent to what in it has been perfected to concrete auto-intuition. In other words, it aims at making itself be and be a fact. Acting on this view, it is self-uttering, intuition-producing: the imagination which creates signs.

Productive imagination is the centre in which the universal and being, one's own and what is picked up, internal and external, are completely welded into one. The preceding "syntheses" of intuition, recollection, &c., are unifications of the same factors, but they are "syntheses"; it is not till creative imagination that intelligence ceases to be the vague mine and the universal, and becomes an individuality, a concrete subjectivity, in which the self-reference is defined both to being and to universality. The creations of imagination are on all hands recognised as such combinations of the mind's own and inward with the matter of intuition; what further and more definite aspects they have is a matter for other departments. For the present this internal studio of intelligence is only to be looked at in these abstract aspects.—Imagination, when regarded as the agency of this unification, is reason, but only a nominal reason, because the matter or theme it embodies is to imagination quâ imagination a matter of indifference; whilst reason quâ reason also insists upon the truth of its content.

Another point calling for special notice is that, when imagination elevates the internal meaning to an image and intuition, and this is expressed by saying that it gives the former the character of an existent, the phrase must not seem surprising that intelligence makes itself be as a thing; for its ideal import is itself, and so is the aspect which it imposes upon it. The image produced by imagination of an object is a bare mental or subjective intuition: in the sign or symbol it adds intuitability proper; and in mechanical memory it completes, so far as it is concerned, this form of being.

§ 458. In this unity (initiated by intelligence) of an independent representation with an intuition, the matter of the latter is, in the first instance, something accepted, somewhat immediate or given (e.g. the colour of the cockade, &c.). But in the fusion of the two elements, the intuition does not count positively or as representing itself, but as representative of something else. It is an image, which has received as its soul and meaning an independent mental representation. This intuition is the Sign.

The sign is some immediate intuition, representing a totally different import from what naturally belongs to it; it is the pyramid into which a foreign soul has been conveyed, and where it is conserved. The sign is different from the symbol: for in the symbol the original characters (in essence and conception) of the visible object are more or less identical with the import which it bears as symbol; whereas in the sign, strictly so-called, the natural attributes of the intuition, and the connotation of which it is a sign, have nothing to do with each other. Intelligence therefore gives proof of wider choice and ampler authority in the use of intuitions when it treats them as designatory (significative) rather than as symbolical.

In logic and psychology, signs and language are usually foisted in somewhere as an appendix, without any trouble being taken to display their necessity and systematic place in the economy of intelligence. The right place for the sign is that just given: where intelligence—which as intuiting generates the form of time and space, but is apparently recipient of sensible matter, out of which it forms ideas—now gives its own original ideas a definite existence from itself, treating the intuition (or time and space as filled full) as its own property, deleting the connotation which properly and naturally belongs to it, and conferring on it an other connotation as its soul and import. This sign-creating activity may be distinctively named "productive" Memory (the primarily abstract "Mnemosyne"); since memory, which in ordinary life is often used as interchangeable and synonymous with remembrance (recollection), and even with conception and imagination, has always to do with signs only.

§ 459. The intuition—in its natural phase a something given and given in space—acquires, when employed as a sign, the peculiar characteristic of existing only as superseded and sublimated. Such is the negativity of intelligence; and thus the truer phase of the intuition used as a sign is existence in time (but its existence vanishes in the moment of being), and if we consider the rest of its external psychical quality, its institution by intelligence, but an institution growing out of its (anthropological) own naturalness. This institution of the natural is the vocal note, where the inward idea manifests itself in adequate utterance. The vocal note which receives further articulation to express specific ideas—speech and, its system, language—gives to sensations, intuitions, conceptions, a second and higher existence than they naturally possess,—invests them with the right of existence in the ideational realm.

Language here comes under discussion only in the special aspect of a product of intelligence for manifesting its ideas in an external medium. If language had to be treated in its concrete nature, it would be necessary for its vocabulary or material part to recall the anthropological or psycho-physiological point of view (§ 401), and for the grammar or formal portion to anticipate the standpoint of analytic understanding. With regard to the elementary material of language, while on one hand the theory of mere accident has disappeared, on the other the principle of imitation has been restricted to the slight range it actually covers—that of vocal objects. Yet one may still hear the German language praised for its wealth—that wealth consisting in its special expression for special sounds—Rauschen, Sausen, Knarren, &c.;—there have been collected more than a hundred such words, perhaps: the humour of the moment creates fresh ones when it pleases. Such superabundance in the realm of sense and of triviality contributes nothing to form the real wealth of a cultivated language. The strictly raw material of language itself depends more upon an inward symbolism than a symbolism referring to external objects; it depends, i.e. on anthropological articulation, as it were the posture in the corporeal act of oral utterance. For each vowel and consonant accordingly, as well as for their more abstract elements (the posture of lips, palate, tongue in each) and for their combinations, people have tried to find the appropriate signification. But these dull sub-conscious beginnings are deprived of their original importance and prominence by new influences, it may be by external agencies or by the needs of civilisation. Having been originally sensuous intuitions, they are reduced to signs, and thus have only traces left of their original meaning, if it be not altogether extinguished. As to the formal element, again, it is the work of analytic intellect which informs language with its categories: it is this logical instinct which gives rise to grammar. The study of languages still in their original state, which we have first really begun to make acquaintance with in modern times, has shown on this point that they contain a very elaborate grammar and express distinctions which are lost or have been largely obliterated in the languages of more civilised nations. It seems as if the language of the most civilised nations has the most imperfect grammar, and that the same language has a more perfect grammar when the nation is in a more uncivilised state than when it reaches a higher civilisation. (Cf. W. von Humboldt's Essay on the Dual.)

In speaking of vocal (which is the original) language, we may touch, only in passing, upon written language,—a further development in the particular sphere of language which borrows the help of an externally practical activity. It is from the province of immediate spatial intuition to which written language proceeds that it takes and produces the signs (§ 454). In particular, hieroglyphics uses spatial figures to designate ideas; alphabetical writing, on the other hand, uses them to designate vocal notes which are already signs. Alphabetical writing thus consists of signs of signs,—the words or concrete signs of vocal language being analysed into their simple elements, which severally receive designation.—Leibnitz's practical mind misled him to exaggerate the advantages which a complete written language, formed on the hieroglyphic method (and hieroglyphics are used even where there is alphabetic writing, as in our signs for the numbers, the planets, the chemical elements, &c.), would have as a universal language for the intercourse of nations and especially of scholars. But we may be sure that it was rather the intercourse of nations (as was probably the case in Phoenicia, and still takes place in Canton—see Macartney's Travels by Staunton) which occasioned the need of alphabetical writing and led to its formation. At any rate a comprehensive hieroglyphic language for ever completed is impracticable. Sensible objects no doubt admit of permanent signs; but, as regards signs for mental objects, the progress of thought and the continual development of logic lead to changes in the views of their internal relations and thus also of their nature; and this would involve the rise of a new hieroglyphical denotation. Even in the case of sense-objects it happens that their names, i.e. their signs in vocal language, are frequently changed, as e.g. in chemistry and mineralogy. Now that it has been forgotten what names properly are, viz. externalities which of themselves have no sense, and only get signification as signs, and now that, instead of names proper, people ask for terms expressing a sort of definition, which is frequently changed capriciously and fortuitously, the denomination, i.e. the composite name formed of signs of their generic characters or other supposed characteristic properties, is altered in accordance with the differences of view with regard to the genus or other supposed specific property. It is only a stationary civilisation, like the Chinese, which admits of the hieroglyphic language of that nation; and its method of writing moreover can only be the lot of that small part of a nation which is in exclusive possession of mental culture.—The progress of the vocal language depends most closely on the habit of alphabetical writing; by means of which only does vocal language acquire the precision and purity of its articulation. The imperfection of the Chinese vocal language is notorious: numbers of its words possess several utterly different meanings, as many as ten and twenty, so that, in speaking, the distinction is made perceptible merely by accent and intensity, by speaking low and soft or crying out. The European, learning to speak Chinese, falls into the most ridiculous blunders before he has mastered these absurd refinements of accentuation. Perfection here consists in the opposite of that *parler sans accent* which in Europe is justly required of an educated speaker. The hieroglyphic mode of writing keeps the Chinese vocal language from reaching that objective precision which is gained in articulation by alphabetic writing.

Alphabetic writing is on all accounts the more intelligent: in it the word—the mode, peculiar to the intellect, of uttering its ideas most worthily—is brought to consciousness and made an object of reflection. Engaging the attention of intelligence, as it does, it is analysed; the work of sign-making is reduced to its few simple elements (the primary postures of articulation) in which the sense-factor in speech is brought to the form of universality, at the same time that in this elementary phase it acquires complete precision and purity. Thus alphabetic writing retains at the same time the advantage of vocal language, that the ideas have names strictly so called: the name is the simple sign for the exact idea, i.e. the simple plain idea, not decomposed into its features and compounded out of them. Hieroglyphics, instead of springing from the direct analysis of sensible signs, like alphabetic writing, arise from an antecedent analysis of ideas. Thus a theory readily arises that all ideas may be reduced to their elements, or simple logical terms, so that from the elementary signs chosen to express these (as, in the case of the Chinese Koua, the simple straight stroke, and the stroke broken into two parts) a hieroglyphic system would be generated by their composition. This feature of hieroglyphic—the analytical designations of ideas—which misled Leibnitz to regard it as preferable to alphabetic writing is rather in antagonism with the fundamental desideratum of language,—the name. To want a name means that for the immediate idea (which, however ample a connotation it may include, is still for the mind simple in the name), we require a simple immediate sign which for its own sake does not suggest anything, and has for its sole function to signify and represent sensibly the simple idea as such. It is not merely the image-loving and image-limited intelligence that lingers over the simplicity of ideas and redintegrates them from the more abstract factors into which they have been analysed: thought too reduces to the form of a simple thought the concrete connotation which it "resumes" and reunites from the mere aggregate of attributes to which analysis has reduced it. Both alike require such signs, simple in respect of their meaning: signs, which though consisting of several letters or syllables and even decomposed into such, yet do not exhibit a combination of several ideas.—What has been stated is the principle for settling the value of these written languages. It also follows that in hieroglyphics the relations of concrete mental ideas to one another must necessarily be tangled and perplexed, and that the analysis of these (and the proximate results of such analysis must again be analysed) appears to be possible in the most various and divergent ways. Every divergence in analysis would give rise to another formation of the written name; just as in modern times (as already noted, even in the region of sense) muriatic acid has undergone several changes of name. A hieroglyphic written language would require a philosophy as stationary as is the civilisation of the Chinese.

What has been said shows the inestimable and not sufficiently appreciated educational value of learning to read and write an alphabetic character. It leads the mind from the sensibly concrete image to attend to the more formal structure of the vocal word and its abstract elements, and contributes much to give stability and independence to the inward realm of mental life. Acquired habit subsequently effaces the peculiarity by which alphabetic writing appears, in the interest of vision, as a roundabout way to ideas by means of audibility; it makes them a sort of hieroglyphic to us, so that in using them we need not consciously realise them by means of tones, whereas people unpractised in reading utter aloud what they read in order to catch its meaning in the sound. Thus, while (with the faculty which transformed alphabetic writing into hieroglyphics) the capacity of abstraction gained by the first practice remains, hieroglyphic reading is of itself a deaf reading and a dumb writing. It is true that the audible (which is in time) and the visible (which is in space), each have their own basis, one no less authoritative than the other. But in the case of alphabetic writing there is only a single basis: the two aspects occupy their rightful relation to each other: the visible language is related to the vocal only as a sign, and intelligence expresses itself immediately and unconditionally by speaking.—The instrumental function of the comparatively non-sensuous element of tone for all ideational work shows itself further as peculiarly important in memory which forms the passage from representation to thought.

§ 460. The name, combining the intuition (an intellectual production) with its signification, is primarily a single transient product; and conjunction of the idea (which is inward) with the intuition (which is outward) is itself outward. The reduction of this outwardness to inwardness is (verbal) Memory.

(γγ) *Memory[141]*.

§ 461. Under the shape of memory the course of intelligence passes through the same inwardising (recollecting) functions, as regards the intuition of the word, as representation in general does in dealing with the first immediate intuition (§ 451). [1] Making its own the synthesis achieved in the sign, intelligence, by this inwardising (memorising) elevates the single synthesis to a universal, i.e. permanent, synthesis, in which name and meaning are for it objectively united, and renders the intuition (which the name originally is) a representation. Thus the import (connotation) and sign, being identified, form one representation: the representation in its inwardness is rendered concrete and gets existence for its import: all this being the work of memory which retains names (retentive Memory).

§ 462. The name is thus the thing so far as it exists and counts in the ideational realm. [2] In the name, Reproductive memory has and recognises the thing, and with the thing it has the name, apart from intuition and image. The name, as giving an existence to the content in intelligence, is the externality of intelligence to itself; and the inwardising or recollection of the name, i.e. of an intuition of intellectual origin, is at the same time a self-externalisation to which intelligence reduces itself on its own ground. The association of the particular names lies in the meaning of the features sensitive, representative, or cogitant,—series of which the intelligence traverses as it feels, represents, or thinks.

Given the name lion, we need neither the actual vision of the animal, nor its image even: the name alone, if we understand it, is the unimaged simple representation. We think in names.

The recent attempts—already, as they deserved, forgotten—to rehabilitate the Mnemonic of the ancients, consist in transforming names into images, and thus again deposing memory to the level of imagination. The place of the power of memory is taken by a permanent tableau of a series of images, fixed in the imagination, to which is then attached the series of ideas forming the composition to be learned by rote. Considering the heterogeneity between the import of these ideas and those permanent images, and the speed with which the attachment has to be made, the attachment cannot be made otherwise than by shallow, silly, and utterly accidental links. Not merely is the mind put to the torture of being worried by idiotic stuff, but what is thus learnt by rote is just as quickly forgotten, seeing that the same tableau is used for getting by rote every other series of ideas, and so those previously attached to it are effaced. What is mnemonically impressed is not like what is retained in memory really got by heart, i.e. strictly produced from within outwards, from the deep pit of the ego, and thus recited, but is, so to speak, read off the tableau of fancy.—Mnemonic is connected with the common prepossession about memory, in comparison with fancy and imagination; as if the latter were a higher and more intellectual activity than memory. On the contrary, memory has ceased to deal with an image derived from intuition,—the immediate and incomplete mode of intelligence; it has rather to do with an object which is the product of intelligence itself,—such a without book[142] as remains locked up in the within-book[143] of intelligence, and is, within intelligence, only its outward and existing side.

§ 463. [3] As the interconnexion of the names lies in the meaning, the conjunction of their meaning with the reality as names is still an (external) synthesis; and intelligence in this its externality has not made a complete and simple return into self. But intelligence is the universal,—the single plain truth of its particular self-divestments; and its consummated appropriation of them abolishes that distinction between meaning and name. This extreme inwardising of representation is the supreme self-divestment of intelligence, in which it renders itself the mere being, the universal space of names as such, i.e. of meaningless words. The ego, which is this abstract being, is, because subjectivity, at the same time the power over the different names,—the link which, having nothing in itself, fixes in itself series of them and keeps them in stable order. So far as they merely are, and intelligence is here itself this being of theirs, its power is a merely abstract subjectivity,—memory; which, on account of the complete externality in which the members of such series stand to one another, and because it is itself this externality (subjective though that be), is called mechanical (§ 195).

A composition is, as we know, not thoroughly conned by rote, until one attaches no meaning to the words. The recitation of what has been thus got by heart is therefore of course accentless. The correct accent, if it is introduced, suggests the meaning: but this introduction of the signification of an idea disturbs the mechanical nexus and therefore easily throws out the reciter. The faculty of conning by rote series of words, with no principle governing their succession, or which are separately meaningless, e.g. a series of proper names, is so supremely marvellous, because it is the very essence of mind to have its wits about it; whereas in this case the mind is estranged in itself, and its action is like machinery. But it is only as uniting subjectivity with objectivity that the mind has its wits about it. Whereas in the case before us, after it has in intuition been at first so external as to pick up its facts ready-made, and in representation inwardises or recollects this datum and makes it its own,—it proceeds as memory to make itself external in itself, so that what is its own assumes the guise of something found. Thus one of the two dynamic factors of thought, viz. objectivity, is here put in intelligence itself as a quality of it.— It is only a step further to treat memory as mechanical—the act implying no intelligence—in which case it is only justified by its uses, its indispensability perhaps for other purposes and functions of mind. But by so doing we overlook the proper signification it has in the mind.

§ 464. If it is to be the fact and true objectivity, the mere name as an existent requires something else,—to be interpreted by the representing intellect. Now in the shape of mechanical memory, intelligence is at once that external objectivity and the meaning. In this way intelligence is explicitly made an existence of this identity, i.e. it is explicitly active as such an identity which as reason it is implicitly. Memory is in this manner the passage into the function of thought, which no longer has a meaning, i.e. its objectivity is no longer severed from the subjective, and its inwardness does not need to go outside for its existence.

The German language has etymologically assigned memory (Gedächtniß), of which it has become a foregone conclusion to speak contemptuously, the high position of direct kindred with thought (Gedanke).—It is not matter of chance that the young have a better memory than the old, nor is their memory solely exercised for the sake of utility. The young have a good memory because they have not yet reached the stage of reflection; their memory is exercised with or without design so as to level the ground of their inner life to pure being or to pure space in which the fact, the implicit content, may reign and unfold itself with no antithesis to a subjective inwardness. Genuine ability is in youth generally combined with a good memory. But empirical statements of this sort help little towards a knowledge of what memory intrinsically is. To comprehend the position and meaning of memory and to understand its organic interconnexion with thought is one of the hardest points, and hitherto one quite unregarded in the theory of mind. Memory quâ memory is itself the merely external mode, or merely existential aspect of thought, and thus needs a complementary element. The passage from it to thought is to our view and implicitly the identity of reason with this existential mode: an identity from which it follows that reason only exists in a subject, and as the function of that subject. Thus active reason is Thinking.

(γ) *Thinking*[144].

§ 465. Intelligence is recognitive: it cognises an intuition, but only because that intuition is already its own (§ 454); and in the name it re-discovers the fact (§ 462): but now it finds its universal in the double signification of the universal as such, and of the universal as immediate or as being,—finds i.e. the genuine universal which is its own unity overlapping and including its other, viz. being. Thus intelligence is explicitly, and on its own part cognitive: virtually it is the universal,—its product (the thought) is the thing: it is a plain identity of subjective and objective. It knows that what is thought, is, and that what is, only is in so far as it is a thought (§ 521); the thinking of intelligence is to have thoughts: these are as its content and object.

§ 466. But cognition by thought is still in the first instance formal: the universality and its being is the plain subjectivity of intelligence. The thoughts therefore are not yet fully and freely determinate, and the representations which have been inwardised to thoughts are so far still the given content.

§ 467. As dealing with this given content, thought is (α) understanding with its formal identity, working up the representations, that have been memorised, into species, genera, laws, forces, &c., in short into categories,—thus indicating that the raw material does not get the truth of its being save in these thought-forms. As intrinsically infinite negativity, thought is (β) essentially an act of partition,—judgment, which however does not break up the concept again into the old antithesis of universality and being, but distinguishes on the lines supplied by the interconnexions peculiar to the concept. Thirdly (γ), thought supersedes the formal distinction and institutes at the same time an identity of the differences,—thus being nominal reason or inferential understanding. Intelligence, as the act of thought, cognises. And (α) understanding out of its generalities (the categories) explains the individual, and is then said to comprehend or understand itself: (β) in the judgment it explains the individual to be an universal (species, genus). In these forms the content appears as given: (γ) but in inference (syllogism) it characterises a content from itself, by superseding that form-difference. With the perception of the necessity, the last immediacy still attaching to formal thought has vanished.

In Logic there was thought, but in its implicitness, and as reason develops itself in this distinction-lacking medium. So in consciousness thought occurs as a stage (§ 437 note). Here reason is as the truth of the antithetical distinction, as it had taken shape within the mind's own limits. Thought thus recurs again and again in these different parts of philosophy, because these parts are different only through the medium they are in and the antithesis they imply; while thought is this one and the same centre, to which as to their truth the antithesis return.

§ 468. Intelligence which as theoretical appropriates an immediate mode of being, is, now that it has completed taking possession, in its own property: the last negation of immediacy has implicitly required that the intelligence shall itself determine its content. Thus thought, as free notion, is now also free in point of content. But when intelligence is aware that it is determinative of the content, which is its mode no less than it is a mode of being, it is Will.

(b) *Mind Practical*[145].

§ 469. As will, the mind is aware that it is the author of its own conclusions, the origin of its self-fulfilment. Thus fulfilled, this independency or individuality form the side of existence or of reality for the Idea of mind. As will, the mind steps into actuality; whereas as cognition it is on the soil of notional generality. Supplying its own content, the will is self-possessed, and in the widest sense free: this is its characteristic trait. Its finitude lies in the formalism that the spontaneity of its self-fulfilment means no more than a general and abstract ownness, not yet identified with matured reason. It is the function of the essential will to bring liberty to exist in the formal will, and it is therefore the aim of that formal will to fill itself with its essential nature, i.e. to make liberty its pervading character, content, and aim, as well as its sphere of existence. The essential freedom of will is, and must always be, a thought: hence the way by which will can make itself objective mind is to rise to be a thinking will,—to give itself the content which it can only have as it thinks itself.

True liberty, in the shape of moral life, consists in the will finding its purpose in a universal content, not in subjective or selfish interests. But such a content is only possible in thought and through thought: it is nothing short of absurd to seek to banish thought from the moral, religious, and law-abiding life.

§ 470. Practical mind, considered at first as formal or immediate will, contains a double ought—[1] in the contrast which the new mode of being projected outward by the will offers to the immediate positivity of its old existence and condition,—an antagonism which in consciousness grows to correlation with external objects. [2] That first self-determination, being itself immediate, is not at once elevated into a thinking universality: the latter, therefore, virtually constitutes an obligation on the former in point of form, as it may also constitute it in point of matter;—a distinction which only exists for the observer.

(α) *Practical Sense or Feeling*[146].

§ 471. The autonomy of the practical mind at first is immediate and therefore formal, i.e. it finds itself as an individuality determined in its inward nature. It is thus "practical feeling," or instinct of action. In this phase, as it is at bottom a subjectivity simply identical with reason, it has no doubt a rational content, but a content which as it stands is individual, and for that reason also natural, contingent and subjective,—a content which may be determined quite as much by mere personalities of want and opinion, &c., and by the subjectivity which selfishly sets itself against the universal, as it may be virtually in conformity with reason.

An appeal is sometimes made to the sense (feeling) of right and morality, as well as of religion, which man is alleged to possess,—to his benevolent dispositions,—and even to his heart generally,—i.e. to the subject so far as the various practical feelings are in it all combined. So far as this appeal implies [1] that these ideas are immanent in his own self, and [2] that when feeling is opposed to the logical understanding, it, and not the partial abstractions of the latter, may be the totality—the appeal has a legitimate meaning. But on the other hand feeling too may be onesided, unessential and bad. The rational, which exists in the shape of rationality when it is apprehended by thought, is the same content as the good practical feeling has, but presented in its universality and necessity, in its objectivity and truth.

Thus it is on the one hand silly to suppose that in the passage from feeling to law and duty there is any loss of import and excellence; it is this passage which lets feeling first reach its truth. It is equally silly to consider intellect as superfluous or even harmful to feeling, heart, and will; the truth and, what is the same thing, the actual rationality of the heart and will can only be at home in the universality of intellect, and not in the singleness of feeling as feeling. If feelings are of the right sort, it is because of their quality or content,—which is right only so far as it is intrinsically universal or has its source in the thinking mind. The difficulty for the logical intellect consists in throwing off the separation it has arbitrarily imposed between the several faculties of feeling and thinking mind, and coming to see that in the human being there is only one reason, in feeling, volition, and thought. Another difficulty connected with this is found in the fact that the Ideas which are the special property of the thinking mind, viz. God, law and morality, can also be felt. But feeling is only the form of the immediate and peculiar individuality of the subject, in which these facts, like any other objective facts (which consciousness also sets over against itself), may be placed.

On the other hand, it is suspicious or even worse to cling to feeling and heart in place of the intelligent rationality of law, right and duty; because all that the former holds more than the latter is only the particular subjectivity with its vanity and caprice. For the same reason it is out of place in a scientific treatment of the feelings to deal with anything beyond their form, and to discuss their content; for the latter, when thought, is precisely what constitutes, in their universality and necessity, the rights and duties which are the true works of mental autonomy. So long as we study practical feelings and dispositions specially, we have only to deal with the selfish, bad, and evil; it is these alone which belong to the individuality which retains its opposition to the universal: their content is the reverse of rights and duties, and precisely in that way do they—but only in antithesis to the latter—retain a speciality of their own.

§ 472. The "Ought" of practical feeling is the claim of its essential autonomy to control some existing mode of fact—which is assumed to be worth nothing save as adapted to that claim. But as both, in their immediacy, lack objective determination, this relation of the requirement to existent fact is the utterly subjective and superficial feeling of pleasant or unpleasant.

Delight, joy, grief, &c., shame, repentance, contentment, &c., are partly only modifications of the formal "practical feeling" in general, but are partly different in the features that give the special tone and character mode to their "Ought."

The celebrated question as to the origin of evil in the world, so far at least as evil is understood to mean what is disagreeable and painful merely, arises on this stage of the formal practical feeling. Evil is nothing but the incompatibility between what is and what ought to be. "Ought" is an ambiguous term,—indeed infinitely so, considering that casual aims may also come under the form of Ought. But where the objects sought are thus casual, evil only executes what is rightfully due to the vanity and nullity of their planning: for they themselves were radically evil. The finitude of life and mind is seen in their judgment: the contrary which is separated from them they also have as a negative in them, and thus they are the contradiction called evil. In the dead there is neither evil nor pain: for in inorganic nature the intelligible unity (concept) does not confront its existence and does not in the difference at the same time remain its permanent subject. Whereas in life, and still more in mind, we have this immanent distinction present: hence arises the Ought: and this negativity, subjectivity, ego, freedom are the principles of evil and pain. Jacob Böhme viewed egoity (selfhood) as pain and torment, and as the fountain of nature and of spirit.

(β) *The Impulses and Choice[147]*.

§ 473. The practical ought is a "real" judgment. Will, which is essentially self-determination, finds in the conformity—as immediate and merely found to hand—of the existing mode to its requirement a negation, and something inappropriate to it. If the will is to satisfy itself, if the implicit unity of the universality and the special mode is to be realised, the conformity of its inner requirement and of the existent thing ought to be its act and institution. The will, as regards the form of its content, is at first still a natural will, directly identical with its specific mode:—natural impulse and inclination. Should, however, the totality of the practical spirit throw itself into a single one of the many restricted forms of impulse, each being always in conflict to another, it is passion.

§ 474. Inclinations and passions embody the same constituent features as the practical feeling. Thus, while on one hand they are based on the rational nature of the mind; they on the other, as part and parcel of the still subjective and single will, are infected with contingency, and appear as particular to stand to the individual and to each other in an external relation and with a necessity which creates bondage.

The special note in passion is its restriction to one special mode of volition, in which the whole subjectivity of the individual is merged, be the value of that mode what it may. In consequence of this formalism, passion is neither good nor bad; the title only states that a subject has thrown his whole soul,—his interests of intellect, talent, character, enjoyment,—on one aim and object. Nothing great has been and nothing great can be accomplished without passion. It is only a dead, too often, indeed, a hypocritical moralising which inveighs against the form of passion as such.

But with regard to the inclinations, the question is directly raised, Which are good and bad?—Up to what degree the good continue good;—and (as there are many, each with its private range) In what way have they, being all in one subject and hardly all, as experience shows, admitting of gratification, to suffer at least reciprocal restriction? And, first of all, as regards the numbers of these impulses and propensities, the case is much the same as with the psychical powers, whose aggregate is to form the mind theoretical,—an aggregate which is now increased by the host of impulses. The nominal rationality of impulse and propensity lies merely in their general impulse not to be subjective merely, but to get realised, overcoming the subjectivity by the subject's own agency. Their genuine rationality cannot reveal its secret to a method of outer reflection which pre-supposes a number of independent innate tendencies and immediate instincts, and therefore is wanting in a single principle and final purpose for them. But the immanent "reflection" of mind itself carries it beyond their particularity and their natural immediacy, and gives their contents a rationality and objectivity, in which they exist as necessary ties of social relation, as rights and duties. It is this objectification which evinces their real value, their mutual connexions, and their truth. And thus it was a true perception when Plato (especially including as he did the mind's whole nature under its right) showed that the full reality of justice could be exhibited only in the objective phase of justice, viz. in the construction of the State as the ethical life.

The answer to the question, therefore, What are the good and rational propensities, and how they are to be co-ordinated with each other? resolves itself into an exposition of the laws and forms of common life produced by the mind when developing itself as objective mind—a development in which the content of autonomous action loses its contingency and optionality. The discussion of the true intrinsic worth of the impulses, inclinations, and passions is thus essentially the theory of legal, moral, and social duties.

§ 475. The subject is the act of satisfying impulses, an act of (at least) formal rationality, as it translates them from the subjectivity of content (which so far is purpose) into objectivity, where the subject is made to close with itself. If the content of the impulse is distinguished as the thing or business from this act of carrying it out, and we regard the thing which has been brought to pass as containing the element of subjective individuality and its action, this is what is called the interest. Nothing therefore is brought about without interest.

An action is an aim of the subject, and it is his agency too which executes this aim: unless the subject were in this way in the most disinterested action, i.e. unless he had an interest in it, there would be no action at all.—The impulses and inclinations are sometimes depreciated by being contrasted with the baseless chimera of a happiness, the free gift of nature, where wants are supposed to find their satisfaction without the agent doing anything to produce a conformity between immediate existence and his own inner requirements. They are sometimes contrasted, on the whole to their disadvantage, with the morality of duty for duty's sake. But impulse and passion are the very life-blood of all action: they are needed if the agent is really to be in his aim and the execution thereof. The morality concerns the content of the aim, which as such is the universal, an inactive thing, that finds its actualising in the agent; and finds it only when the aim is immanent in the agent, is his interest and—should it claim to engross his whole efficient subjectivity—his passion.

§ 476. The will, as thinking and implicitly free, distinguishes itself from the particularity of the impulses, and places itself as simple subjectivity of thought above their diversified content. It is thus "reflecting" will.

§ 477. Such a particularity of impulse has thus ceased to be a mere datum: the reflective will now sees it as its own, because it closes with it and thus gives itself specific individuality and actuality. It is now on the standpoint of choosing between inclinations, and is option or choice.

§ 478. Will as choice claims to be free, reflected into itself as the negativity of its merely immediate autonomy. However, as the content, in which its former universality concludes itself to actuality, is nothing but the content of the impulses and appetites, it is actual only as a subjective and contingent will. It realises itself in a particularity, which it regards at the same time as a nullity, and finds a satisfaction in what it has at the same time emerged from. As thus contradictory, it is the process of distracting and suspending one desire or enjoyment by another,—and one satisfaction, which is just as much no satisfaction, by another, without end. But the truth of the particular satisfactions is the universal, which under the name of happiness the thinking will makes its aim.

(γ) *Happiness*[148].

§ 479. In this idea, which reflection and comparison have educed, of a universal satisfaction, the impulses, so far as their particularity goes, are reduced to a mere negative; and it is held that in part they are to be sacrificed to each other for the behoof that aim, partly sacrificed to that aim directly, either altogether or in part. Their mutual limitation, on one hand, proceeds from a mixture of qualitative and quantitative considerations: on the other hand, as happiness has its sole affirmative contents in the springs of action, it is on them that the decision turns, and it is the subjective feeling and good pleasure which must have the casting vote as to where happiness is to be placed.

§ 480. Happiness is the mere abstract and merely imagined universality of things desired,—a universality which only ought to be. But the particularity of the satisfaction which just as much is as it is abolished, and the abstract singleness, the option which gives or does not give itself (as it pleases) an aim in happiness, find their truth in the intrinsic universality of the will, i.e. its very autonomy or freedom. In this way choice is will only as pure subjectivity, which is pure and concrete at once, by having for its contents and aim only that infinite mode of being—freedom itself. In this truth of its autonomy, where concept and object are one, the will is an actually free will.

Free Mind[149]

§ 481. Actual free will is the unity of theoretical and practical mind: a free will, which realises its own freedom of will now that the formalism, fortuitousness, and contractedness of the practical content up to this point have been superseded. By superseding the adjustments of means therein contained, the will is the immediate individuality self-instituted,—an individuality, however, also purified of all that interferes with its universalism, i.e. with freedom itself. This universalism the will has as its object and aim, only so far as it thinks itself, knows this its concept, and is will as free intelligence.

§ 482. The mind which knows itself as free and wills itself as this its object, i.e. which has its true being for characteristic and aim, is in the first instance the rational will in general, or implicit Idea, and because implicit only the notion of absolute mind. As abstract Idea again, it is existent only in the immediate will—it is the existential side of reason,—the single will as aware of this its universality constituting its contents and aim, and of which it is only the formal activity. If the will, therefore, in which the Idea thus appears is only finite, that will is also the act of developing the Idea, and of investing its self-unfolding content with an existence which, as realising the idea, is actuality. It is thus "Objective" Mind.

No Idea is so generally recognised as indefinite, ambiguous, and open to the greatest misconceptions (to which therefore it actually falls a victim) as the idea of Liberty: none in common currency with so little appreciation of its meaning. Remembering that free mind is actual mind, we can see how misconceptions about it are of tremendous consequence in practice. When individuals and nations have once got in their heads the abstract concept of full-blown liberty, there is nothing like it in its uncontrollable strength, just because it is the very essence of mind, and that as its very actuality. Whole continents, Africa and the East, have never had this idea, and are without it still. The Greeks and Romans, Plato and Aristotle, even the Stoics, did not have it. On the contrary, they saw that it is only by birth (as e.g. an Athenian or Spartan citizen), or by strength of character, education, or philosophy (— the sage is free even as a slave and in chains) that the human being is actually free. It was through Christianity that this idea came into the world. According to Christianity, the individual as such has an infinite value as the object and aim of divine love, destined as mind to live in absolute relationship with God himself, and have God's mind dwelling in him: i.e. man is implicitly destined to supreme freedom. If, in religion as such, man is aware of this relationship to the absolute mind as his true being, he has also, even when he steps into the sphere of secular existence, the divine mind present with him, as the substance of the state of the family, &c. These institutions are due to the guidance of that spirit, and are constituted after its measure; whilst by their existence the moral temper comes to be indwelling in the individual, so that in this sphere of particular existence, of present sensation and volition, he is actually free.

If to be aware of the idea—to be aware, i.e. that men are aware of freedom as their essence, aim, and object—is matter of speculation, still this very idea itself is the actuality of men—not something which they have, as men, but which they are. Christianity in its adherents has realised an ever-present sense that they are not and cannot be slaves; if they are made slaves, if the decision as regards their property rests with an arbitrary will, not with laws or courts of justice, they would find the very substance of their life outraged. This will to liberty is no longer an impulse which demands its satisfaction, but the permanent character—the spiritual consciousness grown into a non-impulsive nature. But this freedom, which the content and aim of freedom has, is itself only a notion—a principle of the mind and heart, intended to develope into an objective phase, into legal, moral, religious, and not less into scientific actuality.

SECTION II – MIND OBJECTIVE

§ 483. The objective Mind is the absolute Idea, but only existing in posse: and as it is thus on the territory of finitude, its actual rationality retains the aspect of external apparency. The free will finds itself immediately confronted by differences which arise from the circumstance that freedom is its inward function and aim, and is in relation to an external and already subsisting objectivity, which splits up into different heads: viz. anthropological data (i.e. private and personal needs), external things of nature which exist for consciousness, and the ties of relation between individual wills which are conscious of their own diversity and particularity. These aspects constitute the external material for the embodiment of the will.

§ 484. But the purposive action of this will is to realise its concept, Liberty, in these externally-objective aspects, making the latter a world moulded by the former, which in it is thus at home with itself, locked together with it: the concept accordingly perfected to the Idea. Liberty, shaped into the actuality of a world, receives the form of Necessity the deeper substantial nexus of which is the system or organisation of the principles of liberty, whilst its phenomenal nexus is power or authority, and the sentiment of obedience awakened in consciousness.

§ 485. This unity of the rational will with the single will (this being the peculiar and immediate medium in which the former is actualised) constitutes the simple actuality of liberty. As it (and its content) belongs to thought, and is the virtual universal, the content has its right and true character only in the form of universality. When invested with this character for the intelligent consciousness, or instituted as an authoritative power, it is a Law[150]. When, on the other hand, the content is freed from the mixedness and fortuitousness, attaching to it in the practical feeling and in impulse, and is set and grafted in the individual will, not in the form of impulse, but in its universality, so as to become its habit, temper and character, it exists as manner and custom, or Usage[151].

§ 486. This "reality," in general, where free will has existence, is the Law (Right),—the term being taken in a comprehensive sense not merely as the limited juristic law, but as the actual body of all the conditions of freedom. These conditions, in relation to the subjective will, where they, being universal, ought to have and can only have their existence, are its Duties; whereas as its temper and habit they are Manners. What is a right is also a duty, and what is a duty, is also a right. For a mode of existence is a right, only as a consequence of the free substantial will: and the same content of fact, when referred to the will distinguished as subjective and individual, is a duty. It is the same content which the subjective consciousness recognises as a duty, and brings into existence in these several wills. The finitude of the objective will thus creates the semblance of a distinction between rights and duties.

In the phenomenal range right and duty are correlata, at least in the sense that to a right on my part corresponds a duty in some one else. But, in the light of the concept, my right to a thing is not merely possession, but as possession by a person it is property, or legal possession, and it is a duty to possess things as property, i.e. to be as a person. Translated into the phenomenal relationship, viz. relation to another person—this grows into the duty of some one else to respect my right. In the morality of the conscience, duty in general is in me—a free subject—at the same time a right of my subjective will or disposition. But in this individualist moral sphere, there arises the division between what is only inward purpose (disposition or intention), which only has its being in me and is merely subjective duty, and the actualisation of that purpose: and with this division a contingency and imperfection which makes the inadequacy of mere individualistic morality. In social ethics these two parts have reached their truth, their absolute unity; although even right and duty return to one another and combine by means of certain adjustments and under the guise of necessity. The rights of the father of the family over its members are equally duties towards them; just as the children's duty of obedience is their right to be educated to the liberty of manhood. The penal judicature of a government, its rights of administration, &c., are no less its duties to punish, to administer, &c.; as the services of the members of the State in dues, military services, &c., are duties and yet their right to the protection of their private property and of the general substantial life in which they have their root. All the aims of society and the State are the private aim of the individuals. But the set of adjustments, by which their duties come back to them as the exercise and enjoyment of right, produces an appearance of diversity: and this diversity is increased by the variety of shapes which value assumes in the course of exchange, though it remains intrinsically the same. Still it holds fundamentally good that he who has no rights has no duties and vice versa.

Distribution.

§ 487. The free will is

A. itself at first immediate, and hence as a single being—the person: the existence which the person gives to its liberty is property. The Right as right (law) is formal, abstract right.

B. When the will is reflected into self, so as to have its existence inside it, and to be thus at the same time characterised as a particular, it is the right of the subjective will, morality of the individual conscience.

C. When the free will is the substantial will, made actual in the subject and conformable to its concept and rendered a totality of necessity,—it is the ethics of actual life in family, civil society, and state.

Sub-Section A. Law.[152]

(a) *Property.*

§ 488. Mind, in the immediacy of its self-secured liberty, is an individual, but one that knows its individuality as an absolutely free will: it is a person, in whom the inward sense of this freedom, as in itself still abstract and empty, has its particularity and fulfilment not yet on its own part, but on an external thing. This thing, as something devoid of will, has no rights against the subjectivity of intelligence and volition, and is by that subjectivity made adjectival to it, the external sphere of its liberty;—possession.

§ 489. By the judgment of possession, at first in the outward appropriation, the thing acquires the predicate of "mine." But this predicate, on its own account merely "practical," has here the signification that I import my personal will into the thing. As so characterised, possession is property, which as possession is a means, but as existence of the personality is an end.

§ 490. In his property the person is brought into union with itself. But the thing is an abstractly external thing, and the I in it is abstractly external. The concrete return of me into me in the externality is that I, the infinite self-relation, am as a person the repulsion of me from myself, and have the existence of my personality in the being of other persons, in my relation to them and in my recognition by them, which is thus mutual.

§ 491. The thing is the mean by which the extremes meet in one. These extremes are the persons who, in the knowledge of their identity as free, are simultaneously mutually independent. For them my will has its definite recognisable existence in the thing by the immediate bodily act of taking possession, or by the formation of the thing or, it may be, by mere designation of it.

§ 492. The casual aspect of property is that I place my will in this thing: so far my will is arbitrary, I can just as well put it in it as not,—just as well withdraw it as not. But so far as my will lies in a thing, it is only I who can withdraw it: it is only with my will that the thing can pass to another, whose property it similarly becomes only with his will:—Contract.

(b) *Contract.*

§ 493. The two wills and their agreement in the contract are as an internal state of mind different from its realisation in the performance. The comparatively "ideal" utterance (of contract) in the stipulation contains the actual surrender of a property by the one, its changing hands, and its acceptance by the other will. The contract is thus thoroughly binding: it does not need the performance of the one or the other to become so—otherwise we should have an infinite regress or infinite division of thing, labour, and time. The utterance in the stipulation is complete and exhaustive. The inwardness of the will which surrenders and the will which accepts the property is in the realm of ideation, and in that realm the word is deed and thing (§ 462)—the full and complete deed, since here the conscientiousness of the will does not come under consideration (as to whether the thing is meant in earnest or is a deception), and the will refers only to the external thing.

§ 494. Thus in the stipulation we have the substantial being of the contract standing out in distinction from its real utterance in the performance, which is brought down to a mere sequel. In this way there is put into the thing or performance a distinction between its immediate specific quality and its substantial being or value, meaning by value the quantitative terms into which that qualitative feature has been translated. One piece of property is thus made comparable with another, and may be made equivalent to a thing which is (in quality) wholly heterogeneous. It is thus treated in general as an abstract, universal thing or commodity.

§ 495. The contract, as an agreement which has a voluntary origin and deals with a casual commodity, involves at the same time the giving to this "accidental" will a positive fixity. This will may just as well not be conformable to law (right), and, in that case, produces a wrong: by which however the absolute law (right) is not superseded, but only a relationship originated of right to wrong.

(c) *Right versus Wrong.*

§ 496. Law (right) considered as the realisation of liberty in externals, breaks up into a multiplicity of relations to this external sphere and to other persons (§§ 491, 493 seqq.). In this way there are [1] several titles or grounds at law, of which (seeing that property both on the personal and the real side is exclusively individual) only one is the right, but which, because they face each other, each and all are invested with a show of right, against which the former is defined as the intrinsically right.

§ 497. Now so long as (compared against this show) the one intrinsically right, still presumed identical with the several titles, is affirmed, willed, and recognised, the only diversity lies in this, that the special thing is subsumed under the one law or right by the particular will of these several persons. This is naïve, non-malicious wrong. Such wrong in the several claimants is a simple negative judgment, expressing the civil suit. To settle it there is required a third judgment, which, as the judgment of the intrinsically right, is disinterested, and a power of giving the one right existence as against that semblance.

§ 498. But [2] if the semblance of right is willed as such against right intrinsical by the particular will, which thus becomes wicked, then the external recognition of right is separated from the right's true value; and while the former only is respected, the latter is violated. This gives the wrong of fraud—the infinite judgment as identical (§ 173),—where the nominal relation is retained, but the sterling value is let slip.

§ 499. [3] Finally, the particular will sets itself in opposition to the intrinsic right by negating that right itself as well as its recognition or semblance. [Here there is a negatively infinite judgment (§ 173) in which there is denied the class as a whole, and not merely the particular mode—in this case the apparent recognition.] Thus the will is violently wicked, and commits a crime.

§ 500. As an outrage on right, such an action is essentially and actually null. In it the agent, as a volitional and intelligent being, sets up a law—a law however which is nominal and recognised by him only—a universal which holds good for him, and under which he has at the same time subsumed himself by his action. To display the nullity of such an act, to carry out simultaneously this nominal law and the intrinsic right, in the first instance by means of a subjective individual will, is the work of Revenge. But, revenge, starting from the interest of an immediate particular personality, is at the same time only a new outrage; and so on without end. This progression, like the last, abolishes itself in a third judgment, which is disinterested—punishment.

§ 501. The instrumentality by which authority is given to intrinsic right is (α) that a particular will, that of the judge, being conformable to the right, has an interest to turn against the crime (—which in the first instance, in revenge, is a matter of chance), and (β) that an executive power (also in the first instance casual) negates the negation of right that was created by the criminal. This negation of right has its existence in the will of the criminal; and consequently revenge or punishment directs itself against the person or property of the criminal and exercises coercion upon him. It is in this legal sphere that coercion in general has possible scope,—compulsion against the thing, in seizing and maintaining it against another's seizure: for in this sphere the will has its existence immediately in externals as such, or in corporeity, and can be seized only in this quarter. But more than possible compulsion is not, so long as I can withdraw myself as free from every mode of existence, even from the range of all existence, i.e. from life. It is legal only as abolishing a first and original compulsion.

§ 502. A distinction has thus emerged between the law (right) and the subjective will. The "reality" of right, which the personal will in the first instance gives itself in immediate wise, is seen to be due to the instrumentality of the subjective will,—whose influence as on one hand it gives existence to the essential right, so may on the other cut itself off from and oppose itself to it. Conversely, the claim of the subjective will to be in this abstraction a power over the law of right is null and empty of itself: it gets truth and reality essentially only so far as that will in itself realises the reasonable will. As such it is morality[153] proper.

The phrase "Law of Nature," or Natural Right[154], in use for the philosophy of law involves the ambiguity that it may mean either right as something existing ready-formed in nature, or right as governed by the nature of things, i.e. by the notion. The former used to be the common meaning, accompanied with the fiction of a state of nature, in which the law of nature should hold sway; whereas the social and political state rather required and implied a restriction of liberty and a sacrifice of natural rights. The real fact is that the whole law and its every article are based on free personality alone,—on self-determination or autonomy, which is the very contrary of determination by nature. The law of nature—strictly so called—is for that reason the predominance of the strong and the reign of force, and a state of nature a state of violence and wrong, of which nothing truer can be said than that one ought to depart from it. The social state, on the other hand, is the condition in which alone right has its actuality: what is to be restricted and sacrificed is just the wilfulness and violence of the state of nature.

Sub-Section B - The Morality Of Conscience[155].

§ 503. The free individual, who, in mere law, counts only as a person, is now characterised as a subject, a will reflected into itself so that, be its affection what it may, it is distinguished (as existing in it) as its own from the existence of freedom in an external thing. Because the affection of the will is thus inwardised, the will is at the same time made a particular, and there arise further particularisations of it and relations of these to one another. This affection is partly the essential and implicit will, the reason of the will, the essential basis of law and moral life: partly it is the existent volition, which is before us and throws itself into actual deeds, and thus comes into relationship with the former. The subjective will is morally free, so far as these features are its inward institution, its own, and willed by it. Its utterance in deed with this freedom is an action, in the externality of which it only admits as its own, and allows to be imputed to it, so much as it has consciously willed.

This subjective or "moral" freedom is what a European especially calls freedom. In virtue of the right thereto a man must possess a personal knowledge of the distinction between good and evil in general: ethical and religious principles shall not merely lay their claim on him as external laws and precepts of authority to be obeyed, but have their assent, recognition, or even justification in his heart, sentiment, conscience, intelligence, &c. The subjectivity of the will in itself is its supreme aim and absolutely essential to it.

The "moral" must be taken in the wider sense in which it does not signify the morally good merely. In French le moral is opposed to le physique, and means the mental or intellectual in general. But here the moral signifies volitional mode, so far as it is in the interior of the will in general; it thus includes purpose and intention,—and also moral wickedness.

a. *Purpose*[156].

§ 504. So far as the action comes into immediate touch with existence, my part in it is to this extent formal, that external existence is also independent of the agent. This externality can pervert his action and bring to light something else than lay in it. Now, though any alteration as such, which is set on foot by the subject's action, is its deed[157], still the subject does not for that reason recognise it as its action[158], but only admits as its own that existence in the deed which lay in its knowledge and will, which was its purpose. Only for that does it hold itself responsible.

b. *Intention and Welfare*[159].

§ 505. As regards its empirically concrete content [1] the action has a variety of particular aspects and connexions. In point of form, the agent must have known and willed the action in its essential feature, embracing these individual points. This is the right of intention. While purpose affects only the immediate fact of existence, intention regards the underlying essence and aim thereof. [2] The agent has no less the right to see that the particularity of content in the action, in point of its matter, is not something external to him, but is a particularity of his own,—that it contains his needs, interests, and aims. These aims, when similarly comprehended in a single aim, as in happiness (§ 479), constitute his well-being. This is the right to well-being. Happiness (good fortune) is distinguished from well-being only in this, that happiness implies no more than some sort of immediate existence, whereas well-being regards it as also justified as regards morality.

§ 506. But the essentiality of the intention is in the first instance the abstract form of generality. Reflection can put in this form this and that particular aspect in the empirically-concrete action, thus making it essential to the intention or restricting the intention to it. In this way the supposed essentiality of the intention and the real essentiality of the action may be brought into the greatest contradiction— e.g. a good intention in case of a crime. Similarly well-being is abstract and may be set on this or that: as appertaining to this single agent, it is always something particular.

c. *Goodness and Wickedness*[160].

§ 507. The truth of these particularities and the concrete unity of their formalism is the content of the universal, essential and actual, will,—the law and underlying essence of every phase of volition, the essential and actual good. It is thus the absolute final aim of the world, and duty for the agent who ought to have insight into the good, make it his intention and bring it about by his activity.

§ 508. But though the good is the universal of will—a universal determined in itself,—and thus including in it particularity,—still so far as this particularity is in the first instance still abstract, there is no principle at hand to determine it. Such determination therefore starts up also outside that universal; and as heteronomy or determinance of a will which is free and has rights of its own, there awakes here the deepest contradiction. (α) In consequence of the indeterminate determinism of the good, there are always several sorts of good and many kinds of duties, the variety of which is a dialectic of one against another and brings them into collision. At the same time because good is one, they ought to stand in harmony; and yet each of them, though it is a particular duty, is as good and as duty absolute. It falls upon the agent to be the dialectic which, superseding this absolute claim of each, concludes such a combination of them as excludes the rest.

§ 509. (β) To the agent, who in his existent sphere of liberty is essentially as a particular, his interest and welfare must, on account of that existent sphere of liberty, be essentially an aim and therefore a duty. But at the same time in aiming at the good, which is the not-particular but only universal of the will, the particular interest ought not to be a constituent motive. On account of this independency of the two principles of action, it is likewise an accident whether they harmonise. And yet they ought to harmonise, because the agent, as individual and universal, is always fundamentally one identity.

(γ) But the agent is not only a mere particular in his existence; it is also a form of his existence to be an abstract self-certainty, an abstract reflection of freedom into himself. He is thus distinct from the reason in the will, and capable of making the universal itself a particular and in that way a semblance. The good is thus reduced to the level of a mere "may happen" for the agent, who can therefore resolve itself to somewhat opposite to the good, can be wicked.

§ 510. (δ) The external objectivity, following the distinction which has arisen in the subjective will (§ 503), constitutes a peculiar world of its own,—another extreme which stands in no rapport with the internal will-determination. It is thus a matter of chance, whether it harmonises with the subjective aims, whether the good is realised, and the wicked, an aim essentially and actually null, nullified in it: it is no less matter of chance whether the agent finds in it his well-being, and more precisely whether in the world the good agent is happy and the wicked unhappy. But at the same time the world ought to allow the good action, the essential thing, to be carried out in it; it ought to grant the good agent the satisfaction of his particular interest, and refuse it to the wicked; just as it ought also to make the wicked itself null and void.

§ 511. The all-round contradiction, expressed by this repeated ought, with its absoluteness which yet at the same time is not—contains the most abstract 'analysis' of the mind in itself, its deepest descent into itself. The only relation the self-contradictory principles have to one another is in the abstract certainty of self; and for this infinitude of subjectivity the universal will, good, right, and duty, no more exist than not. The subjectivity alone is aware of itself as choosing and deciding. This pure self-certitude, rising to its pitch, appears in the two directly inter-changing forms—of Conscience and Wickedness. The former is the will of goodness; but a goodness which to this pure subjectivity is the non-objective, non-universal, the unutterable; and over which the agent is conscious that he in his individuality has the decision. Wickedness is the same awareness that the single self possesses the decision, so far as the single self does not merely remain in this abstraction, but takes up the content of a subjective interest contrary to the good.

§ 512. This supreme pitch of the "phenomenon" of will,—sublimating itself to this absolute vanity—to a goodness, which has no objectivity, but is only sure of itself, and a self-assurance which involves the nullification of the universal—collapses by its own force. Wickedness, as the most intimate reflection of subjectivity itself, in opposition to the objective and universal, (which it treats as mere sham,) is the same as the good sentiment of abstract goodness, which reserves to the subjectivity the determination thereof:—the utterly abstract semblance, the bare perversion and annihilation of itself. The result, the truth of this semblance, is, on its negative side, the absolute nullity of this volition which would fain hold its own against the good, and of the good, which would only be abstract. On the affirmative side, in the notion, this semblance thus collapsing is the same simple universality of the will, which is the good. The subjectivity, in this its identity with the good, is only the infinite form, which actualises and developes it. In this way the standpoint of bare reciprocity between two independent sides,—the standpoint of the ought, is abandoned, and we have passed into the field of ethical life.

Sub-Section C - The Moral Life, Or Social Ethics[161].

§ 513. The moral life is the perfection of spirit objective—the truth of the subjective and objective spirit itself. The failure of the latter consists—partly in having its freedom immediately in reality, in something external therefore, in a thing,—partly in the abstract universality of its goodness. The failure of spirit subjective similarly consists in this, that it is, as against the universal, abstractly self-determinant in its inward individuality. When these two imperfections are suppressed, subjective freedom exists as the covertly and overtly universal rational will, which is sensible of itself and actively disposed in the consciousness of the individual subject, whilst its practical operation and immediate universal actuality at the same time exist as moral usage, manner and custom,—where self-conscious liberty has become nature.

§ 514. The consciously free substance, in which the absolute "ought" is no less an "is," has actuality as the spirit of a nation. The abstract disruption of this spirit singles it out into persons, whose independence it however controls and entirely dominates from within. But the person, as an intelligent being, feels that underlying essence to be his own very being—ceases when so minded to be a mere accident of it—looks upon it as his absolute final aim. In its actuality he sees not less an achieved present, than somewhat he brings it about by his action,—yet somewhat which without all question is. Thus, without any selective reflection, the person performs its duty as his own and as something which is; and in this necessity he has himself and his actual freedom.

§ 515. Because the substance is the absolute unity of individuality and universality of freedom, it follows that the actuality and action of each individual to keep and to take care of his own being, while it is on one hand conditioned by the pre-supposed total in whose complex alone he exists, is on the other a transition into a universal product.—The social disposition of the individuals is their sense of the substance, and of the identity of all their interests with the total; and that the other individuals mutually know each other and are actual only in this identity, is confidence (trust)—the genuine ethical temper.

§ 516. The relations between individuals in the several situations to which the substance is particularised form their ethical duties. The ethical personality, i.e. the subjectivity which is permeated by the substantial life, is virtue. In relation to the bare facts of external being, to destiny, virtue does not treat them as a mere negation, and is thus a quiet repose in itself: in relation to substantial objectivity, to the total of ethical actuality, it exists as confidence, as deliberate work for the community, and the capacity of sacrificing self thereto; whilst in relation to the incidental relations of social circumstance, it is in the first instance justice and then benevolence. In the latter sphere, and in its attitude to its own visible being and corporeity, the individuality expresses its special character, temperament, &c. as personal virtues.

§ 517. The ethical substance is

AA. as "immediate" or natural mind,—the Family.

BB. The "relative" totality of the "relative" relations of the individuals as independent persons to one another in a formal univérsality—Civil Society.

CC. The self-conscious substance, as the mind developed to an organic actuality—the Political Constitution.

AA. *The Family.*

§ 518. The ethical spirit, in its immediacy, contains the natural factor that the individual has its substantial existence in its natural universal, i.e. in its kind. This is the sexual tie, elevated however to a spiritual significance,—the unanimity of love and the temper of trust. In the shape of the family, mind appears as feeling.

§ 519. [1] The physical difference of sex thus appears at the same time as a difference of intellectual and moral type. With their exclusive individualities these personalities combine to form a single person: the subjective union of hearts, becoming a "substantial" unity, makes this union an ethical tie— Marriage. The 'substantial' union of hearts makes marriage an indivisible personal bond—monogamic marriage: the bodily conjunction is a sequel to the moral attachment. A further sequel is community of personal and private interests.

§ 520. [2] By the community in which the various members constituting the family stand in reference to property, that property of the one person (representing the family) acquires an ethical interest, as do also its industry, labour, and care for the future.

§ 521. The ethical principle which is conjoined with the natural generation of the children, and which was assumed to have primary importance in first forming the marriage union, is actually realised in the second or spiritual birth of the children,—in educating them to independent personality.

§ 522. [3] The children, thus invested with independence, leave the concrete life and action of the family to which they primarily belong, acquire an existence of their own, destined however to found anew such an actual family. Marriage is of course broken up by the natural element contained in it, the death of husband and wife: but even their union of hearts, as it is a mere "substantiality" of feeling, contains the germ of liability to chance and decay. In virtue of such fortuitousness, the members of the family take up to each other the status of persons; and it is thus that the family finds introduced into it for the first time the element, originally foreign to it, of legal regulation.

BB. *Civil Society*[162].

§ 523. As the substance, being an intelligent substance, particularises itself abstractly into many persons (the family is only a single person), into families or individuals, who exist independent and free, as private persons, it loses its ethical character: for these persons as such have in their consciousness and as their aim not the absolute unity, but their own petty selves and particular interests. Thus arises the system of atomistic: by which the substance is reduced to a general system of adjustments to connect self-subsisting extremes and their particular interests. The developed totality of this connective system is the state as civil society, or state external.

a. *The System of Wants*[163].

§ 524. (α) The particularity of the persons includes in the first instance their wants. The possibility of satisfying these wants is here laid on the social fabric, the general stock from which all derive their satisfaction. In the condition of things in which this method of satisfaction by indirect adjustment is realised, immediate seizure (§ 488) of external objects as means thereto exists barely or not at all: the objects are already property. To acquire them is only possible by the intervention, on one hand, of the possessors' will, which as particular has in view the satisfaction of their variously defined interests; while on the other hand it is conditioned by the ever continued production of fresh means of exchange by the exchangers' own labour. This instrument, by which the labour of all facilitates satisfaction of wants, constitutes the general stock.

§ 525. (β) The glimmer of universal principle in this particularity of wants is found in the way intellect creates differences in them, and thus causes an indefinite multiplication both of wants and of means for their different phases. Both are thus rendered more and more abstract. This "morcellement" of their content by abstraction gives rise to the division of labour. The habit of this abstraction in enjoyment, information, feeling and demeanour, constitutes training in this sphere, or nominal culture in general.

§ 526. The labour which thus becomes more abstract tends on one hand by its uniformity to make labour easier and to increase production,—on another to limit each person to a single kind of technical skill, and thus produce more unconditional dependence on the social system. The skill itself becomes in this way mechanical, and gets the capability of letting the machine take the place of human labour.

§ 527. (γ) But the concrete division of the general stock—which is also a general business (of the whole society)—into particular masses determined by the factors of the notion,—masses each of which possesses its own basis of subsistence, and a corresponding mode of labour, of needs, and of means for satisfying them, besides of aims and interests, as well as of mental culture and habit—constitutes the difference of Estates (orders or ranks). Individuals apportion themselves to these according to natural talent, skill, option and accident. As belonging to such a definite and stable sphere, they have their actual existence, which as existence is essentially a particular; and in it they have their social morality, which is honesty, their recognition and their honour.

Where civil society, and with it the State, exists, there arise the several estates in their difference: for the universal substance, as vital, exists only so far as it organically particularises itself. The history of constitutions is the history of the growth of these estates, of the legal relationships of individuals to them, and of these estates to one another and to their centre.

§ 528. To the "substantial," natural estate the fruitful soil and ground supply a natural and stable capital; its action gets direction and content through natural features, and its moral life is founded on faith and trust. The second, the "reflected" estate has as its allotment the social capital, the medium created by the action of middlemen, of mere agents, and an ensemble of contingencies, where the individual has to depend on his subjective skill, talent, intelligence and industry. The third, "thinking" estate has for its business the general interests; like the second it has a subsistence procured by means of its own skill, and like the first a certain subsistence, certain however because guaranteed through the whole society.

b. Administration of Justice[164].

§ 529. When matured through the operation of natural need and free option into a system of universal relationships and a regular course of external necessity, the principle of casual particularity gets that stable articulation which liberty requires in the shape of formal right. [1] The actualisation which right gets in this sphere of mere practical intelligence is that it be brought to consciousness as the stable universal, that it be known and stated in its specificity with the voice of authority—the Law[165].

The positive element in laws concerns only their form of publicity and authority—which makes it possible for them to be known by all in a customary and external way. Their content per se may be reasonable—or it may be unreasonable and so wrong. But when right, in the course of definite manifestation, is developed in detail, and its content analyses itself to gain definiteness, this analysis, because of the finitude of its materials, falls into the falsely infinite progress: the final definiteness, which is absolutely essential and causes a break in this progress of unreality, can in this sphere of finitude be attained only in a way that savours of contingency and arbitrariness. Thus whether three years, ten thalers, or only 2-1/2, 2-3/4, 2-4/5 years, and so on ad infinitum, be the right and just thing, can by no means be decided on intelligible principles,—and yet it should be decided. Hence, though of course only at the final points of deciding, on the side of external existence, the "positive" principle naturally enters law as contingency and arbitrariness. This happens and has from of old happened in all legislations: the only thing wanted is clearly to be aware of it, and not be misled by the talk and the pretence as if the ideal of law were, or could be, to be, at every point, determined through reason or legal intelligence, on purely reasonable and intelligent grounds. It is a futile perfectionism to have such expectations and to make such requirements in the sphere of the finite.

There are some who look upon laws as an evil and a profanity, and who regard governing and being governed from natural love, hereditary, divinity or nobility, by faith and trust, as the genuine order of life, while the reign of law is held an order of corruption and injustice. These people forget that the stars—and the cattle too—are governed and well governed too by laws;—laws however which are only internally in these objects, not for them, not as laws set to them:—whereas it is man's privilege to know his law. They forget therefore that he can truly obey only such known law,—even as his law can only be a just law, as it is a known law;—though in other respects it must be in its essential content contingency and caprice, or at least be mixed and polluted with such elements.

The same empty requirement of perfection is employed for an opposite thesis—viz. to support the opinion that a code is impossible or impracticable. In this case there comes in the additional absurdity of putting essential and universal provisions in one class with the particular detail. The finite material is definable on and on to the false infinite: but this advance is not, as in the mental images of space, a generation of new spatial characteristics of the same quality as those preceding them, but an advance into greater and ever greater speciality by the acumen of the analytic intellect, which discovers new distinctions, which again make new decisions necessary. To provisions of this sort one may give the name of new decisions or new laws; but in proportion to the gradual advance in specialisation the interest and value of these provisions declines. They fall within the already subsisting "substantial," general laws, like improvements on a floor or a door, within the house—which though something new, are not a new house. But there is a contrary case. If the legislation of a rude age began with single provisos, which go on by their very nature always increasing their number, there arises, with the advance in multitude, the need of a simpler code,—the need i.e. of embracing that lot of singulars in their general features. To find and be able to express these principles well beseems an intelligent and civilised nation. Such a gathering up of single rules into general forms, first really deserving the name of laws, has lately been begun in some directions by the English Minister Peel, who has by so doing gained the gratitude, even the admiration, of his countrymen.

§ 530. [2] The positive form of Laws—to be promulgated and made known as laws—is a condition of the external obligation to obey them; inasmuch as, being laws of strict right, they touch only the abstract will,—itself at bottom external—not the moral or ethical will. The subjectivity to which the will has in this direction a right is here only publicity. This subjective existence is as existence of the essential and developed truth in this sphere of Right at the same time an externally objective existence, as universal authority and necessity.

The legality of property and of private transactions concerned therewith—in consideration of the principle that all law must be promulgated, recognised, and thus become authoritative—gets its universal guarantee through formalities.

§ 531. [3] Legal forms get the necessity, to which objective existence determines itself, in the judicial system. Abstract right has to exhibit itself to the court—to the individualised right—as proven:—a process in which there may be a difference between what is abstractly right and what is provably right. The court takes cognisance and action in the interest of right as such, deprives the existence of right of its contingency, and in particular transforms this existence,—as this exists as revenge—into punishment (§ 500).

The comparison of the two species, or rather two elements in the judicial conviction, bearing on the actual state of the case in relation to the accused,—[1] according as that conviction is based on mere circumstances and other people's witness alone,—or [2] in addition requires the confession of the accused, constitutes the main point in the question of the so-called jury-courts. It is an essential point that the two ingredients of a judicial cognisance, the judgment as to the state of the fact, and the judgment as application of the law to it, should, as at bottom different sides, be exercised as different functions. By the said institution they are allotted even to bodies differently qualified,—from the one of which individuals belonging to the official judiciary are expressly excluded. To carry this separation of functions up to this separation in the courts rests rather on extra-essential considerations: the main point remains only the separate performance of these essentially different functions.—It is a more important point whether the confession of the accused is or is not to be made a condition of penal judgment. The institution of the jury-court loses sight of this condition. The point is that on this ground certainty is completely inseparable from truth: but the confession is to be regarded as the very acmé of certainty-giving which in its nature is subjective. The final decision therefore lies with the confession. To this therefore the accused has an absolute right, if the proof is to be made final and the judges to be convinced. No doubt this factor is incomplete, because it is only one factor; but still more incomplete is the other when no less abstractly taken,—viz. mere circumstantial evidence. The jurors are essentially judges and pronounce a judgment. In so far, then, as all they have to go on are such objective proofs, whilst at the same time their defect of certainty (incomplete in so far as it is only in them) is admitted, the jury-court shows traces of its barbaric origin in a confusion and admixture between objective proofs and subjective or so-called "moral" conviction.—It is easy to call extraordinary punishments an absurdity; but the fault lies rather with the shallowness which takes offence at a mere name. Materially the principle involves the difference of objective probation according as it goes with or without the factor of absolute certification which lies in confession.

§ 532. The function of judicial administration is only to actualise to necessity the abstract side of personal liberty in civil society. But this actualisation rests at first on the particular subjectivity of the judge, since here as yet there is not found the necessary unity of it with right in the abstract. Conversely, the blind necessity of the system of wants is not lifted up into the consciousness of the universal, and worked from that period of view.

c. *Police and Corporation*[166].

§ 533. Judicial administration naturally has no concern with such part of actions and interests as belongs only to particularity, and leaves to chance not only the occurrence of crimes but also the care for public weal. In civil society the sole end is to satisfy want—and that, because it is man's want, in a uniform general way, so as to secure this satisfaction. But the machinery of social necessity leaves in many ways a casualness about this satisfaction. This is due to the variability of the wants themselves, in which opinion and subjective good-pleasure play a great part. It results also from circumstances of locality, from the connexions between nation and nation, from errors and deceptions which can be foisted upon single members of the social circulation and are capable of creating disorder in it,—as also and especially from the unequal capacity of individuals to take advantage of that general stock. The onward march of this necessity also sacrifices the very particularities by which it is brought about, and does not itself contain the affirmative aim of securing the satisfaction of individuals. So far as concerns them, it may be far from beneficial: yet here the individuals are the morally-justifiable end.

§ 534. To keep in view this general end, to ascertain the way in which the powers composing that social necessity act, and their variable ingredients, and to maintain that end in them and against them, is the work of an institution which assumes on one hand, to the concrete of civil society, the position of an external universality. Such an order acts with the power of an external state, which, in so far as it is rooted in the higher or substantial state, appears as state "police." On the other hand, in this sphere of particularity the only recognition of the aim of substantial universality and the only carrying of it out is restricted to the business of particular branches and interests. Thus we have the corporation, in which the particular citizen in his private capacity finds the securing of his stock, whilst at the same time he in it emerges from his single private interest, and has a conscious activity for a comparatively universal end, just as in his legal and professional duties he has his social morality.

CC. The State.

§ 535. The State is the self-conscious ethical substance, the unification of the family principle with that of civil society. The same unity, which is in the family as a feeling of love, is its essence, receiving however at the same time through the second principle of conscious and spontaneously active volition the form of conscious universality. This universal principle, with all its evolution in detail, is the absolute aim and content of the knowing subject, which thus identifies itself in its volition with the system of reasonableness.

§ 536. The state is (α) its inward structure as a self-relating development—constitutional (inner-state) law: (β) a particular individual, and therefore in connexion with other particular individuals,—international (outer-state) law; (γ) but these particular minds are only stages in the general development of mind in its actuality: universal history.

α. *Constitutional Law*[167].

§ 537. The essence of the state is the universal, self-originated and self-developed,—the reasonable spirit of will; but, as self-knowing and self-actualising, sheer subjectivity, and—as an actuality—one individual. Its work generally—in relation to the extreme of individuality as the multitude of individuals—consists in a double function. First it maintains them as persons, thus making right a necessary actuality, then it promotes their welfare, which each originally takes care of for himself, but which has a thoroughly general side; it protects the family and guides civil society. Secondly, it carries back both, and the whole disposition and action of the individual—whose tendency is to become a centre of his own—into the life of the universal substance; and, in this direction, as a free power it interferes with those subordinate spheres and retains them in substantial immanence.

§ 538. The laws express the special provisions for objective freedom. First, to the immediate agent, his independent self-will and particular interest, they are restrictions. But, secondly, they are an absolute final end and the universal work: hence they are a product of the "functions" of the various orders which parcel themselves more and more out of the general particularising, and are a fruit of all the acts and private concerns of individuals. Thirdly, they are the substance of the volition of individuals—which volition is thereby free—and of their disposition: being as such exhibited as current usage.

§ 539. As a living mind, the state only is as an organised whole, differentiated into particular agencies, which, proceeding from the one notion (though not known as notion) of the reasonable will, continually produce it as their result. The constitution is this articulation or organisation of state-power. It provides for the reasonable will,—in so far as it is in the individuals only implicitly the universal will,—coming to a consciousness and an understanding of itself and being found; also for that will being put in actuality, through the action of the government and its several branches, and not left to perish, but protected both against their casual subjectivity and against that of the individuals. The constitution is existent justice,—the actuality of liberty in the development all its reasonable provisions.

Liberty and Equality are the simple rubrics into which is frequently concentrated what should form the fundamental principle, the final aim and result of the constitution. However true this is, the defect of these terms is their utter abstractness: if stuck to in this abstract form, they are principles which either prevent the rise of the concreteness of the state, i.e. its articulation into a constitution and a government in general, or destroy them. With the state there arises inequality, the difference of governing powers and of governed, magistracies, authorities, directories, &c. The principle of equality, logically carried out, rejects all differences, and thus allows no sort of political condition to exist. Liberty and equality are indeed the foundation of the state, but as the most abstract also the most superficial, and for that very reason naturally the most familiar. It is important therefore to study them closer.

As regards, first, Equality, the familiar proposition, All men are by nature equal, blunders by confusing the "natural" with the "notion." It ought rather to read: By nature men are only unequal. But the notion of liberty, as it exists as such, without further specification and development, is abstract subjectivity, as a person capable of property (§ 488). This single abstract feature of personality constitutes the actual equality of human beings. But that this freedom should exist, that it should be man (and not as in Greece, Rome, &c. some men) that is recognised and legally regarded as a person, is so little by nature, that it is rather only a result and product of the consciousness of the deepest principle of mind, and of the universality and expansion of this consciousness. That the citizens are equal before the law contains a great truth, but which so expressed is a tautology: it only states that the legal status in general exists, that the laws rule. But, as regards the concrete, the citizens—besides their personality—are equal before the law only in these points when they are otherwise equal outside the law. Only that equality which (in whatever way it be) they, as it happens, otherwise have in property, age, physical strength, talent, skill, &c.—or even in crime, can and ought to make them deserve equal treatment before the law:—only it can make them—as regards taxation, military service, eligibility to office, &c.—punishment, &c.—equal in the concrete. The laws themselves, except in so far as they concern that narrow circle of personality, presuppose unequal conditions, and provide for the unequal legal duties and appurtenances resulting therefrom.

As regards Liberty, it is originally taken partly in a negative sense against arbitrary intolerance and lawless treatment, partly in the affirmative sense of subjective freedom; but this freedom is allowed great latitude both as regards the agent's self-will and action for his particular ends, and as regards his claim to have a personal intelligence and a personal share in general affairs. Formerly the legally defined rights, private as well as public rights of a nation, town, &c. were called its "liberties." Really, every genuine law is a liberty: it contains a reasonable principle of objective mind; in other words, it embodies a liberty. Nothing has become, on the contrary, more familiar than the idea that each must restrict his liberty in relation to the liberty of others: that the state is a condition of such reciprocal restriction, and that the laws are restrictions. To such habits of mind liberty is viewed as only casual good-pleasure and self-will. Hence it has also been said that "modern" nations are only susceptible of equality, or of equality more than liberty: and that for no other reason than that, with an assumed definition of liberty (chiefly the participation of all in political affairs and actions), it was impossible to make ends meet in actuality—which is at once more reasonable and more powerful than abstract presuppositions. On the contrary, it should be said that it is just the great development and maturity of form in modern states which produces the supreme concrete inequality of individuals in actuality: while, through the deeper reasonableness of laws and the greater stability of the legal state, it gives rise to greater and more stable liberty, which it can without incompatibility allow. Even the superficial distinction of the words liberty and equality points to the fact that the former tends to inequality: whereas, on the contrary, the current notions of liberty only carry us back to equality. But the more we fortify liberty,—as security of property, as possibility for each to develop and make the best of his talents and good qualities, the more it gets taken for granted: and then the sense and appreciation of liberty especially turns in a subjective direction. By this is meant the liberty to attempt action on every side, and to throw oneself at pleasure in action for particular and for general intellectual interests, the removal of all checks on the individual particularity, as well as the inward liberty in which the subject has principles, has an insight and conviction of his own, and thus gains moral independence. But this liberty itself on one hand implies that supreme differentiation in which men are unequal and make themselves more unequal by education; and on another it only grows up under conditions of that objective liberty, and is and could grow to such height only in modern states. If, with this development of particularity, there be simultaneous and endless increase of the number of wants, and of the difficulty of satisfying them, of the lust of argument and the fancy of detecting faults, with its insatiate vanity, it is all but part of that indiscriminating relaxation of individuality in this sphere which generates all possible complications, and must deal with them as it can. Such a sphere is of course also the field of restrictions, because liberty is there under the taint of natural self-will and self-pleasing, and has therefore to restrict itself: and that, not merely with regard to the naturalness, self-will and self-conceit, of others, but especially and essentially with regard to reasonable liberty.

The term political liberty, however, is often used to mean formal participation in the public affairs of state by the will and action even of those individuals who otherwise find their chief function in the particular aims and business of civil society. And it has in part become usual to give the title constitution only to the side of the state which concerns such participation of these individuals in general affairs, and to regard a state, in which this is not formally done, as a state without a constitution. On this use of the term, the only thing to remark is that by constitution must be understood the determination of rights, i.e. of liberties in general, and the organisation of the actualisation of them; and that political freedom in the above sense can in any case only constitute a part of it. Of it the following paragraphs will speak.

§ 540. The guarantee of a constitution (i.e. the necessity that the laws be reasonable, and their actualisation secured) lies in the collective spirit of the nation,—especially in the specific way in which it is itself conscious of its reason. (Religion is that consciousness in its absolute substantiality.) But the guarantee lies also at the same time in the actual organisation or development of that principle in suitable institutions. The constitution presupposes that consciousness of the collective spirit, and conversely that spirit presupposes the constitution: for the actual spirit only has a definite consciousness of its principles, in so far as it has them actually existent before it.

The question—To whom (to what authority and how organised) belongs the power to make a constitution? is the same as the question, Who has to make the spirit of a nation? Separate our idea of a constitution from that of the collective spirit, as if the latter exists or has existed without a constitution, and your fancy only proves how superficially you have apprehended the nexus between the spirit in its self-consciousness and in its actuality. What is thus called "making" a "constitution," is—just because of this inseparability—a thing that has never happened in history, just as little as the making of a code of laws. A constitution only develops from the national spirit identically with that spirit's own development, and runs through at the same time with it the grades of formation and the alterations required by its concept. It is the indwelling spirit and the history of the nation (and, be it added, the history is only that spirit's history) by which constitutions have been and are made.

§ 541. The really living totality,—that which preserves, in other words continually produces the state in general and its constitution, is the government. The organisation which natural necessity gives is seen in the rise of the family and of the 'estates' of civil society. The government is the universal part of the constitution, i.e. the part which intentionally aims at preserving those parts, but at the same time gets hold of and carries out those general aims of the whole which rise above the function of the family and of civil society. The organisation of the government is likewise its differentiation into powers, as their peculiarities have a basis in principle; yet without that difference losing touch with the actual unity they have in the notion's subjectivity.

As the most obvious categories of the notion are those of universality and individuality and their relationship that of subsumption of individual under universal, it has come about that in the state the legislative and executive power have been so distinguished as to make the former exist apart as the absolute superior, and to subdivide the latter again into administrative (government) power and judicial power, according as the laws are applied to public or private affairs. The division of these powers has been treated as the condition of political equilibrium, meaning by division their independence one of another in existence,—subject always however to the above-mentioned subsumption of the powers of the individual under the power of the general. The theory of such "division" unmistakably implies the elements of the notion, but so combined by "understanding" as to result in an absurd collocation, instead of the self-redintegration of the living spirit. The one essential canon to make liberty deep and real is to give every business belonging to the general interests of the state a separate organisation wherever they are essentially distinct. Such real division must be: for liberty is only deep when it is differentiated in all its fullness and these differences manifested in existence. But to make the business of legislation an independent power—to make it the first power, with the further proviso that all citizens shall have part therein, and the government be merely executive and dependent, presupposes ignorance that the true idea, and therefore the living and spiritual actuality, is the self-redintegrating notion, in other words, the subjectivity which contains in it universality as only one of its moments. (A mistake still greater, if it goes with the fancy that the constitution and the fundamental laws were still one day to make,—in a state of society, which includes an already existing development of differences.) Individuality is the first and supreme principle which makes itself fall through the state's organisation. Only through the government, and by its embracing in itself the particular businesses (including the abstract legislative business, which taken apart is also particular), is the state one. These, as always, are the terms on which the different elements essentially and alone truly stand towards each other in the logic of "reason," as opposed to the external footing they stand on in 'understanding,' which never gets beyond subsuming the individual and particular under the universal. What disorganises the unity of logical reason, equally disorganises actuality.

§ 542. In the government—regarded as organic totality—the sovereign power (principate) is (a) subjectivity as the infinite self-unity of the notion in its development;—the all-sustaining, all-decreeing will of the state, its highest peak and all-pervasive unity. In the perfect form of the state, in which each and every element of the notion has reached free existence, this subjectivity is not a so-called "moral person," or a decree issuing from a majority (forms in which the unity of the decreeing will has not an actual existence), but an actual individual,—the will of a decreeing individual,—monarchy. The monarchical constitution is therefore the constitution of developed reason: all other constitutions belong to lower grades of the development and realisation of reason.

The unification of all concrete state-powers into one existence, as in the patriarchal society,—or, as in a democratic constitution, the participation of all in all affairs—impugns the principle of the division of powers, i.e. the developed liberty of the constituent factors of the Idea. But no whit less must the division (the working out of these factors each to a free totality) be reduced to "ideal" unity, i.e. to subjectivity. The mature differentiation or realisation of the Idea means, essentially, that this subjectivity should grow to be a real "moment," an actual existence; and this actuality is not otherwise than as the individuality of the monarch—the subjectivity of abstract and final decision existent in one person. All those forms of collective decreeing and willing,—a common will which shall be the sum and the resultant (on aristocratical or democratical principles) of the atomistic of single wills, have on them the mark of the unreality of an abstraction. Two points only are all-important, first to see the necessity of each of the notional factors, and secondly the form in which it is actualised. It is only the nature of the speculative notion which can really give light on the matter. That subjectivity—being the "moment" which emphasises the need of abstract deciding in general—partly leads on to the proviso that the name of the monarch appear as the bond and sanction under which everything is done in the government;—partly, being simple self-relation, has attached to it the characteristic of immediacy, and then of nature—whereby the destination of individuals for the dignity of the princely power is fixed by inheritance.

§ 543. (b) In the particular government-power there emerges, first, the division of state-business into its branches (otherwise defined), legislative power, administration of justice or judicial power, administration and police, and its consequent distribution between particular boards or offices, which having their business appointed by law, to that end and for that reason, possess independence of action, without at the same time ceasing to stand under higher supervision. Secondly, too, there arises the participation of several in state-business, who together constitute the "general order" (§ 528) in so far as they take on themselves the charge of universal ends as the essential function of their particular life;—the further condition for being able to take individually part in this business being a certain training, aptitude, and skill for such ends.

§ 544. The estates-collegium or provincial council is an institution by which all such as belong to civil society in general, and are to that degree private persons, participate in the governmental power, especially in legislation—viz. such legislation as concerns the universal scope of those interests which do not, like peace and war, involve the, as it were, personal interference and action of the State as one man, and therefore do not belong specially to the province of the sovereign power. By virtue of this participation subjective liberty and conceit, with their general opinion, can show themselves palpably efficacious and enjoy the satisfaction of feeling themselves to count for something.

The division of constitutions into democracy, aristocracy and monarchy, is still the most definite statement of their difference in relation to sovereignty. They must at the same time be regarded as necessary structures in the path of development,—in short, in the history of the State. Hence it is superficial and absurd to represent them as an object of choice. The pure forms—necessary to the process of evolution—are, in so far as they are finite and in course of change, conjoined both with forms of their degeneration,—such as ochlocracy, &c., and with earlier transition-forms. These two forms are not to be confused with those legitimate structures. Thus, it may be—if we look only to the fact that the will of one individual stands at the head of the state—oriental despotism is included under the vague name monarchy,—as also feudal monarchy, to which indeed even the favourite name of "constitutional monarchy" cannot be refused. The true difference of these forms from genuine monarchy depends on the true value of those principles of right which are in vogue and have their actuality and guarantee in the state-power. These principles are those expounded earlier, liberty of property, and above all personal liberty, civil society, with its industry and its communities, and the regulated efficiency of the particular bureaux in subordination to the laws.

The question which is most discussed is in what sense we are to understand the participation of private persons in state affairs. For it is as private persons that the members of bodies of estates are primarily to be taken, be they treated as mere individuals, or as representatives of a number of people or of the nation. The aggregate of private persons is often spoken of as the nation: but as such an aggregate it is vulgus, not populus: and in this direction, it is the one sole aim of the state that a nation should not come to existence, to power and action, as such an aggregate. Such a condition of a nation is a condition of lawlessness, demoralisation, brutishness: in it the nation would only be a shapeless, wild, blind force, like that of the stormy, elemental sea, which however is not self-destructive, as the nation—a spiritual element—would be. Yet such a condition may be often heard described as that of true freedom. If there is to be any sense in embarking upon the question of the participation of private persons in public affairs, it is not a brutish mass, but an already organised nation—one in which a governmental power exists—which should be presupposed. The desirability of such participation however is not to be put in the superiority of particular intelligence, which private persons are supposed to have over state officials—the contrary may be the case—nor in the superiority of their good will for the general best. The members of civil society as such are rather people who find their nearest duty in their private interest and (as especially in the feudal society) in the interest of their privileged corporation. Take the case of England which, because private persons have a predominant share in public affairs, has been regarded as having the freest of all constitutions. Experience shows that that country—as compared with the other civilised states of Europe—is the most backward in civil and criminal legislation, in the law and liberty of property, in arrangements for art and science, and that objective freedom or rational right is rather sacrificed to formal right and particular private interest; and that this happens even in the institutions and possessions supposed to be dedicated to religion. The desirability of private persons taking part in public affairs is partly to be put in their concrete, and therefore more urgent, sense of general wants. But the true motive is the right of the collective spirit to appear as an externally universal will, acting with orderly and express efficacy for the public concerns. By this satisfaction of this right it gets its own life quickened, and at the same time breathes fresh life in the administrative officials; who thus have it brought home to them that not merely have they to enforce duties but also to have regard to rights. Private citizens are in the state the incomparably greater number, and form the multitude of such as are recognised as persons. Hence the will-reason exhibits its existence in them as a preponderating majority of freemen, or in its "reflectional" universality, which has its actuality vouchsafed it as a participation in the sovereignty. But it has already been noted as a "moment" of civil society (§§ 527, 534) that the individuals rise from external into substantial universality, and form a particular kind,—the Estates: and it is not in the inorganic form of mere individuals as such (after the democratic fashion of election), but as organic factors, as estates, that they enter upon that participation. In the state a power or agency must never appear and act as a formless, inorganic shape, i.e. basing itself on the principle of multeity and mere numbers.

Assemblies of Estates have been wrongly designated as the legislative power, so far as they form only one branch of that power,—a branch in which the special government-officials have an ex officio share, while the sovereign power has the privilege of final decision. In a civilised state moreover legislation can only be a further modification of existing law, and so-called new laws can only deal with minutiae of detail and particularities (cf. § 529, note), the main drift of which has been already prepared or preliminarily settled by the practice of the law-courts. The so-called financial law, in so far as it requires the assent of the estates, is really a government affair: it is only improperly called a law, in the general sense of embracing a wide, indeed the whole, range of the external means of government. The finances deal with what in their nature are only particular needs, ever newly recurring, even if they touch on the sum total of such needs. If the main part of the requirement were—as it very likely is— regarded as permanent, the provision for it would have more the nature of a law: but to be a law, it would have to be made once for all, and not be made yearly, or every few years, afresh. The part which varies according to time and circumstances concerns in reality the smallest part of the amount, and the provisions with regard to it have even less the character of a law: and yet it is and may be only this slight variable part which is matter of dispute, and can be subjected to a varying yearly estimate. It is this last then which falsely bears the high-sounding name of the "Grant" of the Budget, i.e. of the whole of the finances. A law for one year and made each year has even to the plain man something palpably absurd: for he distinguishes the essential and developed universal, as content of a true law, from the reflectional universality which only externally embraces what in its nature is many. To give the name of a law to the annual fixing of financial requirements only serves—with the presupposed separation of legislative from executive—to keep up the illusion of that separation having real existence, and to conceal the fact that the legislative power, when it makes a decree about finance, is really engaged with strict executive business. But the importance attached to the power of from time to time granting "supply," on the ground that the assembly of estates possesses in it a check on the government, and thus a guarantee against injustice and violence,—this importance is in one way rather plausible than real. The financial measures necessary for the state's subsistence cannot be made conditional on any other circumstances, nor can the state's subsistence be put yearly in doubt. It would be a parallel absurdity if the government were e.g. to grant and arrange the judicial institutions always for a limited time merely; and thus, by the threat of suspending the activity of such an institution and the fear of a consequent state of brigandage, reserve for itself a means of coercing private individuals. Then again, the pictures of a condition of affairs, in which it might be useful and necessary to have in hand means of compulsion, are partly based on the false conception of a contract between rulers and ruled, and partly presuppose the possibility of such a divergence in spirit between these two parties as would make constitution and government quite out of the question. If we suppose the empty possibility of getting help by such compulsive means brought into existence, such help would rather be the derangement and dissolution of the state, in which there would no longer be a government, but only parties, and the violence and oppression of one party would only be helped away by the other. To fit together the several parts of the state into a constitution after the fashion of mere understanding—i.e. to adjust within it the machinery of a balance of powers external to each other—is to contravene the fundamental idea of what a state is.

§ 545. The final aspect of the state is to appear in immediate actuality as a single nation marked by physical conditions. As a single individual it is exclusive against other like individuals. In their mutual relations, waywardness and chance have a place; for each person in the aggregate is autonomous: the universal of law is only postulated between them, and not actually existent. This independence of a central authority reduces disputes between them to terms of mutual violence, a state of war, to meet which the general estate in the community assumes the particular function of maintaining the state's independence against other states, and becomes the estate of bravery.

§ 546. This state of war shows the omnipotence of the state in its individuality—an individuality that goes even to abstract negativity. Country and fatherland then appear as the power by which the particular independence of individuals and their absorption in the external existence of possession and in natural life is convicted of its own nullity,—as the power which procures the maintenance of the general substance by the patriotic sacrifice on the part of these individuals of this natural and particular existence,—so making nugatory the nugatoriness that confronts it.

β. *External Public Law*[168].

§ 547. In the game of war the independence of States is at stake. In one case the result may be the mutual recognition of free national individualities (§ 430): and by peace-conventions supposed to be for ever, both this general recognition, and the special claims of nations on one another, are settled and fixed. External state-rights rest partly on these positive treaties, but to that extent contain only rights falling short of true actuality (§ 545): partly on so-called international law, the general principle of which is its presupposed recognition by the several States. It thus restricts their otherwise unchecked action against one another in such a way that the possibility of peace is left; and distinguishes individuals as private persons (non-belligerents) from the state. In general, international law rests on social usage.

γ. Universal History[169].

§ 548. As the mind of a special nation is actual and its liberty is under natural conditions, it admits on this nature-side the influence of geographical and climatic qualities. It is in time; and as regards its range and scope, has essentially a particular principle on the lines of which it must run through a development of its consciousness and its actuality. It has, in short, a history of its own. But as a restricted mind its independence is something secondary; it passes into universal world-history, the events of which exhibit the dialectic of the several national minds,—the judgment of the world.

§ 549. This movement is the path of liberation for the spiritual substance, the deed by which the absolute final aim of the world is realised in it, and the merely implicit mind achieves consciousness and self-consciousness. It is thus the revelation and actuality of its essential and completed essence, whereby it becomes to the outward eye a universal spirit—a world-mind. As this development is in time and in real existence, as it is a history, its several stages and steps are the national minds, each of which, as single and endued by nature with a specific character, is appointed to occupy only one grade, and accomplish one task in the whole deed.

The presupposition that history has an essential and actual end, from the principles of which certain characteristic results logically flow, is called an a priori view of it, and philosophy is reproached with a priori history-writing. On this point, and on history-writing in general, this note must go into further detail. That history, and above all universal history, is founded on an essential and actual aim, which actually is and will be realised in it—the plan of Providence; that, in short, there is Reason in history, must be decided on strictly philosophical ground, and thus shown to be essentially and in fact necessary. To presuppose such aim is blameworthy only when the assumed conceptions or thoughts are arbitrarily adopted, and when a determined attempt is made to force events and actions into conformity with such conceptions. For such a priori methods of treatment at the present day, however, those are chiefly to blame who profess to be purely historical, and who at the same time take opportunity expressly to raise their voice against the habit of philosophising, first in general, and then in history. Philosophy is to them a troublesome neighbour: for it is an enemy of all arbitrariness and hasty suggestions. Such a priori history-writing has sometimes burst out in quarters where one would least have expected it, especially on the philological side, and in Germany more than in France and England, where the art of historical writing has gone through a process of purification to a firmer and maturer character. Fictions, like that of a primitive age and its primitive people, possessed from the first of the true knowledge of God and all the sciences,—of sacerdotal races,—and, when we come to minutiae, of a Roman epic, supposed to be the source of the legends which pass current for the history of ancient Rome, &c., have taken the place of the pragmatising which detected psychological motives and associations. There is a wide circle of persons who seem to consider it incumbent on a learned and ingenious historian drawing from the original sources to concoct such baseless fancies, and form bold combinations of them from a learned rubbish-heap of out-of-the-way and trivial facts, in defiance of the best-accredited history.

Setting aside this subjective treatment of history, we find what is properly the opposite view forbidding us to import into history an objective purpose. This is after all synonymous with what seems to be the still more legitimate demand that the historian should proceed with impartiality. This is a requirement often and especially made on the history of philosophy: where it is insisted there should be no prepossession in favour of an idea or opinion, just as a judge should have no special sympathy for one of the contending parties. In the case of the judge it is at the same time assumed that he would administer his office ill and foolishly, if he had not an interest, and an exclusive interest in justice, if he had not that for his aim and one sole aim, or if he declined to judge at all. This requirement which we may make upon the judge may be called partiality for justice; and there is no difficulty here in distinguishing it from subjective partiality. But in speaking of the impartiality required from the historian, this self-satisfied insipid chatter lets the distinction disappear, and rejects both kinds of interest. It demands that the historian shall bring with him no definite aim and view by which he may sort out, state and criticise events, but shall narrate them exactly in the casual mode he finds them, in their incoherent and unintelligent particularity. Now it is at least admitted that a history must have an object, e.g. Rome and its fortunes, or the Decline of the grandeur of the Roman empire. But little reflection is needed to discover that this is the presupposed end which lies at the basis of the events themselves, as of the critical examination into their comparative importance, i.e. their nearer or more remote relation to it. A history without such aim and such criticism would be only an imbecile mental divagation, not as good as a fairy tale, for even children expect a motif in their stories, a purpose at least dimly surmiseable with which events and actions are put in relation.

In the existence of a nation the substantial aim is to be a state and preserve itself as such. A nation with no state formation, (a mere nation), has strictly speaking no history,—like the nations which existed before the rise of states and others which still exist in a condition of savagery. What happens to a nation, and takes place within it, has its essential significance in relation to the state: whereas the mere particularities of individuals are at the greatest distance from the true object of history. It is true that the general spirit of an age leaves its imprint in the character of its celebrated individuals, and even their particularities are but the very distant and the dim media through which the collective light still plays in fainter colours. Ay, even such singularities as a petty occurrence, a word, express not a subjective particularity, but an age, a nation, a civilisation, in striking portraiture and brevity; and to select such trifles shows the hand of a historian of genius. But, on the other hand, the main mass of singularities is a futile and useless mass, by the painstaking accumulation of which the objects of real historical value are overwhelmed and obscured. The essential characteristic of the spirit and its age is always contained in the great events. It was a correct instinct which sought to banish such portraiture of the particular and the gleaning of insignificant traits, into the Novel (as in the celebrated romances of Walter Scott, &c.). Where the picture presents an unessential aspect of life it is certainly in good taste to conjoin it with an unessential material, such as the romance takes from private events and subjective passions. But to take the individual pettinesses of an age and of the persons in it, and, in the interest of so-called truth, weave them into the picture of general interests, is not only against taste and judgment, but violates the principles of objective truth. The only truth for mind is the substantial and underlying essence, and not the trivialities of external existence and contingency. It is therefore completely indifferent whether such insignificancies are duly vouched for by documents, or, as in the romance, invented to suit the character and ascribed to this or that name and circumstances.

The point of interest of Biography—to say a word on that here—appears to run directly counter to any universal scope and aim. But biography too has for its background the historical world, with which the individual is intimately bound up: even purely personal originality, the freak of humour, &c. suggests by allusion that central reality and has its interest heightened by the suggestion. The mere play of sentiment, on the contrary, has another ground and interest than history.

The requirement of impartiality addressed to the history of philosophy (and also, we may add, to the history of religion, first in general, and secondly, to church history) generally implies an even more decided bar against presupposition of any objective aim. As the State was already called the point to which in political history criticism had to refer all events, so here the "Truth" must be the object to which the several deeds and events of the spirit would have to be referred. What is actually done is rather to make the contrary presupposition. Histories with such an object as religion or philosophy are understood to have only subjective aims for their theme, i.e. only opinions and mere ideas, not an essential and realised object like the truth. And that with the mere excuse that there is no truth. On this assumption the sympathy with truth appears as only a partiality of the usual sort, a partiality for opinion and mere ideas, which all alike have no stuff in them, and are all treated as indifferent. In that way historical truth means but correctness—an accurate report of externals, without critical treatment save as regards this correctness—admitting, in this case, only qualitative and quantitative judgments, no judgments of necessity or notion (cf. notes to §§ 172 and 175). But, really, if Rome or the German empire, &c. are an actual and genuine object of political history, and the aim to which the phenomena are to be related and by which they are to be judged; then in universal history the genuine spirit, the consciousness of it and of its essence, is even in a higher degree a true and actual object and theme, and an aim to which all other phenomena are essentially and actually subservient. Only therefore through their relationship to it, i.e. through the judgment in which they are subsumed under it, while it inheres in them, have they their value and even their existence. It is the spirit which not merely broods over history as over the waters, but lives in it and is alone its principle of movement: and in the path of that spirit, liberty, i.e. a development determined by the notion of spirit, is the guiding principle and only its notion its final aim, i.e. truth. For Spirit is consciousness. Such a doctrine—or in other words that Reason is in history—will be partly at least a plausible faith, partly it is a cognition of philosophy.

§ 550. This liberation of mind, in which it proceeds to come to itself and to realise its truth, and the business of so doing, is the supreme right, the absolute Law. The self-consciousness of a particular nation is a vehicle for the contemporary development of the collective spirit in its actual existence: it is the objective actuality in which that spirit for the time invests its will. Against this absolute will the other particular natural minds have no rights: that nation dominates the world: but yet the universal will steps onward over its property for the time being, as over a special grade, and then delivers it over to its chance and doom.

§ 551. To such extent as this business of actuality appears as an action, and therefore as a work of individuals, these individuals, as regards the substantial issue of their labour, are instruments, and their subjectivity, which is what is peculiar to them, is the empty form of activity. What they personally have gained therefore through the individual share they took in the substantial business (prepared and appointed independently of them) is a formal universality or subjective mental idea—Fame, which is their reward.

§ 552. The national spirit contains nature-necessity, and stands in external existence (§ 423): the ethical substance, potentially infinite, is actually a particular and limited substance (§§ 549, 550); on its subjective side it labours under contingency, in the shape of its unreflective natural usages, and its content is presented to it as something existing in time and tied to an external nature and external world. The spirit, however, (which thinks in this moral organism) overrides and absorbs within itself the finitude attaching to it as national spirit in its state and the state's temporal interests, in the system of laws and usages. It rises to apprehend itself in its essentiality. Such apprehension, however, still has the immanent limitedness of the national spirit. But the spirit which thinks in universal history, stripping off at the same time those limitations of the several national minds and its own temporal restrictions, lays hold of its concrete universality, and rises to apprehend the absolute mind, as the eternally actual truth in which the contemplative reason enjoys freedom, while the necessity of nature and the necessity of history are only ministrant to its revelation and the vessels of its honour.

The strictly technical aspects of the Mind's elevation to God have been spoken of in the Introduction to the Logic (cf. especially § 51, note). As regards the starting-point of that elevation, Kant has on the whole adopted the most correct, when he treats belief in God as proceeding from the practical Reason. For that starting-point contains the material or content which constitutes the content of the notion of God. But the true concrete material is neither Being (as in the cosmological) nor mere action by design (as in the physico-theological proof) but the Mind, the absolute characteristic and function of which is effective reason, i.e. the self-determining and self-realising notion itself,—Liberty. That the elevation of subjective mind to God which these considerations give is by Kant again deposed to a postulate—a mere "ought"—is the peculiar perversity, formerly noticed, of calmly and simply reinstating as true and valid that very antithesis of finitude, the supersession of which into truth is the essence of that elevation.

As regards the "mediation" which, as it has been already shown (§ 192, cf. § 204 note), that elevation to God really involves, the point specially calling for note is the "moment" of negation through which the essential content of the starting-point is purged of its finitude so as to come forth free. This factor, abstract in the formal treatment of logic, now gets its most concrete interpretation. The finite, from which the start is now made, is the real ethical self-consciousness. The negation through which that consciousness raises its spirit to its truth, is the purification, actually accomplished in the ethical world, whereby its conscience is purged of subjective opinion and its will freed from the selfishness of desire. Genuine religion and genuine religiosity only issue from the moral life: religion is that life rising to think, i.e. becoming aware of the free universality of its concrete essence. Only from the moral life and by the moral life is the Idea of God seen to be free spirit: outside the ethical spirit therefore it is vain to seek for true religion and religiosity.

But—as is the case with all speculative process—this development of one thing out of another means that what appears as sequel and derivative is rather the absolute prius of what it appears to be mediated by, and what is here in mind known as its truth.

Here then is the place to go more deeply into the reciprocal relations between the state and religion, and in doing so to elucidate the terminology which is familiar and current on the topic. It is evident and apparent from what has preceded that moral life is the state retracted into its inner heart and substance, while the state is the organisation and actualisation of moral life; and that religion is the very substance of the moral life itself and of the state. At this rate, the state rests on the ethical sentiment, and that on the religious. If religion then is the consciousness of "absolute" truth, then whatever is to rank as right and justice, as law and duty, i.e. as true in the world of free will, can be so esteemed only as it is participant in that truth, as it is subsumed under it and is its sequel. But if the truly moral life is to be a sequel of religion, then perforce religion must have the genuine content; i.e. the idea of God it knows must be the true and real. The ethical life is the divine spirit as indwelling in self-consciousness, as it is actually present in a nation and its individual members. This self-consciousness retiring upon itself out of its empirical actuality and bringing its truth to consciousness, has in its faith and in its conscience only what it has consciously secured in its spiritual actuality. The two are inseparable: there cannot be two kinds of conscience, one religious and another ethical, differing from the former in body and value of truth. But in point of form, i.e. for thought and knowledge—(and religion and ethical life belong to intelligence and are a thinking and knowing)—the body of religious truth, as the pure self-subsisting and therefore supreme truth, exercises a sanction over the moral life which lies in empirical actuality. Thus for self-consciousness religion is the "basis" of moral life and of the state. It has been the monstrous blunder of our times to try to look upon these inseparables as separable from one another, and even as mutually indifferent. The view taken of the relationship of religion and the state has been that, whereas the state had an independent existence of its own, springing from some force and power, religion was a later addition, something desirable perhaps for strengthening the political bulwarks, but purely subjective in individuals:—or it may be, religion is treated as something without effect on the moral life of the state, i.e. its reasonable law and constitution which are based on a ground of their own.

As the inseparability of the two sides has been indicated, it may be worth while to note the separation as it appears on the side of religion. It is primarily a point of form: the attitude which self-consciousness takes to the body of truth. So long as this body of truth is the very substance or indwelling spirit of self-consciousness in its actuality, then self-consciousness in this content has the certainty of itself and is free. But if this present self-consciousness is lacking, then there may be created, in point of form, a condition of spiritual slavery, even though the implicit content of religion is absolute spirit. This great difference (to cite a specific case) comes out within the Christian religion itself, even though here it is not the nature-element in which the idea of God is embodied, and though nothing of the sort even enters as a factor into its central dogma and sole theme of a God who is known in spirit and in truth. And yet in Catholicism this spirit of all truth is in actuality set in rigid opposition to the self-conscious spirit. And, first of all, God is in the "host" presented to religious adoration as an external thing. (In the Lutheran Church, on the contrary, the host as such is not at first consecrated, but in the moment of enjoyment, i.e. in the annihilation of its externality, and in the act of faith, i.e. in the free self-certain spirit: only then is it consecrated and exalted to be present God.) From that first and supreme status of externalisation flows every other phase of externality,—of bondage, non-spirituality, and superstition. It leads to a laity, receiving its knowledge of divine truth, as well as the direction of its will and conscience from without and from another order—which order again does not get possession of that knowledge in a spiritual way only, but to that end essentially requires an external consecration. It leads to the non-spiritual style of praying—partly as mere moving of the lips, partly in the way that the subject foregoes his right of directly addressing God, and prays others to pray—addressing his devotion to miracle-working images, even to bones, and expecting miracles from them. It leads, generally, to justification by external works, a merit which is supposed to be gained by acts, and even to be capable of being transferred to others. All this binds the spirit under an externalism by which the very meaning of spirit is perverted and misconceived at its source, and law and justice, morality and conscience, responsibility and duty are corrupted at their root.

Along with this principle of spiritual bondage, and these applications of it in the religious life, there can only go in the legislative and constitutional system a legal and moral bondage, and a state of lawlessness and immorality in political life. Catholicism has been loudly praised and is still often praised—logically enough—as the one religion which secures the stability of governments. But in reality this applies only to governments which are bound up with institutions founded on the bondage of the spirit (of that spirit which should have legal and moral liberty), i.e. with institutions that embody injustice and with a morally corrupt and barbaric state of society. But these governments are not aware that in fanaticism they have a terrible power, which does not rise in hostility against them, only so long as and only on condition that they remain sunk in the thraldom of injustice and immorality. But in mind there is a very different power available against that externalism and dismemberment induced by a false religion. Mind collects itself into its inward free actuality. Philosophy awakes in the spirit of governments and nations the wisdom to discern what is essentially and actually right and reasonable in the real world. It was well to call these products of thought, and in a special sense Philosophy, the wisdom of the world[170]; for thought makes the spirit's truth an actual present, leads it into the real world, and thus liberates it in its actuality and in its own self.

Thus set free, the content of religion assumes quite another shape. So long as the form, i.e. our consciousness and subjectivity, lacked liberty, it followed necessarily that self-consciousness was conceived as not immanent in the ethical principles which religion embodies, and these principles were set at such a distance as to seem to have true being only as negative to actual self-consciousness. In this unreality ethical content gets the name of Holiness. But once the divine spirit introduces itself into actuality, and actuality emancipates itself to spirit, then what in the world was a postulate of holiness is supplanted by the actuality of moral life. Instead of the vow of chastity, marriage now ranks as the ethical relation; and, therefore, as the highest on this side of humanity stands the family. Instead of the vow of poverty (muddled up into a contradiction of assigning merit to whosoever gives away goods to the poor, i.e. whosoever enriches them) is the precept of action to acquire goods through one's own intelligence and industry,—of honesty in commercial dealing, and in the use of property,—in short moral life in the socio-economic sphere. And instead of the vow of obedience, true religion sanctions obedience to the law and the legal arrangements of the state—an obedience which is itself the true freedom, because the state is a self-possessed, self-realising reason—in short, moral life in the state. Thus, and thus only, can law and morality exist. The precept of religion, "Give to Caesar what is Caesar's and to God what is God's" is not enough: the question is to settle what is Caesar's, what belongs to the secular authority: and it is sufficiently notorious that the secular no less than the ecclesiastical authority have claimed almost everything as their own. The divine spirit must interpenetrate the entire secular life: whereby wisdom is concrete within it, and it carries the terms of its own justification. But that concrete indwelling is only the aforesaid ethical organisations. It is the morality of marriage as against the sanctity of a celibate order;—the morality of economic and industrial action against the sanctity of poverty and its indolence;—the morality of an obedience dedicated to the law of the state as against the sanctity of an obedience from which law and duty are absent and where conscience is enslaved. With the growing need for law and morality and the sense of the spirit's essential liberty, there sets in a conflict of spirit with the religion of unfreedom. It is no use to organise political laws and arrangements on principles of equity and reason, so long as in religion the principle of unfreedom is not abandoned. A free state and a slavish religion are incompatible. It is silly to suppose that we may try to allot them separate spheres, under the impression that their diverse natures will maintain an attitude of tranquillity one to another and not break out in contradiction and battle. Principles of civil freedom can be but abstract and superficial, and political institutions deduced from them must be, if taken alone, untenable, so long as those principles in their wisdom mistake religion so much as not to know that the maxims of the reason in actuality have their last and supreme sanction in the religious conscience in subsumption under the consciousness of "absolute" truth. Let us suppose even that, no matter how, a code of law should arise, so to speak a priori, founded on principles of reason, but in contradiction with an established religion based on principles of spiritual unfreedom; still, as the duty of carrying out the laws lies in the hands of individual members of the government, and of the various classes of the administrative personnel, it is vain to delude ourselves with the abstract and empty assumption that the individuals will act only according to the letter or meaning of the law, and not in the spirit of their religion where their inmost conscience and supreme obligation lies. Opposed to what religion pronounces holy, the laws appear something made by human hands: even though backed by penalties and externally introduced, they could offer no lasting resistance to the contradiction and attacks of the religious spirit. Such laws, however sound their provisions may be, thus founder on the conscience, whose spirit is different from the spirit of the laws and refuses to sanction them. It is nothing but a modern folly to try to alter a corrupt moral organisation by altering its political constitution and code of laws without changing the religion,—to make a revolution without having made a reformation, to suppose that a political constitution opposed to the old religion could live in peace and harmony with it and its sanctities, and that stability could be procured for the laws by external guarantees, e.g. so-called "chambers," and the power given them to fix the budget, &c. (cf. § 544 note). At best it is only a temporary expedient—when it is obviously too great a task to descend into the depths of the religious spirit and to raise that same spirit to its truth—to seek to separate law and justice from religion. Those guarantees are but rotten bulwarks against the consciences of the persons charged with administering the laws—among which laws these guarantees are included. It is indeed the height and profanity of contradiction to seek to bind and subject to the secular code the religious conscience to which mere human law is a thing profane.

The perception had dawned upon Plato with great clearness of the gulf which in his day had commenced to divide the established religion and the political constitution, on one hand, from those deeper requirements which, on the other hand, were made upon religion and politics by liberty which had learnt to recognise its inner life. Plato gets hold of the thought that a genuine constitution and a sound political life have their deeper foundation on the Idea,—on the essentially and actually universal and genuine principles of eternal righteousness. Now to see and ascertain what these are is certainly the function and the business of philosophy. It is from this point of view that Plato breaks out into the celebrated or notorious passage where he makes Socrates emphatically state that philosophy and political power must coincide, that the Idea must be regent, if the distress of nations is to see its end. What Plato thus definitely set before his mind was that the Idea—which implicitly indeed is the free self-determining thought—could not get into consciousness save only in the form of a thought; that the substance of the thought could only be true when set forth as a universal, and as such brought to consciousness under its most abstract form.

To compare the Platonic standpoint in all its definiteness with the point of view from which the relationship of state and religion is here regarded, the notional differences on which everything turns must be recalled to mind. The first of these is that in natural things their substance or genus is different from their existence in which that substance is as subject: further that this subjective existence of the genus is distinct from that which it gets, when specially set in relief as genus, or, to put it simply, as the universal in a mental concept or idea. This additional "individuality"—the soil on which the universal and underlying principle freely and expressly exists,—is the intellectual and thinking self. In the case of natural things their truth and reality does not get the form of universality and essentiality through themselves, and their "individuality" is not itself the form: the form is only found in subjective thinking, which in philosophy gives that universal truth and reality an existence of its own. In man's case it is otherwise: his truth and reality is the free mind itself, and it comes to existence in his self-consciousness. This absolute nucleus of man—mind intrinsically concrete—is just this—to have the form (to have thinking) itself for a content. To the height of the thinking consciousness of this principle Aristotle ascended in his notion of the entelechy of thought, (which is νόησις τῆς νοήσεως), thus surmounting the Platonic Idea (the genus, or essential being). But thought always—and that on account of this very principle—contains the immediate self-subsistence of subjectivity no less than it contains universality; the genuine Idea of the intrinsically concrete mind is just as essentially under the one of its terms (subjective consciousness) as under the other (universality): and in the one as in the other it is the same substantial content. Under the subjective form, however, fall feeling, intuition, pictorial representation: and it is in fact necessary that in point of time the consciousness of the absolute Idea should be first reached and apprehended in this form: in other words, it must exist in its immediate reality as religion, earlier than it does as philosophy. Philosophy is a later development from this basis (just as Greek philosophy itself is later than Greek religion), and in fact reaches its completion by catching and comprehending in all its definite essentiality that principle of spirit which first manifests itself in religion. But Greek philosophy could set itself up only in opposition to Greek religion: the unity of thought and the substantiality of the Idea could take up none but a hostile attitude to an imaginative polytheism, and to the gladsome and frivolous humours of its poetic creations. The form in its infinite truth, the subjectivity of mind, broke forth at first only as a subjective free thinking, which was not yet identical with the substantiality itself,—and thus this underlying principle was not yet apprehended as absolute mind. Thus religion might appear as first purified only through philosophy,—through pure self-existent thought: but the form pervading this underlying principle—the form which philosophy attacked—was that creative imagination.

Political power, which is developed similarly, but earlier than philosophy, from religion, exhibits the onesidedness, which in the actual world may infect its implicitly true Idea, as demoralisation. Plato, in common with all his thinking contemporaries, perceived this demoralisation of democracy and the defectiveness even of its principle; he set in relief accordingly the underlying principle of the state, but could not work into his idea of it the infinite form of subjectivity, which still escaped his intelligence. His state is therefore, on its own showing, wanting in subjective liberty (§ 503 note, § 513, &c.). The truth which should be immanent in the state, should knit it together and control it, he, for these reasons, got hold of only the form of thought-out truth, of philosophy; and hence he makes that utterance that "so long as philosophers do not rule in the states, or those who are now called kings and rulers do not soundly and comprehensively philosophise, so long neither the state nor the race of men can be liberated from evils,—so long will the idea of the political constitution fall short of possibility and not see the light of the sun." It was not vouchsafed to Plato to go on so far as to say that so long as true religion did not spring up in the world and hold sway in political life, so long the genuine principle of the state had not come into actuality. But so long too this principle could not emerge even in thought, nor could thought lay hold of the genuine idea of the state,—the idea of the substantial moral life, with which is identical the liberty of an independent self-consciousness. Only in the principle of mind, which is aware of its own essence, is implicitly in absolute liberty, and has its actuality in the act of self-liberation, does the absolute possibility and necessity exist for political power, religion, and the principles of philosophy coinciding in one, and for accomplishing the reconciliation of actuality in general with the mind, of the state with the religious conscience as well as with the philosophical consciousness. Self-realising subjectivity is in this case absolutely identical with substantial universality. Hence religion as such, and the state as such,—both as forms in which the principle exists—each contain the absolute truth: so that the truth, in its philosophic phase, is after all only in one of its forms. But even religion, as it grows and expands, lets other aspects of the Idea of humanity grow and expand also (§ 500 sqq.). As it is left therefore behind, in its first immediate, and so also one-sided phase, Religion may, or rather must, appear in its existence degraded to sensuous externality, and thus in the sequel become an influence to oppress liberty of spirit and to deprave political life. Still the principle has in it the infinite "elasticity" of the "absolute" form, so as to overcome this depraving of the form-determination (and of the content by these means), and to bring about the reconciliation of the spirit in itself. Thus ultimately, in the Protestant conscience the principles of the religious and of the ethical conscience come to be one and the same: the free spirit learning to see itself in its reasonableness and truth. In the Protestant state, the constitution and the code, as well as their several applications, embody the principle and the development of the moral life, which proceeds and can only proceed from the truth of religion, when reinstated in its original principle and in that way as such first become actual. The moral life of the state and the religious spirituality of the state are thus reciprocal guarantees of strength.

SECTION III – ABSOLUTE MIND[171].

§ 553. The notion of mind has its reality in the mind. If this reality in identity with that notion is to exist as the consciousness of the absolute Idea, then the necessary aspect is that the implicitly free intelligence be in its actuality liberated to its notion, if that actuality is to be a vehicle worthy of it. The subjective and the objective spirit are to be looked on as the road on which this aspect of reality or existence rises to maturity.

§ 554. The absolute mind, while it is self-centred identity, is always also identity returning and ever returned into itself: if it is the one and universal substance it is so as a spirit, discerning itself into a self and a consciousness, for which it is as substance. Religion, as this supreme sphere may be in general designated, if it has on one hand to be studied as issuing from the subject and having its home in the subject, must no less be regarded as objectively issuing from the absolute spirit which as spirit is in its community.

That here, as always, belief or faith is not opposite to consciousness or knowledge, but rather to a sort of knowledge, and that belief is only a particular form of the latter, has been remarked already (§ 63 note). If nowadays there is so little consciousness of God, and his objective essence is so little dwelt upon, while people speak so much more of the subjective side of religion, i.e. of God's indwelling in us, and if that and not the truth as such is called for,—in this there is at least the correct principle that God must be apprehended as spirit in his community.

§ 555. The subjective consciousness of the absolute spirit is essentially and intrinsically a process, the immediate and substantial unity of which is the Belief in the witness of the spirit as the certainty of objective truth. Belief, at once this immediate unity and containing it as a reciprocal dependence of these different terms, has in devotion—the implicit or more explicit act of worship (cultus)—passed over into the process of superseding the contrast till it becomes spiritual liberation, the process of authenticating that first certainty by this intermediation, and of gaining its concrete determination, viz. reconciliation, the actuality of the spirit.

Sub-Section A - Art.

§ 556. As this consciousness of the Absolute first takes shape, its immediacy produces the factor of finitude in Art. On one hand that is, it breaks up into a work of external common existence, into the subject which produces that work, and the subject which contemplates and worships it. But, on the other hand, it is the concrete contemplation and mental picture of implicitly absolute spirit as the Ideal. In this ideal, or the concrete shape born of the subjective spirit, its natural immediacy, which is only a sign of the Idea, is so transfigured by the informing spirit in order to express the Idea, that the figure shows it and it alone:—the shape or form of Beauty.

§ 557. The sensuous externality attaching to the beautiful,—the form of immediacy as such,—at the same time qualifies what it embodies: and the God (of art) has with his spirituality at the same time the stamp upon him of a natural medium or natural phase of existence—He contains the so-called unity of nature and spirit—i.e. the immediate unity in sensuously intuitional form—hence not the spiritual unity, in which the natural would be put only as "ideal," as superseded in spirit, and the spiritual content would be only in self-relation. It is not the absolute spirit which enters this consciousness. On the subjective side the community has of course an ethical life, aware, as it is, of the spirituality of its essence: and its self-consciousness and actuality are in it elevated to substantial liberty. But with the stigma of immediacy upon it, the subject's liberty is only a manner of life, without the infinite self-reflection and the subjective inwardness of conscience. These considerations govern in their further developments the devotion and the worship in the religion of fine art.

§ 558. For the objects of contemplation it has to produce, Art requires not only an external given material—(under which are also included subjective images and ideas), but—for the expression of spiritual truth—must use the given forms of nature with a significance which art must divine and possess (cf. § 411). Of all such forms the human is the highest and the true, because only in it can the spirit have its corporeity and thus its visible expression.

This disposes of the principle of the imitation of nature in art: a point on which it is impossible to come to an understanding while a distinction is left thus abstract,—in other words, so long as the natural is only taken in its externality, not as the "characteristic" meaningful nature-form which is significant of spirit.

§ 559. In such single shapes the "absolute" mind cannot be made explicit: in and to art therefore the spirit is a limited natural spirit whose implicit universality, when steps are taken to specify its fullness in detail, breaks up into an indeterminate polytheism. With the essential restrictedness of its content, Beauty in general goes no further than a penetration of the vision or image by the spiritual principle,—something formal, so that the thought embodied, or the idea, can, like the material which it uses to work in, be of the most diverse and unessential kind, and still the work be something beautiful and a work of art.

§ 560. The one-sidedness of immediacy on the part of the Ideal involves the opposite one-sidedness (§ 556) that it is something made by the artist. The subject or agent is the mere technical activity: and the work of art is only then an expression of the God, when there is no sign of subjective particularity in it, and the net power of the indwelling spirit is conceived and born into the world, without admixture and unspotted from its contingency. But as liberty only goes as far as there is thought, the action inspired with the fullness of this indwelling power, the artist's enthusiasm, is like a foreign force under which he is bound and passive; the artistic production has on its part the form of natural immediacy, it belongs to the genius or particular endowment of the artist,—and is at the same time a labour concerned with technical cleverness and mechanical externalities. The work of art therefore is just as much a work due to free option, and the artist is the master of the God.

§ 561. In work so inspired the reconciliation appears so obvious in its initial stage that it is without more ado accomplished in the subjective self-consciousness, which is thus self-confident and of good cheer, without the depth and without the sense of its antithesis to the absolute essence. On the further side of the perfection (which is reached in such reconciliation, in the beauty of classical art) lies the art of sublimity,—symbolic art, in which the figuration suitable to the Idea is not yet found, and the thought as going forth and wrestling with the figure is exhibited as a negative attitude to it, and yet all the while toiling to work itself into it. The meaning or theme thus shows it has not yet reached the infinite form, is not yet known, not yet conscious of itself, as free spirit. The artist's theme only is as the abstract God of pure thought, or an effort towards him,—a restless and unappeased effort which throws itself into shape after shape as it vainly tries to find its goal.

§ 562. In another way the Idea and the sensuous figure it appears in are incompatible; and that is where the infinite form, subjectivity, is not as in the first extreme a mere superficial personality, but its inmost depth, and God is known not as only seeking his form or satisfying himself in an external form, but as only finding himself in himself, and thus giving himself his adequate figure in the spiritual world alone. Romantic art gives up the task of showing him as such in external form and by means of beauty: it presents him as only condescending to appearance, and the divine as the heart of hearts in an externality from which it always disengages itself. Thus the external can here appear as contingent towards its significance.

The Philosophy of Religion has to discover the logical necessity in the progress by which the Being, known as the Absolute, assumes fuller and firmer features; it has to note to what particular feature the kind of cultus corresponds,—and then to see how the secular self-consciousness, the consciousness of what is the supreme vocation of man,—in short how the nature of a nation's moral life, the principle of its law, of its actual liberty, and of its constitution, as well as of its art and science, corresponds to the principle which constitutes the substance of a religion. That all these elements of a nation's actuality constitute one systematic totality, that one spirit creates and informs them, is a truth on which follows the further truth that the history of religions coincides with the world-history.

As regards the close connexion of art with the various religions it may be specially noted that beautiful art can only belong to those religions in which the spiritual principle, though concrete and intrinsically free, is not yet absolute. In religions where the Idea has not yet been revealed and known in its free character, though the craving for art is felt in order to bring in imaginative visibility to consciousness the idea of the supreme being, and though art is the sole organ in which the abstract and radically indistinct content,—a mixture from natural and spiritual sources,—can try to bring itself to consciousness;—still this art is defective; its form is defective because its subject-matter and theme is so,—for the defect in subject-matter comes from the form not being immanent in it. The representations of this symbolic art keep a certain tastelessness and stolidity—for the principle it embodies is itself stolid and dull, and hence has not the power freely to transmute the external to significance and shape. Beautiful art, on the contrary, has for its condition the self-consciousness of the free spirit,—the consciousness that compared with it the natural and sensuous has no standing of its own: it makes the natural wholly into the mere expression of spirit, which is thus the inner form that gives utterance to itself alone.

But with a further and deeper study, we see that the advent of art, in a religion still in the bonds of sensuous externality, shows that such religion is on the decline. At the very time it seems to give religion the supreme glorification, expression and brilliancy, it has lifted the religion away over its limitation. In the sublime divinity to which the work of art succeeds in giving expression the artistic genius and the spectator find themselves at home, with their personal sense and feeling, satisfied and liberated: to them the vision and the consciousness of free spirit has been vouchsafed and attained. Beautiful art, from its side, has thus performed the same service as philosophy: it has purified the spirit from its thraldom. The older religion in which the need of fine art, and just for that reason, is first generated, looks up in its principle to an other-world which is sensuous and unmeaning: the images adored by its devotees are hideous idols regarded as wonder-working talismans, which point to the unspiritual objectivity of that other world,—and bones perform a similar or even a better service than such images. But even fine art is only a grade of liberation, not the supreme liberation itself.—The genuine objectivity, which is only in the medium of thought,—the medium in which alone the pure spirit is for the spirit, and where the liberation is accompanied with reverence,—is still absent in the sensuous beauty of the work of art, still more in that external, unbeautiful sensuousness.

§ 563. Beautiful Art, like the religion peculiar to it, has its future in true religion. The restricted value of the Idea passes utterly and naturally into the universality identical with the infinite form;—the vision in which consciousness has to depend upon the senses passes into a self-mediating knowledge, into an existence which is itself knowledge,—into revelation. Thus the principle which gives the Idea its content is that it embody free intelligence, and as "absolute" spirit it is for the spirit.

Sub-Section B - Revealed Religion[172].

§ 564. It lies essentially in the notion of religion,—the religion i.e. whose content is absolute mind—that it be revealed, and, what is more, revealed by God. Knowledge (the principle by which the substance is mind) is a self-determining principle, as infinite self-realising form,—it therefore is manifestation out and out. The spirit is only spirit in so far as it is for the spirit, and in the absolute religion it is the absolute spirit which manifests no longer abstract elements of its being but itself.

The old conception—due to a one-sided survey of human life—of Nemesis, which made the divinity and its action in the world only a levelling power, dashing to pieces everything high and great,—was confronted by Plato and Aristotle with the doctrine that God is not envious. The same answer may be given to the modern assertions that man cannot ascertain God. These assertions (and more than assertions they are not) are the more illogical, because made within a religion which is expressly called the revealed; for according to them it would rather be the religion in which nothing of God was revealed, in which he had not revealed himself, and those belonging to it would be the heathen "who know not God." If the word of God is taken in earnest in religion at all, it is from Him, the theme and centre of religion, that the method of divine knowledge may and must begin: and if self-revelation is refused Him, then the only thing left to constitute His nature would be to ascribe envy to Him. But clearly if the word Mind is to have a meaning, it implies the revelation of Him.

If we recollect how intricate is the knowledge of the divine Mind for those who are not content with the homely pictures of faith but proceed to thought,—at first only "rationalising" reflection, but afterwards, as in duty bound, to speculative comprehension, it may almost create surprise that so many, and especially theologians whose vocation it is to deal with these Ideas, have tried to get off their task by gladly accepting anything offered them for this behoof. And nothing serves better to shirk it than to adopt the conclusion that man knows nothing of God. To know what God as spirit is—to apprehend this accurately and distinctly in thoughts—requires careful and thorough speculation. It includes, in its fore-front, the propositions: God is God only so far as he knows himself: his self-knowledge is, further, his self-consciousness in man, and man's knowledge of God, which proceeds to man's self-knowledge in God.—See the profound elucidation of these propositions in the work from which they are taken: Aphorisms on Knowing and Not-knowing, &c., by C. F. G—l.: Berlin 1829.

§ 565. When the immediacy and sensuousness of shape and knowledge is superseded, God is, in point of content, the essential and actual spirit of nature and spirit, while in point of form he is, first of all, presented to consciousness as a mental representation. This quasi-pictorial representation gives to the elements of his content, on one hand, a separate being, making them presuppositions towards each other, and phenomena which succeed each other; their relationship it makes a series of events according to finite reflective categories. But, on the other hand, such a form of finite representationalism is also overcome and superseded in the faith which realises one spirit and in the devotion of worship.

§ 566. In this separating, the form parts from the content: and in the form the different functions of the notion part off into special spheres or media, in each of which the absolute spirit exhibits itself; (α) as eternal content, abiding self-centred, even in its manifestation; (β) as distinction of the eternal essence from its manifestation, which by this difference becomes the phenomenal world into which the content enters; (γ) as infinite return, and reconciliation with the eternal being, of the world it gave away—the withdrawal of the eternal from the phenomenal into the unity of its fullness.

§ 567. (α) Under the "moment" of Universality,—the sphere of pure thought or the abstract medium of essence,—it is therefore the absolute spirit, which is at first the presupposed principle, not however staying aloof and inert, but (as underlying and essential power under the reflective category of causality) creator of heaven and earth: but yet in this eternal sphere rather only begetting himself as his son, with whom, though different, he still remains in original identity,—just as, again, this differentiation of him from the universal essence eternally supersedes itself, and, though this mediating of a self-superseding mediation, the first substance is essentially as concrete individuality and subjectivity,—is the Spirit.

§ 568. (β) Under the "moment" of particularity, or of judgment, it is this concrete eternal being which is presupposed: its movement is the creation of the phenomenal world. The eternal "moment" of mediation—of the only Son—divides itself to become the antithesis of two separate worlds. On one hand is heaven and earth, the elemental and the concrete nature,—on the other hand, standing in action and reaction with such nature, the spirit, which therefore is finite. That spirit, as the extreme of inherent negativity, completes its independence till it becomes wickedness, and is that extreme through its connexion with a confronting nature and through its own naturalness thereby investing it. Yet, amid that naturalness, it is, when it thinks, directed towards the Eternal, though, for that reason, only standing to it in an external connexion.

§ 569. (γ) Under the "moment" of individuality as such,—of subjectivity and the notion itself, in which the contrast of universal and particular has sunk to its identical ground, the place of presupposition [1] is taken by the universal substance, as actualised out of its abstraction into an individual self-consciousness. This individual, who as such is identified with the essence,—(in the Eternal sphere he is called the Son)—is transplanted into the world of time, and in him wickedness is implicitly overcome. Further, this immediate, and thus sensuous, existence of the absolutely concrete is represented as putting himself in judgment and expiring in the pain of negativity, in which he, as infinite subjectivity, keeps himself unchanged, and thus, as absolute return from that negativity and as universal unity of universal and individual essentiality, has realised his being as the Idea of the spirit, eternal, but alive and present in the world.

§ 570. [2] This objective totality of the divine man who is the Idea of the spirit is the implicit presupposition for the finite immediacy of the single subject. For such subject therefore it is at first an Other, an object of contemplating vision,—but the vision of implicit truth, through which witness of the spirit in him, he, on account of his immediate nature, at first characterised himself as nought and wicked. But, secondly, after the example of his truth, by means of the faith on the unity (in that example implicitly accomplished) of universal and individual essence, he is also the movement to throw off his immediacy, his natural man and self-will, to close himself in unity with that example (who is his implicit life) in the pain of negativity, and thus to know himself made one with the essential Being. Thus the Being of Beings [3] through this mediation brings about its own indwelling in self-consciousness, and is the actual presence of the essential and self-subsisting spirit who is all in all.

§ 571. These three syllogisms, constituting the one syllogism of the absolute self-mediation of spirit, are the revelation of that spirit whose life is set out as a cycle of concrete shapes in pictorial thought. From this its separation into parts, with a temporal and external sequence, the unfolding of the mediation contracts itself in the result,—where the spirit closes in unity with itself,—not merely to the simplicity of faith and devotional feeling, but even to thought. In the immanent simplicity of thought the unfolding still has its expansion, yet is all the while known as an indivisible coherence of the universal, simple, and eternal spirit in itself. In this form of truth, truth is the object of philosophy.

If the result—the realised Spirit in which all meditation has superseded itself—is taken in a merely formal, contentless sense, so that the spirit is not also at the same time known as implicitly existent and objectively self-unfolding;—then that infinite subjectivity is the merely formal self-consciousness, knowing itself in itself as absolute,—Irony. Irony, which can make every objective reality nought and vain, is itself the emptiness and vanity, which from itself, and therefore by chance and its own good pleasure, gives itself direction and content, remains master over it, is not bound by it,—and, with the assertion that it stands on the very summit of religion and philosophy, falls rather back into the vanity of wilfulness. It is only in proportion as the pure infinite form, the self-centred manifestation, throws off the one-sidedness of subjectivity in which it is the vanity of thought, that it is the free thought which has its infinite characteristic at the same time as essential and actual content, and has that content as an object in which it is also free. Thinking, so far, is only the formal aspect of the absolute content.

Sub-Section C - Philosophy.

§ 572. This science is the unity of Art and Religion. Whereas the vision-method of Art, external in point of form, is but subjective production and shivers the substantial content into many separate shapes, and whereas Religion, with its separation into parts, opens it out in mental picture, and mediates what is thus opened out; Philosophy not merely keeps them together to make a total, but even unifies them into the simple spiritual vision, and then in that raises them to self-conscious thought. Such consciousness is thus the intelligible unity (cognised by thought) of art and religion, in which the diverse elements in the content are cognised as necessary, and this necessary as free.

§ 573. Philosophy thus characterises itself as a cognition of the necessity in the content of the absolute picture-idea, as also of the necessity in the two forms—on one hand, immediate vision and its poetry, and the objective and external revelation presupposed by representation,—on the other hand, first the subjective retreat inwards, then the subjective movement of faith and its final identification with the presupposed object. This cognition is thus the recognition of this content and its form; it is the liberation from the one-sidedness of the forms, elevation of them into the absolute form, which determines itself to content, remains identical with it, and is in that the cognition of that essential and actual necessity. This movement, which philosophy is, finds itself already accomplished, when at the close it seizes its own notion,—i.e. only looks back on its knowledge.

Here might seem to be the place to treat in a definite exposition of the reciprocal relations of philosophy and religion. The whole question turns entirely on the difference of the forms of speculative thought from the forms of mental representation and "reflecting" intellect. But it is the whole cycle of philosophy, and of logic in particular, which has not merely taught and made known this difference, but also criticised it, or rather has let its nature develop and judge itself by these very categories. It is only by an insight into the value of these forms that the true and needful conviction can be gained, that the content of religion and philosophy is the same,—leaving out, of course, the further details of external nature and finite mind which fall outside the range of religion. But religion is the truth for all men: faith rests on the witness of the spirit, which as witnessing is the spirit in man. This witness—the underlying essence in all humanity—takes, when driven to expound itself, its first definite form under those acquired habits of thought which his secular consciousness and intellect otherwise employs. In this way the truth becomes liable to the terms and conditions of finitude in general. This does not prevent the spirit, even in employing sensuous ideas and finite categories of thought, from retaining its content (which as religion is essentially speculative,) with a tenacity which does violence to them, and acts inconsistently towards them. By this inconsistency it corrects their defects. Nothing easier therefore for the "Rationalist" than to point out contradictions in the exposition of the faith, and then to prepare triumphs for its principle of formal identity. If the spirit yields to this finite reflection, which has usurped the title of reason and philosophy—("Rationalism")—it strips religious truth of its infinity and makes it in reality nought. Religion in that case is completely in the right in guarding herself against such reason and philosophy and treating them as enemies. But it is another thing when religion sets herself against comprehending reason, and against philosophy in general, and specially against a philosophy of which the doctrine is speculative, and so religious. Such an opposition proceeds from failure to appreciate the difference indicated and the value of spiritual form in general, and particularly of the logical form; or, to be more precise, still from failure to note the distinction of the content— which may be in both the same—from these forms. It is on the ground of form that philosophy has been reproached and accused by the religious party; just as conversely its speculative content has brought the same charges upon it from a self-styled philosophy—and from a pithless orthodoxy. It had too little of God in it for the former; too much for the latter.

The charge of Atheism, which used often to be brought against philosophy (that it has too little of God), has grown rare: the more wide-spread grows the charge of Pantheism, that it has too much of him:—so much so, that it is treated not so much as an imputation, but as a proved fact, or a sheer fact which needs no proof. Piety, in particular, which with its pious airs of superiority fancies itself free to dispense with proof, goes hand in hand with empty rationalism—(which means to be so much opposed to it, though both repose really on the same habit of mind)—in the wanton assertion, almost as if it merely mentioned a notorious fact, that Philosophy is the All-one doctrine, or Pantheism. It must be said that it was more to the credit of piety and theology when they accused a philosophical system (e.g. Spinozism) of Atheism than of Pantheism, though the former imputation at the first glance looks more cruel and insidious (cf. § 71 note). The imputation of Atheism presupposes a definite idea of a full and real God, and arises because the popular idea does not detect in the philosophical notion the peculiar form to which it is attached. Philosophy indeed can recognise its own forms in the categories of religious consciousness, and even its own teaching in the doctrine of religion—which therefore it does not disparage. But the converse is not true: the religious consciousness does not apply the criticism of thought to itself, does not comprehend itself, and is therefore, as it stands, exclusive. To impute

Pantheism instead of Atheism to Philosophy is part of the modern habit of mind—of the new piety and new theology. For them philosophy has too much of God:—so much so, that, if we believe them, it asserts that God is everything and everything is God. This new theology, which makes religion only a subjective feeling and denies the knowledge of the divine nature, thus retains nothing more than a God in general without objective characteristics. Without interest of its own for the concrete, fulfilled notion of God, it treats it only as an interest which others once had, and hence treats what belongs to the doctrine of God's concrete nature as something merely historical. The indeterminate God is to be found in all religions; every kind of piety (§ 72)—that of the Hindoo to asses, cows,—or to dalai-lamas,—that of the Egyptians to the ox—is always adoration of an object which, with all its absurdities, also contains the generic abstract, God in General. If this theory needs no more than such a God, so as to find God in everything called religion, it must at least find such a God recognised even in philosophy, and can no longer accuse it of Atheism. The mitigation of the reproach of Atheism into that of Pantheism has its ground therefore in the superficial idea to which this mildness has attenuated and emptied God. As that popular idea clings to its abstract universality, from which all definite quality is excluded, all such definiteness is only the non-divine, the secularity of things, thus left standing in fixed undisturbed substantiality. On such a presupposition, even after philosophy has maintained God's absolute universality, and the consequent untruth of the being of external things, the hearer clings as he did before to his belief that secular things still keep their being, and form all that is definite in the divine universality. He thus changes that universality into what he calls the pantheistic:—Everything is— (empirical things, without distinction, whether higher or lower in the scale, are)—all possess substantiality; and so—thus he understands philosophy—each and every secular thing is God. It is only his own stupidity, and the falsifications due to such misconception, which generate the imagination and the allegation of such pantheism.

But if those who give out that a certain philosophy is Pantheism, are unable and unwilling to see this—for it is just to see the notion that they refuse—they should before everything have verified the alleged fact that any one philosopher, or any one man, had really ascribed substantial or objective and inherent reality to all things and regarded them as God:—that such an idea had ever come into the hand of any body but themselves. This allegation I will further elucidate in this exoteric discussion: and the only way to do so is to set down the evidence. If we want to take so-called Pantheism in its most poetical, most sublime, or if you will, its grossest shape, we must, as is well known, consult the oriental poets: and the most copious delineations of it are found in Hindoo literature. Amongst the abundant resources open to our disposal on this topic, I select—as the most authentic statement accessible—the Bhagavat-Gita, and amongst its effusions, prolix and reiterative ad nauseam, some of the most telling passages. In the 10th Lesson (in Schlegel, p. 162) Krishna says of himself[173]:—"I am the self, seated in the hearts of all beings. I am the beginning and the middle and the end also of all beings ... I am the beaming sun amongst the shining ones, and the moon among the lunar mansions.... Amongst the Vedas I am the Sâma-Veda: I am mind amongst the senses: I am consciousness in living beings. And I am Sankara (Siva) among the Rudras, ... Meru among the high-topped mountains, ... the Himalaya among the firmly-fixed (mountains).... Among beasts I am the lord of beasts.... Among letters I am the letter A.... I am the spring among the seasons.... I am also that which is the seed of all things: there is nothing moveable or immoveable which can exist without me."

Even in these totally sensuous delineations, Krishna (and we must not suppose there is, besides Krishna, still God, or a God besides; as he said before he was Siva, or Indra, so it is afterwards said that Brahma too is in him) makes himself out to be—not everything, but only—the most excellent of everything. Everywhere there is a distinction drawn between external, unessential existences, and one essential amongst them, which he is. Even when, at the beginning of the passage, he is said to be the beginning, middle, and end of living things, this totality is distinguished from the living things themselves as single existences. Even such a picture which extends deity far and wide in its existence cannot be called pantheism: we must rather say that in the infinitely multiple empirical world, everything is reduced to a limited number of essential existences, to a polytheism. But even what has been quoted shows that these very substantialities of the externally-existent do not retain the independence entitling them to be named Gods; even Siva, Indra, &c. melt into the one Krishna.

This reduction is more expressly made in the following scene (7th Lesson, p. 7 sqq.). Krishna says: "I am the producer and the destroyer of the whole universe. There is nothing else higher than myself; all this is woven upon me, like numbers of pearls upon a thread. I am the taste in water;... I am the light of the sun and the moon; I am 'Om' in all the Vedas.... I am life in all beings.... I am the discernment of the discerning ones.... I am also the strength of the strong." Then he adds: "The whole universe deluded by these three states of mind developed from the qualities [sc. goodness, passion, darkness] does not know me who am beyond them and inexhaustible: for this delusion of mine," [even the Maya is his, nothing independent], "developed from the qualities is divine and difficult to transcend. Those cross beyond this delusion who resort to me alone." Then the picture gathers itself up in a simple expression: "At the end of many lives, the man possessed of knowledge approaches me, (believing) that

Vasudeva is everything. Such a high-souled mind is very hard to find. Those who are deprived of knowledge by various desires approach other divinities... Whichever form of deity one worships with faith, from it he obtains the beneficial things he desires really given by me. But the fruit thus obtained by those of little judgment is perishable.... The undiscerning ones, not knowing my transcendent and inexhaustible essence, than which there is nothing higher, think me who am unperceived to have become perceptible."

This "All," which Krishna calls himself, is not, any more than the Eleatic One, and the Spinozan Substance, the Every-thing. This every-thing, rather, the infinitely-manifold sensuous manifold of the finite is in all these pictures, but defined as the "accidental," without essential being of its very own, but having its truth in the substance, the One which, as different from that accidental, is alone the divine and God. Hindooism however has the higher conception of Brahma, the pure unity of thought in itself, where the empirical everything of the world, as also those proximate substantialities, called Gods, vanish. On that account Colebrooke and many others have described the Hindoo religion as at bottom a Monotheism. That this description is not incorrect is clear from these short citations. But so little concrete is this divine unity—spiritual as its idea of God is—so powerless its grip, so to speak—that Hindooism, with a monstrous inconsistency, is also the maddest of polytheisms. But the idolatry of the wretched Hindoo, when he adores the ape, or other creature, is still a long way from that wretched fancy of a Pantheism, to which everything is God, and God everything. Hindoo monotheism moreover is itself an example how little comes of mere monotheism, if the Idea of God is not deeply determinate in itself. For that unity, if it be intrinsically abstract and therefore empty, tends of itself to let whatever is concrete, outside it—be it as a lot of Gods or as secular, empirical individuals—keep its independence. That pantheism indeed—on the shallow conception of it—might with a show of logic as well be called a monotheism: for if God, as it says, is identical with the world, then as there is only one world there would be in that pantheism only one God. Perhaps the empty numerical unity must be predicated of the world: but such abstract predication of it has no further special interest; on the contrary, a mere numerical unity just means that its content is an infinite multeity and variety of finitudes. But it is that delusion with the empty unity, which alone makes possible and induces the wrong idea of pantheism. It is only the picture—floating in the indefinite blue—of the world as one thing, the all, that could ever be considered capable of combining with God: only on that assumption could philosophy be supposed to teach that God is the world: for if the world were taken as it is, as everything, as the endless lot of empirical existence, then it would hardly have been even held possible to suppose a pantheism which asserted of such stuff that it is God.

But to go back again to the question of fact. If we want to see the consciousness of the One—not as with the Hindoos split between the featureless unity of abstract thought, on one hand, and on the other, the long-winded weary story of its particular detail, but—in its finest purity and sublimity, we must consult the Mohammedans. If e.g. in the excellent Jelaleddin-Rumi in particular, we find the unity of the soul with the One set forth, and that unity described as love, this spiritual unity is an exaltation above the finite and vulgar, a transfiguration of the natural and the spiritual, in which the externalism and transitoriness of immediate nature, and of empirical secular spirit, is discarded and absorbed[174].

I refrain from accumulating further examples of the religious and poetic conceptions which it is customary to call pantheistic. Of the philosophies to which that name is given, the Eleatic, or Spinozist, it has been remarked earlier (§ 50, note) that so far are they from identifying God with the world and making him finite, that in these systems this "everything" has no truth, and that we should rather call them monotheistic, or, in relation to the popular idea of the world, acosmical. They are most accurately called systems which apprehend the Absolute only as substance. Of the oriental, especially the Mohammedan, modes of envisaging God, we may rather say that they represent the Absolute as the utterly universal genus which dwells in the species or existences, but dwells so potently that these existences have no actual reality. The fault of all these modes of thought and systems is that they stop short of defining substance as subject and as mind.

These systems and modes of pictorial conception originate from the one need common to all philosophies and all religions of getting an idea of God, and, secondly, of the relationship of God and the world. (In philosophy it is specially made out that the determination of God's nature determines his relations with the world.) The "reflective" understanding begins by rejecting all systems and modes of conception, which, whether they spring from heart, imagination or speculation, express the interconnexion of God and the world: and in order to have God pure in faith or consciousness, he is as essence parted from appearance, as infinite from the finite. But, after this partition, the conviction arises also that the appearance has a relation to the essence, the finite to the infinite, and so on: and thus arises the question of reflection as to the nature of this relation. It is in the reflective form that the whole difficulty of the affair lies, and that causes this relation to be called incomprehensible by the agnostic. The close of philosophy is not the place, even in a general exoteric discussion, to waste a word on what a "notion" means. But as the view taken of this relation is closely connected with the view taken of philosophy generally and with all imputations against it, we may still add the remark that though philosophy certainly has to do with unity in general, it is not however with abstract unity, mere identity, and the empty absolute, but with concrete unity (the notion), and that in its whole course it has to do with nothing else;—that each step in its advance is a peculiar term or phase of this concrete unity, and that the deepest and last expression of unity is the unity of absolute mind itself. Would-be judges and critics of philosophy might be recommended to familiarise themselves with these phases of unity and to take the trouble to get acquainted with them, at least to know so much that of these terms there are a great many, and that amongst them there is great variety. But they show so little acquaintance with them—and still less take trouble about it—that, when they hear of unity—and relation ipso facto implies unity—they rather stick fast at quite abstract indeterminate unity, and lose sight of the chief point of interest—the special mode in which the unity is qualified. Hence all they can say about philosophy is that dry identity is its principle and result, and that it is the system of identity. Sticking fast to the undigested thought of identity, they have laid hands on, not the concrete unity, the notion and content of philosophy, but rather its reverse. In the philosophical field they proceed, as in the physical field the physicist; who also is well aware that he has before him a variety of sensuous properties and matters— or usually matters alone, (for the properties get transformed into matters also for the physicist)—and that these matters (elements) also stand in relation to one another. But the question is, Of what kind is this relation? Every peculiarity and the whole difference of natural things, inorganic and living, depend solely on the different modes of this unity. But instead of ascertaining these different modes, the ordinary physicist (chemist included) takes up only one, the most external and the worst, viz. composition, applies only it in the whole range of natural structures, which he thus renders for ever inexplicable.

The aforesaid shallow pantheism is an equally obvious inference from this shallow identity. All that those who employ this invention of their own to accuse philosophy gather from the study of God's relation to the world is that the one, but only the one factor of this category of relation—and that the factor of indeterminateness—is identity. Thereupon they stick fast in this half-perception, and assert— falsely as a fact—that philosophy teaches the identity of God and the world. And as in their judgment either of the two,—the world as much as God—has the same solid substantiality as the other, they infer that in the philosophic Idea God is composed of God and the world. Such then is the idea they form of pantheism, and which they ascribe to philosophy. Unaccustomed in their own thinking and apprehending of thoughts to go beyond such categories, they import them into philosophy, where they are utterly unknown; they thus infect it with the disease against which they subsequently raise an outcry. If any difficulty emerge in comprehending God's relation to the world, they at once and very easily escape it by admitting that this relation contains for them an inexplicable contradiction; and that hence, they must stop at the vague conception of such relation, perhaps under the more familiar names of, e.g. omnipresence, providence, &c. Faith in their use of the term means no more than a refusal to define the conception, or to enter on a closer discussion of the problem. That men and classes of untrained intellect are satisfied with such indefiniteness, is what one expects; but when a trained intellect and an interest for reflective study is satisfied, in matters admitted to be of superior, if not even of supreme interest, with indefinite ideas, it is hard to decide whether the thinker is really in earnest with the subject. But if those who cling to this crude "rationalism" were in earnest, e.g. with God's omnipresence, so far as to realise their faith thereon in a definite mental idea, in what difficulties would they be involved by their belief in the true reality of the things of sense! They would hardly like, as Epicurus does, to let God dwell in the interspaces of things, i.e. in the pores of the physicists,—said pores being the negative, something supposed to exist beside the material reality. This very "Beside" would give their pantheism its spatiality,—their everything, conceived as the mutual exclusion of parts in space. But in ascribing to God, in his relation to the world, an action on and in the space thus filled on the world and in it, they would endlessly split up the divine actuality into infinite materiality. They would really thus have the misconception they call pantheism or all-one-doctrine, only as the necessary sequel of their misconceptions of God and the world. But to put that sort of thing, this stale gossip of oneness or identity, on the shoulders of philosophy, shows such recklessness about justice and truth that it can only be explained through the difficulty of getting into the head thoughts and notions, i.e. not abstract unity, but the many-shaped modes specified. If statements as to facts are put forward, and the facts in question are thoughts and notions, it is indispensable to get hold of their meaning. But even the fulfilment of this requirement has been rendered superfluous, now that it has long been a foregone conclusion that philosophy is pantheism, a system of identity, an All-one doctrine, and that the person therefore who might be unaware of this fact is treated either as merely unaware of a matter of common notoriety, or as prevaricating for a purpose. On account of this chorus of assertions, then, I have believed myself obliged to speak at more length and exoterically on the outward and inward untruth of this alleged fact: for exoteric discussion is the only method available in dealing with the external apprehension of notions as mere facts,—by which notions are perverted into their opposite. The esoteric study of God and identity, as of cognitions and notions, is philosophy itself.

§ 574. This notion of philosophy is the self-thinking Idea, the truth aware of itself (§ 236),—the logical system, but with the signification that it is universality approved and certified in concrete content as in its actuality. In this way the science has gone back to its beginning: its result is the logical system but as a spiritual principle: out of the presupposing judgment, in which the notion was only implicit and the beginning an immediate,—and thus out of the appearance which it had there—it has risen into its pure principle and thus also into its proper medium.

§ 575. It is this appearing which originally gives the motive of the further development. The first appearance is formed by the syllogism, which is based on the Logical system as starting-point, with Nature for the middle term which couples the Mind with it. The Logical principle turns to Nature and Nature to Mind. Nature, standing between the Mind and its essence, sunders itself, not indeed to extremes of finite abstraction, nor itself to something away from them and independent,—which, as other than they, only serves as a link between them: for the syllogism is in the Idea and Nature is essentially defined as a transition-point and negative factor, and as implicitly the Idea. Still the mediation of the notion has the external form of transition, and the science of Nature presents itself as the course of necessity, so that it is only in the one extreme that the liberty of the notion is explicit as a self-amalgamation.

§ 576. In the second syllogism this appearance is so far superseded, that that syllogism is the standpoint of the Mind itself, which—as the mediating agent in the process—presupposes Nature and couples it with the Logical principle. It is the syllogism where Mind reflects on itself in the Idea: philosophy appears as a subjective cognition, of which liberty is the aim, and which is itself the way to produce it.

§ 577. The third syllogism is the Idea of philosophy, which has self-knowing reason, the absolutely-universal, for its middle term: a middle, which divides itself into Mind and Nature, making the former its presupposition, as process of the Idea's subjective activity, and the latter its universal extreme, as process of the objectively and implicitly existing Idea. The self-judging of the Idea into its two appearances (§§ 575, 576) characterises both as its (the self-knowing reason's) manifestations: and in it there is a unification of the two aspects:—it is the nature of the fact, the notion, which causes the movement and development, yet this same movement is equally the action of cognition. The eternal Idea, in full fruition of its essence, eternally sets itself to work, engenders and enjoys itself as absolute Mind.

Ἡ δὲ νόησις ἡ καθ᾿ αὑτὴν τοῦ καθ᾿ αὑτὸ ἀρίστου, καὶ ἡ μάλιστα τοῦ μάλιστα. Αὑτὸν δὲ νοεῖ ὁ νοῦς κατὰ μετάληψιν τοῦ νοητοῦ νοητὸς γὰρ γίγνεται θιγγάνων καὶ νοῶν, ὥστε ταὐτὸν νοῦς καὶ νοητόν. Τὸ γὰρ δεκτικὸν τοῦ νοητοῦ καὶ τῆς οὐσίας νοῦς. Ἐνεργεῖ δὲ ἔχων. Ὥστ᾿ ἐκεῖνο μᾶλλον τούτου ὃ δοκεῖ ὁ νοῦς θεῖον ἔχειν, καὶ ἡ θεωρία τὸ ἥδιστον καὶ ἄριστον. Εἰ οὖν οὕτως εὖ ἔχει, ὡς ἡμεῖς ποτέ, ὁ θεὸς ἀεί, θαυμαστόν· εἰ δὲ μᾶλλον, ἔτι θαυμασιώτερον. Ἔχει δὲ ὡδί. Καὶ ζωὴ δέ γε ὑπάρχει· ἡ γὰρ νοῦ ἐνέργεια ζωή, ἐκεῖνος δὲ ἡ ἐνέργεια· ἐνέργεια δὲ ἡ καθ᾿ αὑτὴν ἐκείνου ζωὴ ἀρίστη καὶ ἀΐδιος. Φαμὲν δὲ τὸν θεὸν εἶναι ζῷον ἀΐδιον ἄριστον, ὥστε ζωὴ αἰὼν συνεχὴς καὶ ἀΐδιος ὑπάρχει τῷ θεῷ· τοῦτο γὰρ ὁ θεός. (ARIST. Met. XI. 7.)

FOOTNOTES

1. Plato, Rep. 527.
2. The prospectus of the System of Synthetic Philosophy is dated 1860. Darwin's Origin of Species is 1859. But such ideas, both in Mr. Spencer and others, are earlier than Darwin's book.
3. Hegel's Verhältniss, the supreme category of what is called actuality: where object is necessitated by outside object.
4. Cf. Herbart, Werke (ed. Kehrbach), iv. 372. This consciousness proper is what Leibniz called « Apperception, » la connaissance réflexive de l'état intérieur (Nouveaux Essais).
5. Herbart, Werke, vi. 55 (ed. Kehrbach).
6. p. 59 (§ 440).
7. p. 63 (§ 440).
8. These remarks refer to four out of the five Herbartian ethical ideas. See also Leibniz, who (in 1693, De Notionibus juris et justitiae) had given the following definitions: "Caritas est benevolentia universalis. Justitia est caritas sapientis. Sapientia est scientia felicitatis." The jus naturae has three grades: the lowest, jus strictum; the second, aequitas (or caritas, in the narrower sense); and the highest, pietas, which is honeste, i.e. pie vivere.
9. To which the Greek πόλις, the Latin civitas or respublica, were only approximations. Hegel is not writing a history. If he were, it would be necessary for him to point out how far the individual instance, e.g. Rome, or Prussia, corresponded to its Idea.
10. Shakespeare's phrase, as in Othello, iii. 2; Lover's Complaint, v. 24.
11. Iliad, xii. 243.
12. See Hegel's Logic, pp. 257 seq.
13. See p. 153 (§ 550).
14. Cf. Prolegomena to the Study of Hegel, chaps. xviii, xxvi.
15. As stated in p. 167 (Encycl. § 554). Cf. Phenom. d. Geistes, cap. vii, which includes the Religion of Art, and the same point of view is explicit in the first edition of the Encyclopaedia.
16. Philosophie der Religion (Werke, xi. 5).
17. Hegel, Phenomenologie des Geistes (Werke, ii. 545). The meeting-ground of the Greek spirit, as it passed through Rome, with Christianity. 18 Ib., p. 584.
19. Phenomenologie des Geistes (Werke, ii. 572). Thus Hegelian idealism claims to be the philosophical counterpart of the central dogma of Christianity.
20. From the old Provençal Lay of Boëthius.
21. It is the doctrine of the intellectus agens, or in actu; the actus purus of the Schoolmen.
22. Einleitung in die Philosophie, §§ 1, 2.
23. Psychologie als Wissenschaft, Vorrede.
24. Einleitung in die Philosophie, §§ 11, 12.
25. Einleitung in die Philosophie, § 18: cf. Werke, ed. Kehrbach, v. 108.
26. Cf. Plato's remarks on the problem in the word Self-control. Republ. 430-1.
27. Lehrbuch der Psychologie, §§ 202, 203.
28. Allgemeine Metaphysik, Vorrede.
29. Hauptpunkte der Metaphysik (1806), § 13.
30. Werke, ed. Kehrbach (Ueber die Möglichkeit, &c), v. 96.
31. Ibid., p. 100.
32. One might almost fancy Herbart was translating into a general philosophic thesis the words in which Goethe has described how he overcame a real trouble by transmuting it into an ideal shape, e.g. Wahrheit und Dichtung, cap. xii.
33. Herbart's language is almost identical with Hegel's: Encycl. § 389 (p. 12). Cf. Spencer, Psychology, i. 192. "Feelings are in all cases the materials out of which the superior tracts of consciousness and intellect are evolved."
34. Prolegomena to the Study of Hegel, ch. xvii.
35. Psychologia Empirica, § 29.
36. As is also the case with Herbart's metaphysical reality of the Soul.
37. Human Nature, vii. 2. "Pleasure, Love, and appetite, which is also called desire, are divers

names for divers considerations of the same thing...." Deliberation is (ch. xii. 1) the "alternate succession of appetite and fears."

38. Eth. ii. 48 Schol.

39. Eth. ii. 43 Schol.: cf. 49 Schol.

40. This wide scope of thinking (cogitatio, penser) is at least as old as the Cartesian school: and should be kept in view, as against a tendency to narrow its range to the mere intellect.

41. e.g. Analysis of the Human Mind, ch. xxiv. "Attention is but another name for the interesting character of the idea;" ch. xix. "Desire and the idea of a pleasurable sensation are convertible terms."

42. As Mr. Spencer says (Psychology, i. 141), "Objective psychology can have no existence as such without borrowing its data from subjective psychology."

43. The same failure to note that experiment is valuable only where general points of view are defined, is a common fault in biology.

44. Münsterberg, Aufgaben und Methoden der Psychologie, p. 144.

45. Lehrbuch der Psychologie, § 54 (2nd ed.), or § 11 (1st ed.).

46. See p. 11 (§ 387).

47. Cf. Nietzsche, Also sprach Zarathustra, i. 43. "There is more reason in thy body than in thy best wisdom."

48. This language is very characteristic of the physicists who dabble in psychology and imagine they are treading in the steps of Kant, if not even verifying what they call his guesswork: cf. Ziehen, Physiol. Psychologie, 2nd ed. p. 212. "In every case there is given us only the psychical series of sensations and their memory-images, and it is only a universal hypothesis if we assume beside this psychical series a material series standing in causal relation to it.... The material series is not given equally originally with the psychical."

49. It is the same radical feature of consciousness which is thus noted by Mr. Spencer, Psychology, i. 475. "Perception and sensation are ever tending to exclude each other but never succeed." "Cognition and feeling are antithetical and inseparable." "Consciousness continues only in virtue of this conflict." Cf. Plato's resolution in the Philebus of the contest between intelligence and feeling (pleasure).

50. It is the quasi-Aristotelian ἀπαγωγή, defined as the step from one proposition to another, the knowledge of which will set the first proposition in a full light.

51. Grundlage des Naturrechts, § 5.

52. System der Sittenlehre, § 8, iv.

53. Even though religion (according to Kant) conceive them as divine commands.

54. Cf. Hegel's Werke, vii. 2, p. 236 (Lecture-note on § 410). "We must treat as utterly empty the fancy of those who suppose that properly man should have no organic body," &c.; and see p. 159 of the present work.

55. Criticism of Pure Reason, Architectonic.

56. Spencer, Psychology, i. 291: "Mind can be understood only by observing how mind is evolved."

57. Cf. Spencer, Principles of Ethics, i. 339: "The ethical sentiment proper is, in the great mass of cases, scarcely discernible."

58. Prolegomena to the Study of Hegel, p. 143.

59. Windelband (W.), Präludien (1884), p. 288.

60. Cf. Plato, Republic, p. 486.

61. Human Nature: Morals, Part III.

62. Emotion and Will, ch. xv. § 23.

63. It is characteristic of the Kantian doctrine to absolutise the conception of Duty and make it express the essence of the whole ethical idea.

64. Which are still, as the Socialist Fourier says, states of social incoherence, specially favourable to falsehood.

65. Rechtsphilosophie, § 4.

66. Cf. Schelling, ii. 12: "There are no born sons of freedom."

67. Simmel (G.), Einleitung in die Moralwissenschaft, i. 184.

68. Jenseits von Gut und Böse, p. 225.

69. Aristot. Polit. i. 6.

70. Plato, Phaedo.

71. Carus, Psyche, p. 1.

72. See Arist., Anal. Post. ii. 19 (ed. Berl. 100, a. 10).

73. Cf. The Logic of Hegel, notes &c., p. 421.

74. "Omnia individua corpora quamvis diversis gradibus animata sunt." Eth. ii. 13. schol.

75. Nanna (1848): Zendavesta (1851): Ueber die Seelenfrage (1861).

76. Described by S. as the rise from mere physical cause to physiological stimulus (Reiz), to

psychical motive.

77. Infra, p. 12.

78. Aristot., De Anima, i. c. 4, 5.

79. Wilhelm Meister's Wanderjahre, i. 10.

80. Wilhelm Meister's Wanderjahre, iv. 18.

81. Works like Preyer's Seele des Kindes illustrate this aspect of mental evolution; its acquirement of definite and correlated functions.

82. Cf. the end of Caleb Balderstone (in The Bride of Lammermoor): "With a fidelity sometimes displayed by the canine race, but seldom by human beings, he pined and died."

83. See Windischmann's letters in Briefe von und an Hegel.

84. Cf. Prolegomena to the Study of Hegel, chaps. xii-xiv.

85. Kieser's Tellurismus is, according to Schopenhauer, "the fullest and most thorough text-book of Animal Magnetism."

86. Cf. Fichte, Nachgelassene Werke, iii. 295 (Tagebuch über den animalischen Magnetismus, 1813), and Schopenhauer, Der Wille in der Natur.

87. Bernheim: La suggestion domine toute l'histoire de l'humanité.

88. An instance from an unexpected quarter, in Eckermann's conversations with Goethe: "In my young days I have experienced cases enough, where on lonely walks there came over me a powerful yearning for a beloved girl, and I thought of her so long till she actually came to meet me." (Conversation of Oct. 7, 1827.)

89. Gleichsam in einer Vorwelt, einer diese Welt schaffenden Welt (Nachgelassene Werke, iii. 321).

90. Selbst-bewusstsein is not self-consciousness, in the vulgar sense of brooding over feelings and self: but consciousness which is active and outgoing, rather than receptive and passive. It is practical, as opposed to theoretical.

91. The more detailed exposition of this Phenomenology of Mind is given in the book with that title: Hegel's Werke, ii. pp. 71-316.

92. System der Sittlichkeit, p. 15 (see Essay V).

93. Hegel's Werke, viii. 313, and cf. the passage quoted in my Logic of Hegel, notes, pp. 384, 385.

94. Hegel's Briefe, i. 15.

95. Kritik der Verfassung Deutschlands, edited by G. Mollat (1893). Parts of this were already given by Haym and Rosenkranz. The same editor has also in this year published, though not quite in full, Hegel's System der Sittlichkeit, to which reference is made in what follows.

96. In which some may find a prophecy of the effects of "blood and iron" in 1866.

97. Die Absolute Regierung: in the System der Sittlichkeit, p. 32: cf. p. 55. Hegel himself compares it to Fichte's Ephorate.

98. Die Absolute Regierung, l.c. pp. 37, 38.

99. Some idea of his meaning may perhaps be gathered by comparison with passages in Wilhelm Meister's Wanderjahre, ii. 1, 2.

100. Kritik der Verfassung, p. 20.

101. In some respects Bacon's attitude in the struggle between royalty and parliament may be compared.

102. Just as Schopenhauer, on the contrary, always says moralisch—never sittlich.

103. Grey (G.), Journals of two Expeditions of Discovery in North-West and Western Australia, ii. 220.

104. With some variation of ownership, perhaps, according to the prevalence of so-called matriarchal or patriarchal households.

105. Cf. the custom in certain tribes which names the father after his child: as if the son first gave his father legitimate position in society.

106. System der Sittlichkeit, p. 8.

107. Aufhebung (positive) as given in absolute Sittlichkeit.

108. System der Sittlichkeit, p. 15.

109. This phraseology shows the influence of Schelling, with whom he was at this epoch associated. See Prolegomena to the Study of Hegel, ch. xiv.

110. Cf. the intermediate function assigned (see above, p. clxxxiii) to the priests and the aged.

111. System der Sittlichkeit, p. 19.

112. See infra, p. 156.

113. Wordsworth's Laodamia.

114. "For it's Tommy this, an' Tommy that, an' 'Chuck him out, the brute!' But it's 'Saviour of 'is country' when the guns begin to shoot."

115. "I can assure you," said Werner (the merchant), "that I never reflected on the State in my life.

My tolls, charges and dues I have paid for no other reason than that it was established usage." (Wilh. Meisters Lehrjahre, viii. 2.)

116. System der Sittlichkeit, p. 40.
117. System der Sittlichkeit, p. 65.
118. Ibid. p. 46.
119. Natürliche Seele.
120. Natürliche Qualitäten.
121. Empfindung.
122. Die fühlende Seele.
123. Plato had a better idea of the relation of prophecy generally to the state of sober consciousness than many moderns, who supposed that the Platonic language on the subject of enthusiasm authorised their belief in the sublimity of the revelations of somnambulistic vision. Plato says in the Timaeus (p. 71), "The author of our being so ordered our inferior parts that they too might obtain a measure of truth, and in the liver placed their oracle (the power of divination by dreams). And herein is a proof that God has given the art of divination, not to the wisdom, but, to the foolishness of man; for no man when in his wits attains prophetic truth and inspiration; but when he receives the inspired word, either his intelligence is enthralled by sleep, or he is demented by some distemper or possession (enthusiasm)." Plato very correctly notes not merely the bodily conditions on which such visionary knowledge depends, and the possibility of the truth of the dreams, but also the inferiority of them to the reasonable frame of mind.
124. Selbstgefühl.
125. Gewohnheit.
126. Die wirkliche Seele.
127. Das Bewußtsein als solches: (a) Das sinnliche Bewußtsein.
128. Wahrnehmung.
129. Der Verstand.
130. Selbstbewußtsein.
131. Die Begierde.
132. Das anerkennende Selbstbewußtsein.
133. Die Vernunft.
134. Der Geist.
135. Die Intelligenz.
136. Anschauung.
137. Vorstellung.
138. Die Erinnerung.
139. Die Einbildungskraft.
140. Phantasie.
141. Gedächtniß.
142. Auswendiges.
143. Inwendiges.
144. Das Denken.
145. Der praktische Geist.
146. Der praktische Gefühl.
147. Der Triebe und die Willkühr.
148. Die Glückseligkeit.
149. Der freie Geist.
150. Gesess.
151. Sitte.
152. Das Recht.
153. Moralität.
154. Naturrecht.
155. Moralität.
156. Der Vorsatz.
157. That.
158. Handlung.
159. Die Absicht und das Wohl.
160. Das Gute und das Böse.
161. Die Sittlichkeit.
162. Die bürgerliche Gesellschaft.
163. Das System der Bedürfnisse.
164. Die Rechtspflege.
165. Geseß.

166. Die Polizei und die Corporation.
167. Inneres Staatsrecht.
168. Das äußere Staatsrecht.
169. Die Weltgeschichte.
170. Weltweisheit.
171. Der absolute Geist.
172. Die geoffenbarte Religion.
173. [The citation given by Hegel from Schlegel's translation is here replaced by the version (in one or two points different) in the Sacred Books of the East, vol. viii.]
174. In order to give a clearer impression of it, I cannot refrain from quoting a few passages, which may at the same time give some indication of the marvellous skill of Rückert, from whom they are taken, as a translator. [For Rückert's verses a version is here substituted in which I have been kindly helped by Miss May Kendall.]

III.
I saw but One through all heaven's starry spaces gleaming:
I saw but One in all sea billows wildly streaming.
I looked into the heart, a waste of worlds, a sea,—
I saw a thousand dreams,—yet One amid all dreaming.
And earth, air, water, fire, when thy decree is given,
Are molten into One: against thee none hath striven.
There is no living heart but beats unfailingly
In the one song of praise to thee, from earth and heaven.

V.
As one ray of thy light appears the noonday sun,
But yet thy light and mine eternally are one.
As dust beneath thy feet the heaven that rolls on high:
Yet only one, and one for ever, thou and I.
The dust may turn to heaven, and heaven to dust decay;
Yet art thou one with me, and shalt be one for aye.
How may the words of life that fill heaven's utmost part
Rest in the narrow casket of one poor human heart?
How can the sun's own rays, a fairer gleam to fling,
Hide in a lowly husk, the jewel's covering?
How may the rose-grove all its glorious bloom unfold,
Drinking in mire and slime, and feeding on the mould?
How can the darksome shell that sips the salt sea stream
Fashion a shining pearl, the sunlight's joyous beam?
Oh, heart! should warm winds fan thee, should'st thou floods endure,
One element are wind and flood; but be thou pure.

IX.
I'll tell thee how from out the dust God moulded man,—
Because the breath of Love He breathed into his clay:
I'll tell thee why the spheres their whirling paths began,—
They mirror to God's throne Love's glory day by day:
I'll tell thee why the morning winds blow o'er the grove,—
It is to bid Love's roses bloom abundantly:
I'll tell thee why the night broods deep the earth above,—
Love's bridal tent to deck with sacred canopy:
All riddles of the earth dost thou desire to prove?—
To every earthly riddle is Love alone the key.

XV.
Life shrinks from Death in woe and fear,
Though Death ends well Life's bitter need:
So shrinks the heart when Love draws near,
As though 'twere Death in very deed:
For wheresoever Love finds room,
There Self, the sullen tyrant, dies.
So let him perish in the gloom,—

Thou to the dawn of freedom rise.

In this poetry, which soars over all that is external and sensuous, who would recognise the prosaic ideas current about so-called pantheism—ideas which let the divine sink to the external and the sensuous? The copious extracts which Tholuck, in his work Anthology from the Eastern Mystics, gives us from the poems of Jelaleddin and others, are made from the very point of view now under discussion. In his Introduction, Herr Tholuck proves how profoundly his soul has caught the note of mysticism; and there, too, he points out the characteristic traits of its oriental phase, in distinction from that of the West and Christendom. With all their divergence, however, they have in common the mystical character. The conjunction of Mysticism with so-called Pantheism, as he says (p. 53), implies that inward quickening of soul and spirit which inevitably tends to annihilate that external Everything, which Pantheism is usually held to adore. But beyond that, Herr Tholuck leaves matters standing at the usual indistinct conception of Pantheism; a profounder discussion of it would have had, for the author's emotional Christianity, no direct interest; but we see that personally he is carried away by remarkable enthusiasm for a mysticism which, in the ordinary phrase, entirely deserves the epithet Pantheistic. Where, however, he tries philosophising (p. 12), he does not get beyond the standpoint of the "rationalist" metaphysic with its uncritical categories.

www.ingramcontent.com/pod-product-compliance
Lightning Source LLC
Chambersburg PA
CBHW032004080426
42735CB00007B/502